The Passionate Gardener

IS PUBLISHED IN A FIRST EDITION

OF 1250 NUMBERED COPIES.

COPY 1136

THE PASSIONATE GARDENER

Rudolf Borchardt

English translation by Henry Martin

McPherson & Company

THE PASSIONATE GARDENER

Title of the original: *Der leidenschaftliche Gärtner.*

Published by McPherson & Company, Publishers, P. O. Box 1126, Kingston, New York 12402, with assistance from the Literature Program of the New York State Council on the Arts, a state agency.

Typeset in Columbus with Pastonchi display.

Design by Bruce R. McPherson.

Manufactured in the United States of America.

FIRST EDITION

1 3 5 7 9 10 8 6 4 2 2006 2007 2008 2009 2010

LIBRARY OF CONGRESS CATALOGING-IN-PUBLICATION DATA

Borchardt, Rudolf, 1877-1945.
[Leidenschaftliche Gärtner. English]
The passionate gardener / Rudolf Borchardt ; English translation by Henry Martin.–1st ed.
p. cm.
Includes bibliographical references (p.) and index.
ISBN-13: 978-0-929701-73-8 (alk. paper)
ISBN-10: 0-929701-73-9
1. Gardens–Philosophy. 2. Gardening–Philosophy. I. Title.
SB454.3.P45B67 2006
635–dc22

2006004312

CONTENTS

Preface

RUDOLF BORCHARDT was born in 1877 in Königsberg, in Eastern Prussia, and died in 1945 in the Tyrolean village of Trins, in southern Austria. In the postface to *Rudolf Borchardts Leben von ihm selbst erzählt*—"The Life of Rudolf Borchardt as Told by Himself"—Gustav Seibt remarks on just how fateful it seems for both of these places to be border regions that relate to the poet's life by barely more than chance. Though his parents were themselves from Königsberg, Borchardt was born unexpectedly in the course of a visit which had brought them there from Moscow, where his father managed the family firm, which imported and distributed tea. Borchardt's presence in Tyrol in 1945 resulted from his forced evacuation from Italy, where he had lived near Lucca since 1906 except for the period of the First World War during which he served in Berlin and Elsace as an officer in the Kaiser's army. The circumstances of his removal from Italy in the fall of 1944, along with his wife and three of his children, remain unclear, and are differently remembered by various members of his family: they may have been seen as a German family which the retreating forces of occupation had the duty to remove to safety from the immediate path of the advancing Allied army; or they may have been slated for deportation to a concentration camp, and then spared by an officer whom Borchardt's moral presence had deeply impressed. Borchardt not only was a vocal anti-Nazi, but as well, in earlier years, had made no secret of his family's Jewish origins. (He dated his family's conversion to Evangelism to the first third of the nineteenth century, though it may partly have taken place in as late as the 1870s.) The relationship of the German-Jewish or Jewish-German intellectual to the overall body of German culture had been much debated in the literary circles of the years before the advent of Nazism, and Borchardt had been a part of that debate, and often had been pointed out as the voice of one of the most difficult and controversial attitudes to be found among Jewish intellectuals. The notion of "race" was alien to him, and he looked upon the whole of German culture, and German national identity, as a vast work in progress that would finally absorb, transform and elevate the regional, historical, and ethnic identities of all the groups—whether Jews, Bavarians, or Alsatians—who lived within it, and offer them a rich and multifaceted, but shared, cohesive and cosmopolitan identity that all of them would have helped to create, to their common and mutual benefit, and to the health of the nation as a whole. His Jewish origins were also known to the community in which he lived in Italy. In any case, Borchardt and his wife were vastly surprised when the officer whose convoy they had been forced to join informed them in Innsbruck of their release from custody. He died a few months later, from causes which his eldest son, Kaspar, describes as "a broken heart."

Borchardt writes in his autobiography that the story of his life was the story of the collapse of German tradition, and he somehow shaped the desperate idea that he himself might rescue it. He was educated in archaeology, theology, and classical and oriental philology at universities in Berlin, Bonn and Göttingen, and one of the decisive turning points in his literary career was his meeting in 1898 with Stefan George and Hugo von Hofmannsthal. His friendship with Hugo von Hofmannsthal was in fact to endure until the latter's death, in 1929. It was also through Hofmannsthal and *Insel* magazine that he made the acquaintance of his other lifelong friend and colleague, Rudolf Alexander Schröder.

Borchardt while alive was both famous and obscure. He was intensely involved with the ins and outs and conflicting directions of German literary life, especially in the period before the 1930s, and he was a valued interlocutor, as is also seen in his copious correspondence not only with Hofmannsthal, but as well with a range of notable thinkers from Benedetto Croce to Martin Buber. His thinking was always conservative—he was a part of what was known as "the conservative revolution," though he himself preferred to speak of a need for a "creative restoration"—but in ways that are very much aloof from what we now most generally understand the word "conservative" to imply: the terms on which he looked at life, history, and literature clearly belong to perspectives that lay outside the great conflicts of modern or twentieth-century thought, or its most conspicuous theses and antitheses. Borchardt hailed much further back than that: he discerned and defended a notion of culture that was rooted in classical antiquity, and which he saw as having continued throughout the Middle Ages, and on into the heart of German Romanticism. Borchardt was less in opposition to any one part of his times than indeed to the whole of them. The world in which he believed, and the ideal aspirations he felt it to contain, lost all hope of political practicability and effectively came to an end with the First World War and the demise of the Prussian and Austrian monarchies, and he could only view the political life of the Germany that came in its wake as a base conflict of complementary barbarisms, of which national socialism was the final tragic denouement. Borchardt, in the world of Germany's disintegration at the end of the First World War, has been described as an inveterate partisan of already lost causes, but the tone in which he defended them is less tainted by nostalgia than enlightened by a will to continue to honor a vision.

Borchardt's work is currently found in print in many places. Suhrkamp, in addition to the autobiography mentioned above, has published a volume of *Ausgewählte Gedichte* ("Selected Poems") chosen and with a preface by Theodor W. Adorno.

But the fundamental edition for all of Borchardt's work is the sixteen-volume *Gesammelte Werke* ("Collected Works") published by Klett/Cotta, Stuttgart, 1957-1999, flanked by the volumes of correspondence (seven, to date) which since 1994 have been appearing with Edition Tenschert, Hanser Verlag, Munich. The Klett edition of Borchardt's works includes poetry, drama, novellas, speeches, and several volumes of prose essays on a vast variety of subjects, in addition to Borchardt's translations, the most celebrated of which is his version of Dante's *Divina Commedia*, written in a personal re-invention of the Middle High-German speech which would in fact have been contemporary with Dante's Tuscan vernacular. He also translated the Homeric hymns, Pindar, Plato, Horace and Tacitus, as well as a good deal of verse by Provence's troubadours, various nineteenth-century English poets, and Edna St. Vincent Millay. Of all of Borchardt's writings, the work most frequently republished has been *Der leidenschaftliche Gärtner* ("The Passionate Gardener"). A first and somewhat incomplete edition was published by Nymphenburger Verlagshandlung, Munich, in 1951, followed by the full Klett edition (as a part of the *Gesammelte Werke*) of 1968, and then by two special editions jointly published in 1998 by Hans Magnus Enzenberger's Die Andere Bibliothek and Eichborn Verlag, Frankfurt am Main. It has also appeared in Italy (Adelphi, Milan, 1992) as *Il giardiniere appassionato*, in the translation of Manfredo Roncioni. *Der leidenschaftliche Gärtner* was Rudolf Borchardt's last major undertaking, and the book's first chapter, "The Flower and the Human Being," was the last of his works to be published in the course of his lifetime. It appeared in three installments in the Sunday edition of the *Neue Zürcher Zeitung*, Zurich, on August 30, September 6, and September 13, 1942.

Borchardt's history of plants and gardens is a history of shifting and developing human sensibilities. And Borchardt, surely, would have found no reason to shy away from the word "developing." As a man of the nineteenth century, which in fact he always remained, he had a right to notions of progress. His story of plants is the story of the places and conditions they originally came from—of their original climates and continents–and of how they were brought from those original locales to those in which we find them now. It's the story of the travels of plants and of the human beings who escorted them. It's the story of the colonial empires that sent botanists and collectors all across the earth. It's especially the story, for Borchardt, of the cosmopolitan Habsburg Empire, which from Vienna reached out to the east and the Turkish and Persian garden traditions that the Ottoman Sultanate preserved; which from Spain reached out to Central and South America and the importation of plants that to Europeans where wholly new; which in the Netherlands supported the universities that created the science of botany. It's the story of the meeting places of the interests and loves of princes and peasants: of great courtly gardens, and of parti-colored plantings in the dooryards of modest country cottages. It's the story of the breeding of plants, and of the purification of their forms and colors: a story of human respect for natural givens, but as well of the human ability to grasp and further the development of natural possibilities. It's also the story of the natural growth of democracy, and of ever more popular participation in endeavors and sensibilities which were once reserved to a privileged few. It's the story of traditions that collaborate and fuse with one another in the service of a common and higher ideal: of Roman, Persian, Oriental, Medieval, Baroque, Italian, French, Austrian, English, American and African gardens which cross-fertilize and dialogue with one another on terms that can only make humanity ashamed of the tragic political terms on which these cultures have as well and so perversely met.

One of the wonderful things about this book is that it never reduces to a thesis. Borchardt's subject contains a truth for which he is actively seeking, and the reader becomes involved in the drama of that search. Borchardt pursues his notion of the garden—his image of the garden—in much the same way—with similar scope and similar honesty—that Melville pursues his whale.

Borchardt wrote this book in 1938 while living in Italy, and he knew that it couldn't be published in Germany. And there is more to this than the fact that his exile from Germany had ceased to be self-imposed when the Nazis came to power in 1933. *The Passionate Gardener* espouses a notion of international community, harmony and co-operation—and indeed of the cultural equality of the nations and peoples of the world—which in the Germany of 1938 would have made the book entirely unacceptable, if not an open act of treason. While writing this book, Borchardt was extremely interested in the possibility of seeing it published in England or the United States, and the only fully-corrected copy of its manuscript in fact was sent to England, where its loss took place under circumstances which have never been clarified. So, this translation is a belated fulfillment of Borchardt's most intimate desires. And as Borchardt in the darkness of the years at the end of the 1930s contemplated a possible English-speaking audience, it is not at all unlikely that he hoped, at least unconsciously, to present a living and visionary strain of the best of the German Romantic tradition to a world that had growing reason to view his country in entirely different ways.

HENRY MARTIN

THE PASSIONATE GARDENER

CHAPTER I

The Flower and the Human Being

WHEN one asks what a garden is, viewpoints, naturally, will be no fewer than the differences typical everywhere among human beings, gardeners or otherwise; and sober judgments will always be flanked by biases of every kind, and every time, including—why not?—our own. There are peoples even today who have sacred or nearly sacred gardens—sacred to their identity as a people—and who offer them seasonal celebrations, performed as though in honor of gods. This is nothing new to us. And in perfect opposition to these pagan acts of adoration, there is also the desolate superstition—of which we are equally aware—that sees the garden as a luxury, and looks upon active involvement with a garden as a game, a hobby horse, a harmless pastime permissible to women and children, an ornamentation, or a sort a bauble that some might pin to the living of a life; or finally—at the absolute nadir of the scale for such a way of thinking—the garden is seen as a way of indulging a leaning toward aestheticism. But all such opinions, theories and celebrations, along with all truly serious attempts to ascribe the garden to its proper place in the overall structure of human experience, both social and individual, find unshakable, positive convergence in the *economic* life of our societies. The garden is involved with the mobilization of such colossal figures, and its debits and credits in the financial affairs of all peoples—from those still half in savagery to those now ready to return to it—stand in such an immutable relation to the entirety of the volume of exchange as to make one see it first of all—no matter what else it may be—as a real human necessity: as a need which from the very beginning has always been inborn in the human being, and which always under all conditions has found the way to assert itself, like all the other primordial needs, such as prayer, drink and love.

The fact that the rich imbibe champagne and burgundy does nothing to make a luxury of the sailor's rum or the carter's half-and-half in the middle of a sweltering morning. The fact that idle men of lofty station, as they are reputed to do, only toy with women says nothing of the youthful worker who on a dark street corner fervently courts his girl. Consider those heavyset men in the prime of life who return from work to sixth-floor homes in a building at the rear of a courtyard and immediately go to a window sill to water blue petunias, meanwhile taking a look as well at an old cigar box to see if the marigold seeds it holds have begun to sprout. And note the lack of self-consciousness with which they go about their business, while countless others at countless other windows putter with similar aplomb at a few geraniums, or contentedly boast from window to window of successes they have achieved. Such situations hold a great deal more of the essence of the human garden than will ever be found in the highly modern and ready-to-use arrangement of shrubs which "the man on the rise" has had delivered from a garden architect; or in the lawn-like flower beds of the provincial man of private means; or again in the orgies of raw materials where fanatics of single-color gardens turn their gaze to running meters of yellow or lilac—as though swathed with the broadest of brushes—that roll off toward the horizon. Here, yes, we are looking at luxuries; and surely such things are hobby horses; futile game and crass madness. How else could they be explained? Yet, what do they prove if not the very opposite of the arguments they're imagined to support? Where does nonsense flourish more than at the edges of the passions and the places where meaning is most profound? If gardens and love were nothing more than amusements, then never on their borders with obtusity would a paragon of order have planted patches of ice plant into figures of p's and h's, and no Malvolio would ever have cross-gartered his legs.

Humanity was born in a garden. And since those origins, most of its experience has been intimately connected with events that might be termed a desecration of a garden's laws, and indeed—with the profoundest of implications—not once but twice. The disruption of the garden's order through the philistinism of eating symbolic fruits led straight to the even more grievous misuse of handsome vegetation as a simple source of raw materials, in the impermanent service of clothing. Repeal of the right to enjoyment of the garden's hospitality, and consequent withdrawal into the world of the fields and of childbirth, then marked the start for normal lives of a never-ending chain of further expulsions from constantly reinvented gardens: from the gardens which have sprung, in the defiant rhythms of the human heart, from the decision that every breath of relief, caught no matter how momentarily, from the sweat of the fields and the pains of birthing children would find its use—be it only at a sixth-floor window sill of a house at the rear of a courtyard—in the reconstruction of a paradise from which to be expelled again, always newly provoking the angel who bears the fiery sword.

We know enough about the garden that once was humanity's home to be able to picture its architectonic structure. Like all primordial dispositions connected with human life, this garden was perfectly symmetrical, or, more precisely, perfectly geometrical. Since the human spirit is the breath of God, everything human begins as order, and, by way of the path of disorder which God Himself decreed, must once again become an order. The garden of Eden was square, symmetrically divided and watered by a cross of four rivers that sprang from its center. We also know enough about its cultivated plants to be able to say that two of them—the Tree of Life and the Tree of the Knowledge of Good and Evil—have since disappeared from cultivation, whereas one of the plants still commonly grown today was already there of assistance to humankind in dealing with two of our oldest and most bitter afflictions: hunger and shame. Our knowledge is slight, but sufficient; and compared to what we know about Adam and Eve, it is even quite abundant. How could that be denied? God created the world in six days—indeed, basically, in five, since man, as the heir of the act of creation, required the sixth for himself alone; and one of those days, in its perfect entirety, was allotted to the making of a garden, with its trees, herbs and flowers. In terms of time, it equals in worth and majesty the separation of light from darkness.

Let's set aside such pious, pointed jokes. The dreams and memories, the desires and hopes, the image and symbol of the human being present themselves as gardens. Human beings build gardens in order to give real substance, whether passing or enduring, to a lost world that fills the mind with unappeasable longing. A garden is something from which one surely must have been driven out, since, otherwise, how could one possibly have left it? A garden is the world "beyond" for which we long: Paradise, the Elysian Fields, the Hesperides. The meadow, in Homer, over which the shade of Ajax slipped away found its appellation in a somber adjective. From very early on, the Greeks misread it as the name of a flower, and since that time a variety of rigid, melancholy flowers have been known, for no good reason, as asphodels. In the gardens of the Hesperides, the apples on the trees are of pure gold, as in the fairy tales, long before the time when nature kept faith with the powers ascribed her and allowed the importation from China of oranges. Eurypides' *Hippolytos* contains the gracious fable that the spirits of those who in life never broke their word wander through a blessed meadow where the flowers are never bent or broken by the feet that pass among them. A deathless garden blossoms with the sanctity of the word of honor. The Island of Calypso is a garden, since Ithaca, a weeping woman, an oppressed son, a dishonored father, herds of goats and swine, and a mutinous guard of nobles in no way make for a garden, and constitute instead the drama of life. Passionate suffering gives birth to the equally passionate image of its opposite: to a garden where undying, tearless love on the part of a man of prodigious endurance can be its own consolation, since the perfect image of the perfect orchard, each tree called by its name, encircles the couch of forgetfulness. And the passion which had shaped and sings this garden gives birth in turn to a further reversal: its reversal of itself into the hero's nostalgia for the causal world, and for the smoke that rises from a hearth in his bitterly remembered fatherland. These two worlds are each other's opposite poles, and the drama of the man who is split in two takes place in the space between them. In future times which will allow the world no other unblemished reversal of its image than the sky, this is also what the gardens of Kundrie and Armida will be: unallowable longing—sin—will likewise look like a garden.

The garden—which is an order of the human soul and related to all its other orders—is an order of the whole soul and not of any half of it. It can never belong to only the active and not to the indolent half of the soul. And there are no self-righteous aesthetes, if not for strollers, to whom it offers no reproach. The garden must have its gardener. The passion which the notion of a garden discloses in the imagination, in order then to overthrow reality, does not derive from superabundant fantasy, but from the fullness of a vision of grief and affliction; from an undisguised intelligence of the reality of the world of evil; from the need to catch one's breath from the drama of the struggle with such a world. Christ, too, is a gardener, and not only as the speaker of the parable of the sower who went out to sow his seed; or of the grain of mustard seed; or of the lilies of the field, that toil not, neither do they spin, and yet Solomon in all his glory was not arrayed like one of these. The final struggle between creator and creature in Christ's immortal soul does not take place in any chamber, but in a garden. The plants that may have grown in Eden are imagined in the poetry of a pious people. But no eye has dared to dream what sort of Easter blossoms were crushed by the man who knelt in the garden in Gethsemane. We know only that the scene in which he took his pained departure from the world in fact occurred in a garden, it having been remarked as such by the same imagination which sees him in the guise of a gardener at the time of his return from death, a spade on his shoulder and a basket in his hands as he stands before the three Marias. This, indeed, marks the start of the flowering of that grandiose metaphor in which the human soul is itself a garden, strictly and fervently in the care of God: the heart of the child of the world is rife with weeds, and He plucks them up; the heart of the innocent is a pious, modest field full of silent grace, and fragrant with fine perfume; the heart of the virgin—of apartness from the world, and preparation for the world—becomes a new ideal for the garden, where the only thing that speaks is the secret of utter reserve: the *hortus conclusus.* Blossoms ripen and their presence may well be supposed, but the curious eye has no admittance, on the far side of a locked gate. Longing has built an inner ring inside an outer ring, and thinks itself over to within it from out of the outside world, where all doors stand open, and where the soul remains aghast at the accessibility of everything earthly. Purity can only be found within the protection of vegetation, and everything which is not impure is a garden. The Christian implications of these images are not the whole of their story. The warrior who captains the battle for the redemption of the fallen world is not the only figure of a garden's gardener. His opponent on the scene of world history, the athlete clad in purple who led the final defense of its organization as an empire, was to travel the selfsame path through worldly hopes to otherworldly desire. Emperor Diocletian withdrew from the realm he had newly reordered and became a gardener in his garden in Spalato. Shy eyes which on occasion looked on from a distance watched this cruel old man—this man of terror who so rawly had conducted so many wars, and remained so little touched by so much gore—as, dressed in an apron, he bent down daily over his flower beds, sowing, planting, and watering. The world by now is nothing more than a wilderness; what is not the world can be nothing more than a garden.

In historical terms, the garden lies on the threshold which the ancient nomad peoples at some point had to cross into order to turn into the oldest of the settled peoples. The word—*chortos, hortus, gards*—still had nothing to do with flowers. It meant only a space that was marked off and protected, fenced in and held apart from the world through which all could pass; such fenced-in spaces could be equally places of residence or crop-bearing fields, cities no less than tillage. Compounds such as *Baumgarten,* for orchard, *Weingarten,* for vineyard, or "herb garden" and "rose garden" reveal the limitations of the original word in expressing the meanings demanded from it by subsequent levels of culture. The settled peoples were the first to fence in spaces and to draw themselves inwards from an outwards; the first to gather plants, and therefore to need to protect themselves from feathered and burrowing animals. At the start, and then still for quite some time, such measures belonged to a purely practical world, and they led to no gardens, among either the Greeks or the Germans. The garden gods were those of the indigenous peoples who lent their cultures to the invaders who came from abroad, and thus Apollo is a gardener. From the islands where he reigned as the lord of the world, the emigration of his sovereignty over the soul was accompanied by nurseries that supplied the plants for his sacred groves, and we know nearly every species that they planted and cultivated. But this gardener was also a god of healing and a doctor, and his sons, half-sons and priests were healers in his name. The sacred wood soon came to be edged by herbaries and gardens of medicinal plants, which were instruments of no mean service in the hands of proselytizing priests.

Charlemagne's celebrated *Capitulare de villis* was put to similar use, in similar circumstances, among other newly subjected peoples. Here again, a missionary priesthood spread toward the north beneath the protection of the state and carried the seedlings of an old world into a new one. Records still survive of what the Frankish king ordered to be planted in Germany, and it surely was a sorry assortment when compared to the plants Diocletian is said to have cultivated. But no matter how little it in fact had to do with a garden, it still contained an impoverished selection of the medicinal plants and kitchen herbs of the old classical world, along with all the flowering plants demanded by the altar. The ancient custom of floral offerings was not, after all, to be denied, here on this ancient soil, to the now baptized descendants of these ancient peoples. The altars of the new religion were decked with garlands just like those of the old one; feast days simply turned from antiquity's baskets of flowers to bouquets in vases of water, and meeting such a need in this raw and rainy land could only be a question of cultivation, unlike those southern lands where blossoms strive toward the sun from every crack in every cliff or country wall. Lilies, roses and carnations, stock, wallflower and lovage, basil and sage and rosemary migrated from the shores of the Mediterranean and entered the German spirit by way of the monastery garden and church decorations. They were clamorous novelties and gave rise to a body of symbolism which the always symbolic thinking of the church promoted, supported and ever more widely spread. Still, and still for a great deal of time to come in those prosaic and uninventive centuries, there was no possibility for any such thing as a garden, even while flowers came each to be surrounded by its own secret atmosphere, its own peculiar magic, and not only in terms of superstitions. Each flower now assumed a power of its own, and voiced it. The rose glows with impudent fire, whereas the lily belongs to chastity, the mignonette to modesty, the violet to hidden virtue. Every plant, at the very same time, also became officinal, in accordance with the practical frame of mind of a hard, utilitarian time. Every flower was asked to convince reason of its worthiness of cultivation, by virtue of the possession of medicinal properties, and at the very same time to assume an allegorical function in the spiritual world. The assortment of exotic plants was also joined, slowly and very sparingly, by indigenous wild species: the primrose, the violet, the forget-me-not, the *Primula officinalis*, Euphrasia, speedwell,

Tussilago, which is to speak of that stock of medicinal plants which have always been the tools of the herbalist. These too were slowly assigned their place in the canon of floral symbolism and each began to have its "meaning," which inordinately slowed their progress on the path toward "being." But there was also a great compensation, in unexpected quarters. Contact with flowers—no matter how much they remain entrapped in the purposes of spells, medicines, and offerings—exerts a powerful magic on still untutored human souls. And it nearly immediately lifts them to a level of experience which is typical of peoples who have found their way to more stable interior lives, inclusive of some who are also wild and simple peoples.

Flowers excite the attention of language and thought, and encourage the hand and mind to mirror and explore them further: they are the source of metaphor and ornament. Ninety-nine percent of the figurative expressions employed by the human languages have been taken from the world of plants; ninety-nine percent of the decorative forms employed in visual imagery, no matter how ancient or recent, derive from flowers. Why is this? Chance? Or because the world of plants is "more beautiful" than the world of animals, or the skies, or landscape forms, or the world of human life? Any such proposition misunderstands the depths of the human soul. Two lions face to face are no more beautiful than two buffaloes, but buffaloes have never been turned into heraldic ornaments. There are more beautiful flowers than the water lily, and plants more shapely than the palm. The flowers we call "most beautiful," such as the rose, were treated ornamentally only at a later date, sporadically, and somewhat clumsily. Greece's most splendid flowers, such as *Morina longifolia* and *Moltkia petraea*, were never depicted in antiquity. Should we imagine the Greeks not to have known them, since they are high mountain flora? Which still would not be much to the point. The hyacinth, crocus and narcissus, which they exalted in their sagas, are equally absent from the visual arts of the Greeks: the Minoan draughtsmen of the island of Crete, who made naturalistic records of whatever they found impressive—the lily, the iris, no less than polyps and centipedes—found no Greek followers.

What shakes the human mind and leads it so intensely, with such nostalgia, to portrayals of plants and flowers has nothing to do with any thought of their being more beautiful than other creatures. The secret lies in their greater ability—greater than in any other earthly thing—to present themselves as simple figure, evenly developing on both of the sides of a central axis, their mien a law of spatial form, their structure an order, their tendrils, leaves and calyx so many living sisters of the egg, the cone, the ellipse, the circle: regularity lies more or less hidden in the play of their growth. And behind it lies a rule—but what rule? An order—but an order bearing what name?

Kosmos, in Greek, means ornament, order, and structure, all at the very same time; The concepts differ but cluster together as intertwining images. The flower, the leaf, the tendril are miracles of order, and the human being is an absence of order which derives from order and aspires to return to order. This limpid harmony that rises out of the earth is beatified mathematics, and the non-beatific human being takes heed of it, having lost what it continues to hold. If the flower were not charged with memory, it would count for no more than a pretty butterfly, a brightly colored pebble. "Euclid alone has looked on Beauty bare." The poet of every epoch gives rebirth to the human spirit's original sensibility, its responsiveness, its primordial naiveté. So, it makes no difference whether our insight into the human response to the forms of flowers is gleaned from the oldest of humanity's records, or from the poetry of Edna St. Vincent Millay.

The human soul has always known itself to be more related to the flower than to the animal. This alone suffices to explain why metaphors on vegetation course everywhere through human speech and form the hidden scaffold that supports the whole of its imagery. The intention, here, has never lain in the "ornamentation" of language. Yes, the flower is indeed the oldest and most natural ornament of the human body, since nature herself makes a gift of it, and feathers, shells and splinters of rock compete with the flower thanks only to the permanence of their lifeless colors. But this ornament simply assisted the sexes in playing out the game of the arousal and consummation of their longing for one another: torrid south sea days and the heat of the battle of love quickly wilt the fiery calyx behind the dusky ear, and the bed of flowers lies too soon destroyed. The pained senses had to be schooled in endless sublimation before the flowered gown, embroidered and painted, could weave itself into a veil that hangs before desire, prolonging desires which it could not make eternal: prolonging them by giving them meaning. If the flower as ornament speaks to the human spirit of the mysterious conjunction of divine order and perishability, as metaphor it speaks instead of mortality and rebirth. The flower is the kernel of the similes used in human language—"image of the soul, or indeed its shadow"—not because it *is* and *lives*, but because it *still* is, and soon will be *no more*, and then newly lives again. It symbolizes the cyclical destiny of human experience and the law that governs the human soul—"what we have, what we had"—and this makes it inexhaustible, from every point of view. This makes it the natural subject and center of poetry, which is concerned almost entirely with cyclical things and not with outward appearances. This makes the flower's perishability a metaphor of love, which we'd see so gladly as eternal! Therefore—since speech itself is metaphor, and expression itself is love—this makes the human race and the human individual inherently poetic and loving.

Since human beings experience the flower as a divine messenger who brings the intuition of the cyclical nature of human destiny, we are innately predisposed to the use of imagination in the interpretation of what it has to say, and to marvel at it. The hyacinth is a wonder and cannot be only itself. Its riddle holds the unhealable pain of a god, the monument of a death and a lamentation. Those first tazettas which rose from the ground at the order of the lord of the underworld were so overwhelming a wonder that the glorious dancer, Demeter's child, despite all warning on Hades' beguiling blossoms, cried out in delight and plucked one, and fell into the power of the god. The narcissus, which in southern climes grows wild on the banks of streams, is the shadow of a creature of such great beauty that he couldn't resist the gaze of his own reflection in a pool of water, and, fusing with it, met his death within it. The message of the flower is death, the message of the flower is life, is survival, and life after death, and remaining behind. It is the reawakening of a life which has experienced death, which cannot forget death, which in the guise of the human heart bewails it, which as the human soul overcomes it, through a new creativity that transforms pain, by constructing an image of an image. The five crimson spots that initially appear on the petals of the blossoming Prophet flower, the *Arnebia*, only then to disappear, are drops of angel's blood which fell to the earth as heaven and hell struggled for the Prophet's immortal soul, and which came to rest on a flower: they return to heaven. The legends of Hyakinthus, Narcissus and Adonis are famous and illustrious moments from our classical education and its emphasis on the Greeks, but these tales have counterparts among even the simplest peoples, and all of them point to the same kernel of human experience. Not always has a blunted gaze ignored the beauty of the common field bindweed. How the archaic German temperament accepted and finally spiritualized this sharp, sensual experience of beauty is found in one of the loveliest and least-known tales of the Grimm Brothers: "Our Lady's Little Glass." Mistakenly seen as belonging to a genre of "flower sagas," most of our culture's insights into the essence of flowers have now been entirely forgotten: so much so that only a few of the very oldest names of plants, in our own and related languages, allow us to guess at the little stories in which once they must have been recorded. And what names they are! Solomon's seal and "Aaron's staff" (*Aaronstab,* for the calla lily), crown imperial, and "king's candle" (*Königskerze,* for mullein), Christ's thorn and "heaven's key" (*Himmelsschlüssel,* for *Primula officinalis*), leopard's bane, and foxglove! In what deep and forgotten story must Solomon have impressed his seal, and the fox worn gloves, in explanation of the mystery of a woodland flower! Did the leopard choke on those beautiful, yellow, star-shaped flowers, *Doronicum pardalianches*, that so nobly sway in mountain woods, and lie down to die among them? And is the tooth of that dog to be seen as embodied, or rather as ensouled in that quiet, alpine dog's tooth violet, the *Erythronium*, which grows in wild, shady groves.

These stories were not simply spun and invented as a game, no more so than those of Adonis and Narcissus. They mark the discovery within the flower of something related to the human being—since this, instead of any talk of "anthropomorphic thinking," is the way we best refer to the spiritual process from which they spring—and such movements are inextricably intertwined with everything that makes us human, with *Humanitas*, with the oneness of the human soul. And proof will be found—if proof is needed—in their being in no way confined to gray prehistoric times. The discovery of the second life that lies behind the flower—the awe of that discovery and the passionate need to give that awe a form—extends as well into our own times, and will never end until the final disappearance of the human race. Here in our midst, Lenau discovered the primrose, Platen the honeysuckle, Goethe once again the hyacinth. Since truly human human beings have always understood that beautiful thin young trees in secret are beautiful thin young women—immortal, or, more bitterly, demi-mortal—Goethe could close the Helen act with the retransformation before our eyes of its tender chorus into poplars and fruit trees and cypresses: in verses charged with passionate longing lithe bodies and sleek trunks, carriage and bearing, hair and foliage grow so related to one another as finally to become indistinguishable. Möricke discovered the *Datura suaveolens*—since what remains of the scientific botany of this radically exotic tropical plant in his revelation of "Diana's Flower"? Why Diana's? And the pair of lovers who stand before it, inhaling its perfume: how does their own intoxication link to the riot of this drowsy incantation? Do they increase it, fuse with it, or perhaps displace it? Ah, such confusion and delirium! Yet precisely this delirium is what this tiny drama, no more than a few verses long, calls forth from the flower itself, just as with antiquity's interpretations of flowers. It calls it forth by placing Möricke's heart within the flower: Möricke's heart and Möricke's delirium. Because this flower is secretly a new Peregrina: "He seems to bring it up from the bosom's depth, Where such gold abounds in sacred sorrow"—"You desire me boldly to enflame you, you and myself, You smile and offer me death in this chalice full of sin."

Yes, the deep need of the human spirit to express and indeed to experience itself through plants and flowers will not be seen to have found its limits in the discovery of already extant flowers; instead, it has made itself a creative force and torn itself free from nature, thus taking the final step, the step of invention, no less decisively in the world of thought than it has done pictorially with freely developing arabesques. "What doesn't exist" has been known to take the form of a god, a woman, or a hero; and finally, in the very same way, it can also take the form of a flower. The flower belongs to the highest sphere to which the human being can rise: the sphere of his chimeras. Goethe's archetypal plant and Novalis' blue flower appeared in the course of the same decade and in the geographical environment of the same cultural circle. Goethe's "ulterior" rose and Jean Paul's astonished floral faces—which borrow almost nothing from the features of actual plants than their names—burst out in all directions from the sphere of sense perception; and as visionary intuitions in a region of imaginative and pictorial research they transcend into a realm which itself has been freely created. Speculative botany and the longings of imagination reveal their full humanity in new, immortal myths of plants and flowers, repeating now again what once in remote and ancient times took place in India, Egypt, and Greece. *Humanitas* draws its own ring around that circle of mortal images of bare and simple nature which the human mind, in its immortality, perceives to be too narrow. The plant shares the paradox of the human being: both pre-exist the created world. So, human beings, while returning toward their birthright, toward eternity, hold it in their hands, like the women on Grecian urns; like the Samoan girl as she walks toward a friend; like Sappho, who can never be imagined in any other way than with one of the countless flowers which she tirelessly and happily counted in her hands; like Ophelia.

The flower is the form in which the plant prepares for love and holds its bridal feast; and this lifts this stage of its shifting configuration toward the corresponding phase in the cycle of human life, binding both to a season. Spring, the flower, and love are felt by the human soul—with no need for proof or experience—to be a sacred, natural trinity. Science has simply shown the grounds that support such a point of view, whereas the human being has long been fully aware of the fact itself. We look at the colors of the blossom, with its lures that resemble eyes and faces. We regard the gesture of its organs of courtship around the secret seat of the bride; We savor its delicate, powerful perfume, the attire that so peremptorily sets itself apart from leaves, the bashful glances that issue from a chaos of green. These, we know, belong to countless means through which the root-bound creature broadens the range of its power, in compensation for its lack of locomotion, and makes all creatures who enter its area little more than its guests. All this is clear to the human being, who himself is no less the flower's guest than bee, beetle and bird. Because this invitation, this eruption in the year's new season of the primal force of an always self-renewing creation, irresistibly transfigures the world of which he too is a creature and clothes it in a godly mantle of excitement and expectation.

Pedantry has attributed the flower with cunning, intentional systems through which it is reputed in this or that way to compensate the insect, in order to assure its pollination. But the mystery is far more profound, and hinges on the reality of universal communication. The plant's deepest impulse—as with every other creature—is found in the forces through which it opposes and overcomes its deepest shortcomings. The plant is confined to the ground in which it's rooted; but this also means that of all creatures it must be the most itinerant. Whatever has wings or feet becomes its vehicle. But it is only from the nuptial peak of its cycle of life that the plant can unleash this arcane power which it wields far and wide over all mobile creatures; and from there it is by way of a common intoxication that the plant speaks with every living creature, even the greatest: they communicate through the whole etheric network of the plant's enunciation and articulation of what it shares with him. Since, in any case, yes, these are things they share. The flower's bridal chamber recalls our own, and it summons up notions of courtship, yearning, communion and arousal, as directed toward itself; and after arousal the bitter longing for consummation, appeasement and fruit. Since the call is one and the same, it is heard and answered, its excitement overflows and makes itself irresistible, as consonance and communication. The odor of flowers is a dark, powerful excitation that releases the whole of its overwhelming force within the senses of other living creatures. It travels so securely from the organs of transmission that reside in the plant to those of reception in the human being because, in fact, they are the poles of the same charge and discharge. It is not dispatched and taken in as musk or vanilla; it is something serious. The human excitements it encounters, and which it calls into play, inexpressibly, are vegetative excitations which never bow to individuality: they are forces of which odor and color and form in the plant are themselves extreme expressions. What's brewed and distilled over there, burgeoning and taking flight… what it is inside ourselves that drowsily ripens and seethes, thrusts and desires, colors and resounds and effervesces, gleams and assumes a form… these things are driven by the same innermost causes in the chemistry of life, and they bond together the plant and the human being in the same bittersweet riddle of precisely those explosions in which they seem to find their resolution, only then to withdraw again, and to settle down into our roots. Man shares the hunger of the rootless animal, which he resembles in the hunt for food. Yet in loving, he resembles the plants. That first commonality may disgust him, since he is ashamed of hunger. Love, in order that it have no cause to be ashamed of him, is something of which he must only extend the range, carrying it forward from the level of the plants—that noble, ancient race with which he shares it—and placing it beneath the sign of the God who from even remoter times is likewise inborn within him. Yet even where love is most divine, at its highest elevation, he will find no cause to deny or betray the candor of its origins in vegetation and the vegetative joy of the fusion of the sexes. Asexuality and hermaphroditism are animal abominations, as part of the fall from the laws of God's creation.

So, for months at a time the nuptials of the plants become a dizzy, impelling vortex which draws all living creatures toward itself, seducing them and bringing them together, ruling the earth's very atmosphere and promising to raise it closer to the skies. The nectar that sparkles its invitation from the brightly colored corolla, as though it were only food, is a love potion, the perfume an incantation, the pollen a bewitchment. Separations between the forms of life subside, and the human being steps back to behind the scenes of the drama of individuality and enters once again into the Whole, into a hidden yet intuited mode of Being. The flower takes control of his thoughts and speech. He plucks flowers, and makes gifts of them. Flowers become his similes and terms of comparison, and he feels his feelings grow clear to him through the use of such comparisons. Flowers are the language spoken by love. Well over half the names of all our native flowers are the sweet inventions of lovers: a secret language for those who are happy and those who are not, for the lonely and those held apart from them, for the prisoner and the closely guarded: "thousand-fold beauty" (*Tausendschön,* for sweet William), "hold-me-in-your-thoughts" (*Gedenkemein,* for Omphalodes), forget-me-not, "ardent longing" (*Brennede Liebe,* for scarlet lightning), "tearful heart" (*Tränende Herzen,* for bleeding heart), heartsease, "love-grows-with-time" (*Jelängerjelieber,* for honeysuckle), *pensée,* "heart-mate" (*Herzgespan,* for Leonurus), lovage, "male fidelity" (*Mannestreu,* for sea holly), "befitting love" (*Maßlieb,* for the field daisy), "no turning back" (*Wendunmut,* for hellebore), "prize of honor" (*Ehrenpreis,* for speedwell), love-in-a-mist, *belle de nuit,* "ring flower" (*Ringelblume,* for marigold), love-lies-bleeding, "touch-me-not" (*Ruhmichnichtan,* for sensitive plant), fair maids of France. And then those sour, hurtful moments called "step-mother" (*Stiefmütterchen,* for pansy) "foul hauteur" (*Stinkende Hoffart,* for *Tagetes*), "rasper" (*Schabab,* for Nigella), adder's-tongue, "gossip rose" (*Klatschrose,* for corn poppy), "out of favor" (*Ungnad*—an unidentified flower in a poem by Hoffmann), bittersweet, wormwood, nightshade. In the language of archetypal symbols, the violet and the lily are the highest celebration of the female spirit, even to the fancy of the suitor whose aims are neither chaste nor bashful: they symbolize purity and self-concealment. And the act of which words are forbidden to speak is referred to as "plucking the rose." This is our oldest metaphor for victory over that last resistance, as though men were innately predisposed to see the creature they desire hold high her prize in the form of a flower, with everything around it striving to pluck it or snap its stem. This is the origin of "saying it with flowers," of *conter fleurette,* of "florid" language; and this shared, passionate longing dispels all difference between the peasant boy, who on Saturday evening at the garden gate begs for a flower to wear next morning to church, and the highest poet, who exclaims: "How beautiful she was, how good! I would have given my blood as water for her flowers."

Man, woman, and flower is an archetypal scheme of human behavior. Picked, offered, given, and preserved, the flower passes from hand to hand: it is the simplest, plainest and most natural gift, and as well both less and more. Less than a gift, since a transient thing does not enrich, and therefore creates no obligation. More than a gift, since one must have stooped to gather it, and placed one's humility within it. "This nosegay I have picked, Greets you a thousand times, I have bent down to pluck it, A thousand times, And pressed it to my heart, Hundreds of thousand times." Only a flower can witness and vouch for the moment which has seen such feelings demand the gathering of a similar thought from a well-protected heart, so as then to melt into one with it.

So, it's the very *humanity* of poetry, since the poet is only what the human being, just as always in the past, will always be, our immanence and transcendence…it is poetry's most basically human thrust that binds the poet to the flowers below, just as to the stars above. The fact, as said before, that the human soul is more related to the flower than to the animal—from which we do not descend, since instead we have shed the animal…this quietest of secrets lies concealed in poetry. There is also the fact of the flower as the simplest embodiment of the human dilemma of the ceaseless alternation of love and death. And poetry, again, is eternally its fullest witness. For the authentic poetry of love and death, this lies too plainly in the light of day to be denied. The courtship song and the song of mourning have in every epoch found their point of departure in the flower, in its coming and passing away—or at least in a concept of nature in which the image of the plant is predominant. The bond between naive poetry and the seasons of song is intertwined with flowers, and verse that makes a willful attempt to circumvent habitual imagery soon encounters them again, having traced through circles that finally reapproach them from unexplored directions. And the thought that such surrounding frames of decorative floral imagery might only be external collides with the knowledge that all great poetry, by no matter what poet, has also offered an involuntary portrait of the world of the plants of its time. This is to be seen in Ionian epic, no less than in Dante; in Aeolian lyric and again in imperial Augustan verse; in the heroic poetry of the kingdom of Israel, just as in the songs of Provence; and so on, throughout the centuries. We learn more about the flora of the Greek coasts and mountain meadows from Greek poetry than from Theophrastus and Dioscorides. Its bright, unbroken colors bloom where Persephone vanishes beneath the ground; where Sappho plaits garlands with her lost love in her thoughts; where the powerful Pindar's odes celebrate the infant hero who is born in secret and takes the name of a violet, since violets and gillyflower overgrow his hiding place. They're in every place where a surfeit of intoxicating metaphor sees the much loved lips and cheeks of ardent youth to bear the colors and forms of flowers which a manly people of passionate lovers may perhaps have made no attempt to plant, but all the more vigorously strove to pluck.

The young Dante was a city dweller, imprisoned in the hard, flowerless Middle Ages where nearly nothing was cultivated, and where a tree was such a singular sight as to be able to lend its name, wherever it once may have stood, to a street, or even to a whole city quarter. He belonged to an era in which social and poetic excursions into a never fully dangerless "countryside" were always overpainted with an artificial pastoral tone derived from former literature, bare of all fresh perception. And the Dante of the middle period, who lived within the walls of castles, belonged to the epoch of Bertran de Born, when the chivalric code instructed a man just how far he could allow himself to be a human being, and banned to that degree all parks and gardens. But the Dante who lived in exile—poor, heartbroken, and persecuted—derided the protections of castle walls and the strictures of suits of armor, became fully a human being, and gardens and flowers stood immediately open before him. He constructed the garden of hell—haunted and unforgettable—where plants live and bleed, receiving and inflicting lacerations. And the heavenly garden of the enormous Centifolia tree, of which the leaves are alive, and offer benedictions. He built gardens where weighty, fateful wanderings always find a moment of rest: the alpine garden where the shades of princes sit, with the radiant, jewel-like colors of its flora minutiously described; the magnificent grove of earthly paradise; then not only on toward the rain of flowers which angels' hands let drop on the appearance of Beatrice—this renewal of Virgil's *Manibus date lilia plenis*—but also toward that last, singular form of vegetation at the mountain heights where nothing further is allowed to grow, and where the foot can rise no higher if not by treading the air. He places the *Salix glacialis* at the end of the earthly world, between Eünoè and Lethe. Flowers and weeds; plants that germinate true to seed and others that degenerate; the seasons and the intuitive relationships between the stars and the growth of plants. Such things must ceaselessly have run through his mind, since these are the kinds of images in which his imagination lived.

Similar observations, on which it here would be capricious to insist, might continue down the course of the centuries. But they don't again become imperative until the moment—with Goethe—when all possibilities of human relationship with the world of the fourth day of creation were drawn together at a new and different level: the moment when the poet—as a man of passion, as a human being, and also as a gardener—enrolled himself without reserve in the school of plants—seeing it as a place of knowledge, intuition, research and contemplation—and fully entered their world, then later to be reborn from it and to make his way back home with the immeasurable gifts that it alone could have given him. He had discovered organic life to be the God-given impulse for all natural development from out of a concentrated seed; he had learned that the living human spirit is an organism; he had understood the morphology of the phenomenon of the human being and poet. As a practicing gardener, Goethe planted plants and sowed seeds; he constructed parks and gardens, and while doing so plumbed their poetry with all his heart; as Werther he cultivated peas and happily cooked them; like Dürer he stared into the miniature world of grasses and experienced the notion of the microcosm, not with the impertinence of the magnifying glass but by way of the creative eye. In powerful verses and supernally sure and incisive prose, he gave descriptions of the *habitus* of plants such as no one else has done, if not perhaps for Humboldt. The feelings and thoughts which he expressed through likenesses of plants are so keen, clear and beautiful that they might be likenesses of gods. With the *Urpflanze*—the primordial plant—he dreamed one of the greatest dreams which since the time of Plato's mythic thought the world has been privileged to dream. And he closed all the open circles of this relationship to plants, drawing them together into a larger symbolic whole, by using a garden as the setting for the only novel in which he attempted to delineate the inner workings of a group of human beings, rather as though they constituted a stand of vegetation. Externally viewed—yet not so entirely externally—*Elective Affinities* is the story of the construction of a landscape garden by a group of persons who are intimately linked with one another while nonetheless hovering as though in the air and tending to draw apart. He was the historical protagonist and active conclusion of the entirety of an epoch in the understanding of plants, from the scattered Rococo flowers of "Zephyr, take this upon your wings, and carry it to the garment of my beloved" (and from the powerful, underlying drive of the "Rose of the Heath") to the *Ginkgo biloba* which we find in his *Divan*—where he speaks of "the leaves of this tree that enters my garden from the East"—and on to Germany's first exhibition of dahlias, which Humboldt visited at his side. And as a poet he so thoroughly encompassed the man who plucks the flower, the lover who proffers gifts of them, the gardener who grows them, the scientist who researches them, as to leave all his observations on flowering and living plants with the impress of a body of views, convictions and knowledge which are indissolubly intertwined with one another. Those so lacking in gratitude as to call his *scientific research* poetic really ought not even dare to deny the value of the natural-historical discoveries in his *poetry*. And despite all this, what's truly essential still remains to be said.

Goethe—who passionately experienced our vegetive commonality with the plants, and who sang it in "Ganymede"—so powerfully discerned the interdependence of necessity and form, which he learned from the plants, and established it so thoroughly as a fundamental law of the life of every organism, in opposition to the notions of freedom and idea, as finally to temper the force of Kant and Schiller, and the century's dominant German ideal thus held true to the "spirit and garb" of creation. Kant had decreed, "The starry skies above me, and moral law within me." And Goethe emended, even if these words in *"Urworte"* seem directed only to the planets and the sun, "You are as you must be. You have no escape from yourself...internally determined form that in living unfolds and develops." It was the task of poetry to learn the pain of such an order, and precisely at the point where it painlessly and powerfully rises from the ground to declare its opposition to the passionate disorder of freedom, and only then, and still again, to counter the pain of this insight by holding out the offer of hope. The essence of mortality can never be voiced by mortality itself. Only immortality can furnish the measure of the mortal. The flower addresses the human being. In this sense, it blooms for the human being alone. And, again in this sense, only the epitome of the human being, the poet, is the true and fully formed gardener. That Dante, like Goethe, would have been such a gardener if the epoch and destiny of this greatest of mendicants had allowed him something more than a first intuition of a garden is clear to those who see Marco's speech in *Purgatory* to couple necessity and freedom, form and error, conjoining them in a single system in which both will forever and again appear to the poet, no matter the epoch into which his destiny sends him: "O star and flower, spirit and garb, love, pain, time and eternity."

CHAPTER II

The Garden and the Human Being

A GARDENER is a person who plants flowers. Planting flowers depends on having them. There is more than one way to go about that. We have collected them where we have found them; careful not to harm them, we have cut off parts of them, and replanted those cuttings; we have raised them from their wild seed; and the offspring of the plants obtained in these ways has been newly reproduced, and again replanted.

The urge artificially to settle plants in places near our homes, to possess them as living creatures, has many roots, of great antiquity. The oldest reach back into the agriculture of the peoples who work with plots of ground which are irrigated and precisely circumscribed, and where tillage is garden-like; which is to say where cereals, vegetables, grapes, fruit, medicinal plants and seasoning herbs are all grown together—beside, right after, and between one another—and where this multitude must all be bent to an order that descends from prehistoric times, simply to fit them into the space. Roots of similar depth sink down into the customs of religious life. Ever since the third millennium B.C., Near Eastern temples have been acquainted with baskets and vases charged with flowers, presented as votive offerings—as the recent excavations at Bogazköy have once again made clear. The abundant flowers required for the regular observance of such a practice could only have been assured, in Mesopotamia, by raising them. The spaces in which they were grown belonged most probably to the temples themselves, and we know that similar cultivations were found at rulers' palaces. Queen Semiramis' hanging gardens were also famous in the West, and must owe that fame to having stood at the apex of the art of gardening as the whole of antiquity knew it. They were terraces, irrigated by streams of water that descended from one to the next. Such structures are recurrent in southern lands, where conditions of climate and terrain demand them, and we will note them again and again. By nature, they are highly artificial and presuppose systems of rectangular volumes and surfaces; they likewise tend to divide into quarters and to arrange themselves around a center. Fundamentally regular and geometric, they reflect the geometric architecture of the buildings typically adjacent to them.

But this mysterious human need has other roots as well, and they go beyond all questions of utility, no matter how coarse or ennobled. They connect with the possession of nature as such, with the creation of an essence, of an extract of nature, behind walls or a hedge, set off and delimited and qualified, like one's own house, as a property distinct from any common good. The old Persian paradises (the Avestan *pairi-daësa* means only "rampart") were more than hunting reserves for the great. While leading his campaign against the Greeks, Xerxes called his hordes to a halt in front of a magnificent tree. The tree had moved him, and he ordered that a sacrifice be made to its trunk, bewreathed and decked with ribbons, as a thing of sacred beauty. Eastern Asia since time immemorial has known the artful distillate of nature and landscape—in the form of the tiny landscape garden—not as a region of geometry and symmetry, but as a place charged with *meaning*. The old Chinese and Japanese, like the ancient Persians, saw the garden as a place of experience. The Chinese planted trees in it, the Japanese drew together stones, water, hillocks, shrubbed depressions, and a very few, if any at all, solitary flowers—rare and highly meaningful plants—to fashion a landscape of the soul, and then carefully listened to catch the voice of what they had placed within it. Such gardens, too, embody principles of order, no matter how closely they may play at imitating the wilderness. The forest became a royal park by passing through the human spirit. The Orient's gardens for thinkers and dreamers are epigrams that address the longing of the human soul for solitude and repose. One cannot always travel and ride, as a way of finding seclusion. One creates an abode for the experience of travel, for the need to experience seclusion, siting it just before the door to the house, or just outside the palace or castle gates. The flower, the plant, the bush is by no means the enclosure's primary goal, and at most is only one of its many components, even if an indispensable one. Surely, however, the plant—and the flower first of all—accepts no instructions on the measure of its rights within the human soul. The plant's hegemony is limitless, and how most creatively to come to terms with such a power is left to the human imagination. The oldest forms of cultured attention to Asia's magnificent wild flowers developed, after all, in countries where traditional gardening rejects the use of flowers: in China, Japan and Persia. Plants and flowers turned the Chinese and the Japanese into painters; the Persians into carpet weavers; and those carpets are reflections not only of the world of the country's gardens, but also of the world of its plants. The Orient already possessed a range of cultivated varieties of the peony, the mallow and the primrose when beech forests were still reflected in the waters of the Mediterranean coasts, just as they are today in the seas that bathe the shores of Holstein. The original, wild variety of the *Primula sinensis*—like the original variety of wheat—still remains to be discovered, and may indeed have grown extinct in prehistoric times. The search among the wild carnations of the Mediterranean cliffs for the original form of our garden carnation has likewise been in vain. It points, like the rose, toward Persia, but the species from which it derives can no longer be exactly identified. The magnificent *Regelia-Oncocyclus* class of irises, enormous creatures with an otherwise unheard-of scale of colors in cobalt and olive, black and pink, brown and bluish green, silver-gray and crimson—of which we only cultivate a single, "light" form, the *Iris susiana* or "lady in mourning"—stems from Persian wildflowers, and its blossoms are wholly as fabulous as their startling figures on Persian carpets. Their renown was so great that vanquished peoples of the Near East, according to the evidence of mural paintings, could bring them to the Pharaohs as their nation's tribute. Their breeding and cultivation in places outside their homeland is a highly difficult challenge. But the Persians already had crossed them with one another and created more docile varieties, and they portrayed these new creations on their woven carpets.

The first signs of the still today unchanging tension—the eternal tension—between the flower and the garden are just so old and aboriginal. They seek each other out, in order then to fly apart. The human attachment to the flower—at a hypothetical extreme—can dispense with the garden, just as the human attachment to the garden has at times been known to find expression almost wholly without flowers, and indeed with a minimum of plants. The flower embodies an order, but the garden does the same, and its order is different and separate. The order within the flower is prehuman, and governs the flower itself. The garden speaks of human modes of order, where man is master, subduer, and transformer. The human being connects with the flower by way of unreasoned longing; with the garden by way of will. With the flower by way of boundless possibility; with the garden by way of the acceptance of limitation, which is almost the same as renunciation. The man of the garden—the gardener—lives on the wealth of this tension; just as the whole of mankind's garden—the history of the human garden and all its crises—lives on it. This tension has two valences. It not only separates the garden from the flower, despite their mutual attraction; it also cleaves the human being into his contradictory parts, thus bringing him face to face with his truest, most legitimate dialectic. The human being issues orders to himself, but by no means always obeys them, or at least not right away. He acquiesces, as the case may be, either from the bottom of his heart, or not at all. He defies his circumstances, or plays with them. Or perhaps he always plays with everything: he has just renounced, only a moment ago, but already thinks no more about renunciation, and instead turns everything upside down and desires the impossible. Because the garden was, and still remains, the space in which the human being inscribes his relationship with nature into a structure. And how do we describe this relationship? As love, as hate, or as both? Is it a flight *toward* nature or *away* from it? Is it a humanization of nature, or the penitent's return into the riches of chaos? The garden has witnessed and expressed all this throughout the millennia and the centuries. Each of these various attitudes has at some point furnished the coordinates for a particular type of garden. In times as discordant as our own, most of these various kinds of gardens are even to be found beside one another, as contemporaries. There are gardens today which consist of a playing field, a tennis court, a children's playground with a sandbox, a courtyard where the wash is hung, closed in among four walls, one with a fruit tree espaliered against it, the second and third with bushes and trees and provided with an arbor and a bench, and along the fourth a strip of earth that provides the so-called "fillings" for the dwelling's flower vases: a strip of earth that someone or other has planted full with some such thing or another for so and so much the half-dozen. That's a perfectly legitimate arrangement and expresses a legitimately conceived and self-contained relationship with nature no less perfectly than the one on the other side of the road, with its artful imitation of a natural flowered wilderness: planted wild flowers, a marsh garden, a rock garden, blossoms clustered into groups. Or the one at the house next door, with a formal garden where the flower beds show each its particular colors: only blue and yellow, only orange and violet, only rose and white and crimson, tall, medium and low borders. Everything goes. The earth obeys all whims. It's covered with flowers or free from flowers, in accord with whatever its restless master asks of it. It consists of a sand pit, or of twenty running meters of *Verbena venosa*, reddish lilac, all in a row. But whatever it is is finally a human statement, and of a kind that's relentless and inflexible. Because a garden is always a notion of order, and cannot be otherwise; it is the scale that measures the precise proportions of the human relationship with nature, and which gives it coherent expression. As a question of order it is also a question of example, education and redemption, since these are the things with which all notions of order are concerned. What the human being shares with nature, what we demand from nature and entrust to nature, what we long for and reject, this may all become song and poetry, or music and philosophy, or myth and religion; but in the visible world it must sooner or later become a garden, if it desires to make itself visible at all; and the achievement of visibility—as distinct from simple thinkability, and understandability—is its most irresistible drive, as an inherent part, like all the creative drives of the human race, of the one primordial drive to give birth to structure. So the garden is not only *permitted* to the human race; it is also *imposed* upon us. Rather than simply a whim, the garden is also a law. Because rather than only a human creation, it is also, as an instinct, one of the preconditions of human life. It is the reality with which we may surely play, and which we may also avoid, but into which we must return. It is not nature, no matter how much it seems to be; and no matter how much it may appear to scoff at nature, it constitutes the balance sheet that governs the assessment of a relationship in which nature is the secret, invisible, constant principle of orientation. It calculates the sums, and eternally adjusts that orientation. Because the garden—to sum all of this up—is a basic and perpetual human institution which with victorious tenacity always affirms its right to exist, independently of circumstances. Gardens have been crafted beneath a rain of bullets, and while bombs fall from aircraft; they stand on the roofs of skyscrapers; on the window sills of tenth-floor flats; on cactus shelves in sprawling, box-like housing developments; among rusting wrecks of automobiles and heaps of old tin cans on the outskirts of ailing cities. Because the institution which the garden represents—here returning to a concept already employed and giving it greater substance—is an institution of redress, what one calls a "compensation," and in this sense, too, a corrective. The human being embodies a tension between a nature which has since been lost and an unreachable Divine Creator. The garden stands at precisely the center of this tension and displaces itself, in accord with its fluctuations in the epoch and the individual, toward one or toward the other: toward nature or creativity. This is the deepest reason for which the human being dreams that our origins lie in a garden, and that the garden is the place in which we achieve enlightenment; this is why we hope to find redemption in a garden, and why we look for solace there; why we feel the innate desire to love in a garden, to make commitments in a garden; why a betrothal prefers the humblest arbor of calabash to the most elegant bar; why Plato most naturally is thought of as thinking in the garden of Akademos, and Epicurus in the one which was simply known as "garden," *kepos*. This, indeed, is why even in front of his flight into vice the human being will hang up the veil that says "rose garden," or *joshiwara*. So, when times are stark, the garden too will be stark, but a garden will be there. In arid times, charged with anxiety, bleak and insecure like our own, the garden will be a sand pit, but will not be missing. In epochs when the sense of nature is stable, and holds its own particular form as the highest model for *humanitas*, men build Versailles and Bobolis, and sing their praises in verse. And in epochs in which the sense of nature experiences elementary crisis, they go about the felling of hedges, fountains and Oreads while trilling out the tune of Goethe's maiden and its shameless parody of the great excitements of the times: "Dear Mother, my playmates now have been my torture for, oh, so long a time." The extent to which peoples culturally and spiritually conquer one another will also be seen in their reciprocal exchange of these ideal structures through which they adjust their sense of self by way of a relationship with nature. The Hellenistic garden of Alexandria, which itself was an Egyptian version, in Egyptian colors, of the Greek garden, was to cover Rome with visual interpretations of the same small and melancholy idyll that the music of Alexandrian poetry was to breathe over Roman elegy. Italy was to impose its Renaissance garden on the France of the three Louis, and by way of Vienna its Baroque garden on the Germans—just as for a century it imposed on both its northern neighbors the whole of its spirit of form in every field—with an architectural emphasis disinclined to colors, solemnly proud, and vibrantly classical. And when England's still wild freedom and melancholy health did away with continental gardens and poetics, Italy's tradition of fictitious antiquity and eternal Arcadia likewise found itself supplanted. England preferred to plant parks and to force one either to cry with Ossian, or to be stirred by the Vicar of Wakefield, or by the desolate images of Gray and Goldsmith.

All of these gardens and garden forms—just like those of Semiramis and the Syrian Diadochi, of Alexandria, of Lucullus and the Roman Optimates—were ideal worlds in which a since lost nature is seen as mankind's home, and realized anew in the real world: so many islands of Calypso, shot through with reflections of ancient times; paradises; royal, princely, lavish gambles, in pursuit of the impossible. They all communicate with one another, and despite the centuries that separate them, they form a single dynasty that's full of reversions to its own past, and which descends from a single line of ancestors. Each invokes the antiquity of the one before it, and finally they all presuppose one another, which after all is only logical, since the stages of the fall from the "golden age" may be as numerous and reciprocally contradictory as anyone might say, but the golden age itself, the past, the human spirit and nature are one. The Egyptian garden's small abandoned temple and tiny altar to the Faun stood again, as frescos show, in the gardens of imperial Rome; since that time they may just as well have stood anywhere, in the gardens of any century, much as now they stand in Weimar and Muskau. And even though these garden worlds were the realization of compensatory dreams on the part of single, mighty, princely persons—inclusive, quite understandably, of great and powerful soldiers—they also quickly turned into proud national treasures, and their forms left visible traces on even the most modest of the gardens of lesser individuals. There had to be places where money was spent with god-like prodigality—"thrown away" is the common phrase—so that even the poorest provincial corner might capture a golden ray of form and meaning. Only envy is anti-social. Like the peoples and centuries, the social stations too shared their dreams of an ideal world of nature, and gradations from one to the next were gentle and gradual, if not close to imperceptible. The human being and the human spirit are everywhere the same.

But all these forms of the garden drew up their plans on a vast scale, and those plans made no provision for flowers; rather than pull them into their order, they ordered them out. Flowers, to be sure, were always there, as in ancient China and Persia, more or less on the garden's flanks, but modestly, and cramped. The everyman assortment of cultivated flowers remained still everywhere the same, and consisted only of the staples of the old Mediterranean countries: wallflower, Jacob's ladder, the lily, the Greek crocus, the antique rose in a limited number of double forms, the mallow, carnation and snapdragon that grow on southern crags and in southern kitchen gardens. The monasteries, which had brought them over the mountains, held tightly onto them. The bulwark that stood before the flower and assured its survival throughout the centuries in which the garden excluded it consisted of the monastery gardens, or, rather, of the monastery and peasant gardens, which formed a single, indivisible whole. The priests and country folk, a resilient group, extolled by the poets, preserved the most ancient human intuition of the scope and balance of nature, as revealed in the image of the flower. The old assortment of cultivated plants was expanded, fine wildflowers of local growth were transplanted, naïve delight in color and form found symbols and dreams of love in neighboring fields and woods. Monk's hood and primrose, columbine and "Turk's tulip" (*Tulipa greigi*), larkspur and foxglove immigrated into the colorful profusion between the onion and the cabbage: for altar decorations, Sunday bouquets, garlands for girls. The princely garden, which embodies an order, has few if any flowers; the world of these little gardens which overflow with flowers embodies no order and obeys no order: it is simply a drive that derives from a natural need, and it develops skills through which that need can be gratified. These skills were already highly developed. Gardening orders of monks, such as the Carthusians and Capuchins, learned and taught. And southern flora, which nearly without exception is shy of moisture and in need of warmth, was by no means here excluded because "it doesn't survive our winters," and instead marked the point where the arts of cultivation were most cunningly employed. Garden terrains were drained, cold terrains were sheltered. Jacob's ladder and gillyflower, and of course the carnation first of all, become potted plants. In long years of cultivation, double and hybrid forms, large-flowered forms and dwarfs came into existence as a matter of course. Seeds and cuttings traveled from cloister to cloister, from village to village. Myrtle and basil were shielded on sunny window sills. The cowshed revealed its capacity for storing warmth. The northern hotbed protected plants much as during Tacitus' time huts of mud and dung had protected women and children.

This state of affairs, however, was to feel the effects of two groundshaking events: the fall of Constantinople and the discovery of America. The sixteenth century—in which those effects grew slowly ever more undeniable and finally overwhelming, to the point of deciding the tension between the garden and the flower—became the first high point of a process of which the end still today is not in sight. Asia and America, as a second wave, following the flood which had come from the Mediterranean, were to change the ways in which the peoples of Europe understood the flower. Thanks to the Turks, the decorative plants of the East, first of all from Persia, became initially Dutch and Habsburg-Austrian, then French, English and German. The tropical and subtropical plants which arrived from the "West Indies"—of which the bean, the potato, tobacco, maize, and later the tomato, the eggplant, and the garden pepper revolutionized Europe's foods and food-related needs—also consisted of a flood of flowers which burst through every sluice and began an inundation of Europe which even today remains unconcluded. Sunflowers and beauty-of-the-night, from Texas and Peru, were at first imported for the oils and rhizomes that made them dubious pleasures, like the poppy of the East. Once their flowers established their appeal to Western sensibilities, drawing others along in their wake, the cataract was to know no halt.

The exclusion of flowers from the Western garden in the grand style derived from Italy. When the Italics, Latins, Romans and Italians strive to return to nature—which they do with a passion unequaled by any other people—they dream of a lost paradise in which they were allowed to be simple farmers, and they direct the prayers of their tragico-historical condition as a race of suffering city dwellers to the primordial gods of rural worlds of order, rigorously sober and with clear discriminations between the real and the desirable, culture and nature. With Horace, it isn't only that we enter a world where nothing any longer blooms; he speaks, instead, with the archaic voice of his peninsula's religion of rural life and forbids all blossoming flowers. The rose is allowed, where it belongs in the company of wine and anointing oil, since in any case it quickly withers. Rich floral decoration, artfully contrived and displayed, is hateful Asia. A twig of myrtle, snapped from the nearest bush, is enough for you and me. An austere program, for obedient centuries. Yet it didn't apply for the doctor and the apothecary. In the shadow of Salerno's medical school, the world's first botanical garden was founded in 1320 by Matthias Salvaticus, and was thus contemporary to the dream gardens of Dante's courtly poetry. The medical school in Venice, the second heir, after Salerno, of Eastern medicine, received the aid of the Serenissima and established in 1333 the world's first great garden of medicinal plants, full of the rare and exotic. The Italian Renaissance was then to inherit these traditions and institutions, and united such collections of useful plants with its general compendiums of nature's manifold curiosities, both plant and animal. Gardens were annexed to the universities at Padua, Pisa and Bologna, and learned collectors like Mattioli, who clearly had already broken free of habitual Italian premises, had private collections of flowering plants. The great Italian gardens of the fifteenth and sixteenth centuries took in individual specimens as showpieces, oddities, rarities or curiosities to be admired, presenting them in isolation, as accents, or against contrasting backdrops. The strictly geometric hedge garden, obedient to shears that followed the guide of plumb lines and taut horizontal strings, remains the bronze-like scene of a semi-divine Arcadia. Since it begins to grow capricious, it plays with water and stone, with surprise, parody, and sculptural grotesques, with architectural structures and illusions. But it shies away from the flower. Since it has tired of black and green, white and gray, it summons colors from bright rocks, colored sands and artful arrangements of shards of glass, refusing however to paint with the palette of nature. It knew it could not subjugate the flower. The flower owes it no obedience. It its own way, the flower is as little open to compromise as this garden itself. The flower is cyclical, and this garden has assumed its geometric form precisely in order to escape from cyclic sufferings. The flower changes, and the garden wants to peer, at least for once, into immutability. The flower belongs to endlessness, whereas the garden has no desire to set itself adrift, hoping instead for solace in delimitations. Insofar as the flower belongs to an understanding of the fullness of nature, the garden indifferently assigns it a place as far away from itself as possible, at the university. Italian botany was to pay the price for this. The son of a poor German furrier, Konrad Gesner, from Zurich, was the first to examine its collections, along with lesser collections of his time, in the light of a principle of scientific classification. The great systematizers, from Gesner on through Linnaeus, Jussieu and de Candolle to Engler, include no representative of the people who invented the botanical garden. In as early as the sixteenth century, Italy's tradition of collecting plants had spread to Leiden, and was then to find its culmination in the world's first universal institution for the collection of plants. The Jardin des Plantes was founded by Louis XIII and his doctor Hérouard. Tournefort, its first truly authoritative director, was already Europe's first great botanist. But the garden of the time—the French garden—remained nonetheless within the tightly-fitting yoke of Western Roman tradition. Flowers found admittance to the *parterre des pièces coupées*, to the *rabatte*, at most to the *parterre de compartiment*, tightly packed into ornamental alleys, as color effects, treated in the very same way as the lifeless materials that served for similar effects: gravel, sand, clipped lawn, colored splinters of rock, bright slake, red porphyry gravel, coal. Among the pots where propped-up fruit trees grow on the terrace of the *orangerie*, some something here or there may cautiously be allowed to flower in a vase, on condition that it resemble a flower as little as possible. Relating to nature is a question of control, and thus of refuge from feelings that know no bounds or predictability. But in the course of what could see itself as a staunch defense of a circumscribed horizon of pure and colorless order—an order that discovers its secret soul in a lost ideal of culture—the flower had successfully circumvented the garden's proud front gates, and had sent out roots beneath it.

The flower had found a new garden, in historical terms, on the flanks of France. The Orient had conquered the Netherlands and had made them the world's most prominent center of floriculture. The Dutch tradition of landscape painting, starting with Ruysdael, had passed through Flanders and exerted an influence on Claude Lorrain, and would at least momentarily intrigue Poussin. On the other side of the Channel, it encouraged and reconfirmed the English bent for fantasy, while also making the acquaintance of fledgling interpretations of still uncertain notions of the garden of the Far East. The gardens of Austria's princes attracted flowers from the Orient, no less than from America by way of Spain, and their influence pressed forward into Germany, where it coalesced with the peasant and monastery gardens' hot, ingenuous thirst for flowers. Poetry unsealed the lips of the whole of this widely ranging impulse. The restricted spaces of the country homes of two English poets hosted the first free attempts to create a new, ideal structure: the park combined with the flower garden. Pope's small, irregular park near Strawberry Hill above the Thames, and Addison's famous planting were the germ of the first great "English gardens." Brockes, in Hamburg, depicted his flower garden in his *Earthly Pleasure in God*, and previously Spee had appointed new dignity to the monastery garden's world of flowers by employing its colors as the setting of his clerico-pastoral lyrics. Two centuries had to pass before the planet-wide upheaval which marked the eve of the high Renaissance could find its conclusion in the end of Europe's isolation as little more than a hinterland of the world of the Mediterranean and the oldest of its centers. Since the advance of the sultans, the world again had an Eastern as well as a Western Roman face, just as after the Conquistadors its face was Atlantic as well as European.

Byzantium had been the watershed between West and East, and as such the barrier between Europe and Asia: an impenetrable and fruitless barrier, as well as creaky and brittle and almost destined more to crumble than to be set aside. This barrier's collapse—in the same generation that saw Isabella's caravels, with America in tow, land in Spain—put an end to the antiquarianism, which had outlived its history, of the Western Roman Empire and of West Roman Europe—that first truly Western world—and shifted the weights on the balance of time toward the East. This world, which suddenly opened itself to the unpredictable, gravitated toward Vienna, where the artery from the Orient, once broken open, found its port, where Habsburg Spain and Flanders were solidly represented, and where the geopolitical relationships among Austria, England, Holland and Spain promoted uniformity not only in the interests and goods of their peoples, but also in their spiritual evolution. Europe's ideal worlds showed the features of the epoch at an earlier date than its real worlds. The stiff, humanistic garden of

Western Roman tradition—that nearly flowerless garden in which the ever more depleted legacy of Alexandria, Rome, and Italy was repeatedly inherited to death like an estate on its way to bankruptcy court—went under in the moment when Busbecq, traveling as envoy to the Sultan and Caliph from Emperor Ferdinand, first saw blossoming tulips in a garden in Hadrianople and purchased both their seeds and bulbs. No part of these events took place by chance; everything about them is history. The imperial ambassador was no Italian—an Italian would have ridden on—but a Dutchman, which is why he stopped and marveled. The tulip—of which the seed first blossomed five years later in Augsburg, in the patrician garden of Johann Heinrich Herwart, where in April it was seen and described by Zurich's Konrad Gesner, and which then, after eleven more years had passed, would begin to spread out from Mecheln, and already in 1579 from Brussels—had been no wild field flower of the northern Balkans: it was a cultivated flower from Persia, and already highly developed. The likes of this harbinger of the Western flower garden were something of which Europe could not have known. The Persian gardener, at whose side the Persian carpet weaver knotted rugs, had been carried along in the Turkish advance toward the west, just as the whole of the refined, dreamy, age-old Orient had been subsumed and incorporated into the Seljuq Caliphate. Busbecq stood among varieties of flowers which carried him back to Isfahan and Shiraz; and like a true German Dutchman, he collected all the seed he could, from as many possible species of flowers. What stood before him, as will soon grow clear, was a true Persian assortment of improved varieties of flowers, already quite expensive, and jealously guarded and bred. He passed along these seeds of every kind to his countryman Clusius—Charles de l'Ecluse of Arras—whose soul had been fertile ground on which the kernel of Leiden's school of botany had fallen—that science which first had come from Italy—and who in 1573 would assume the chair of the new science of flowers at the University of Vienna. Twenty years later, having returned to his professorship in Leiden, he became the leading apologist of the new world of flowers. He had been in possession of Turkish seeds of the true hyacinth (the hyacinth of the Greeks was *Orchis moro*, not, as is still reported today, *Gladiolus communis*) ever since 1557. Flemish collectors imported its bulbs from Istanbul in the 1580s, but Clusius had seen it in flower at the home of Jean de Brancion even before he moved to Vienna. His stay in Vienna made the flower Austrian. By the end of the century it was already blossoming in all its colors in England, and Gerard, the first English writer on gardening, who in 1596 grew it in his garden in Holborn, describes it in his famous book. It was likewise through Clusius' chair that the first of Persia's truly characteristic flora, obtained by way of Turkey, entered Dutch and Austrian gardens: the crown imperial (*Fritillaria imperialis*) and the *Scilla peruviana* (found all throughout Asia Minor, up to the high plains of Iran, whereas America, in fact, has no *Scillas*). In 1565, Clusius collected various species of narcissus in Spain, and introduced the tazetta, *Narcissus tazetta*, from Gibraltar, the jonquil, *Narcissus jonquilla* from Cadiz and Seville; in 1614, our own narcissus, the Greek *Narcissus poeticus*, flowered as a curiosity, surely imported from Turkey, in a Leiden apothecary's garden. In 1599, the Spanish *Narcissus triandrus* reached Clusius by way of France; and previously, by way of Steiermark, the *Narcissus odorus* had made its way to Frankfurt, where Clusius saw and described it. Thirty years later, the English passion for the narcissus exploded—"Fair daffodils we weep to see"—and in 1629 Parkinson's *Paradisus terrestris* already listed the names of a hundred varieties. By now, however, Europe's change of heart had long since grown complete. The latitudes of Europe's first great flower painters—where painters from Dürer to van der Goes sat before the columbine and rendered it line by line—held enormous expanses of gardenless terrain, wholly given over to the new flowers; and next to them, unreconciled, and flowerless, stood the old patrician gardens. Having grown dispensable, exclusive attention to the flora of foreign lands had died out. The first European wild flower to be discovered with the continent's newly educated eyes was the primrose, *Primula auricula*, which Mattioli held to be medicinal and referred to as *Sanicula*, and which Clusius rendered famous: an entire chapter of the third volume of his epoch-making treatise on plants was dedicated to this noble child of the Alps. In 1597, John Gerard was already able to illustrate the chapter he dedicated to it—chapter 262 of his *Herball*—with six woodcuts of various forms of the flower, and since that time the number of descriptions and varieties has grown to gigantic proportions. Next to come was the extraordinary story of the Flemish and English cultivation of the primrose: two separate traditions that saw it almost exclusively entrusted to the hands of middle-class burghers and artisans who were intoxicated, obsessed, made drunk by this flower: there, the weaver and mystic cobbler of the English Midlands, the Quakers of Walworth and Newcastle: here, the apothecaries and parish priests of Flemish towns and villages. The ripened harvest at the close of the flower's great century was twofold. Dutch flower painting was lending attention to the new world of wonders, displaying it in dizzying arrangements, aided as well by the incomparable draughtsmen who illustrated the Dutch and German treatises which, from the other side of the world, also brought the fabulous forms of American flowers to the notice of European sensibilities. And new scientific investigations, from the great Tournefort in Provence to Geneva's de Candolle, were French and systematic, following the model of all the new natural sciences in France, and thanks to the generous flow of means provided by the nation's kings. Collecting and drawing in the tradition of Clusius, Tournefort traveled through Provence, Savoy and Burgundy, discovered the botany of the Pyrenees, then went like the Flemish to Spain where he took his degree in Barcelona; after further, thoroughgoing explorations of Spain and Portugal, he visited England where breeders were busy with all the new flowers. Next he was drawn to the center of this work in Holland, and then in 1700 to the motherland of so many new excitements: after a two-year voyage to Greece and

Asia Minor, he was to publish the results of his studies in three epoch-making volumes. 1700 was also the year of the appearance of his celebrated *Institutiones*, which established the principles of classification and binomial nomenclature. From that point on, men traveled in pursuit of flowers. "For my heart has a strong and vast desire / To draw into itself and there to abide / With everything the world calls joy / In touch with the universe, like Banks and Solander." The high ranks of English and Dutch nobility stood with means, grounds and the writing of learned works, as will be shown, next to *petits bourgeois* collectors and breeders. By the start of the new century, the Dutch Count Cliffort's world-famous collection in Hartekamp had become a focal point of such initiatives. It was here that Linnaeus, a student and then doctor at Leiden's University, grew to the stature of his historical mission, starting out as the collection's custodian.

Our essay, however, must be careful not to abandon the point of view from which it started out, and must return to the Vienna of Karl and Ferdinand. Its theme is the garden. The flower to which we have diverted attention is still without a garden, and still without spaces and principles that place it within an order. The bulbed plants of the Flanders of Clusius, Sweerts and Passaeus, in Mecheln as in Haarlem, flowered much like field crops on plains traversed by canals. What has come to be known as the "Dutch garden" is a bastard of the French, with the simple addition of potted plants and pitiful monstrosities. The primrose is everywhere cultivated in flower pots, in the limited spaces of homes and dooryard gardens. The flower is a presence in the rooms and minds, in the senses and longings of the whole of a new humanity, but it has no place of its own, and is still at a distance from obtaining one. In England's burgeoning landscape gardens, where grandiose longings and majestic feelings shape the scene, the flower's status is just as uncertain as in flowerless Trianon and Versailles, since these new paradises too were born as great, wide, flowerless expanses. The part of the park called "the pleasure ground," where flowers are cultivated next to the house, separate from the artificial wilderness, is a makeshift measure of uncertain purpose and style. The scattering of flowers through fields must first be slowly learned; in addition, it's only seldom to be practiced, since it rules out proper care for them, thus leading them to degenerate, and go wild. The period's great collections were simply rooms packed full with plants, ready for the studious gaze and its search for particulars; and given the steady growth in the number of new arrivals, their spaces were chronically cramped. Recourse to ever more pots was doubtless the natural expedient, but it also completed the already implicit separation of the garden from the flower. A garden is a structure, and the plants that grow within it are fixed, constituent parts of that structure. Something I carry about as I walk, and can put here or there or set aside as the mood may move me, negates the idea of structure, and at best is a gardenlike decoration of the point at which I finally set it down, like a vase or a basket. What grows in a pot has less been planted in the garden than uprooted from it.

But the oriental seeds which had made their way to Vienna and the Habsburgs had sprouted not only in distant lands, visibly and acclaimed, but also in the nearer vicinity, silently. In doctors' gardens in Breslau—as in Augsburg, Frankfurt, Nürnberg and Lucerne—the new blooms stood tall and still, even previous to 1600, and from there made further inroads. Germany's peasant and monastery gardens (which is to speak of those of all the lands where German and its dialects are spoken) with their pure and simple congregations of every sort of flower—or of every flower which was richly hued, richly shaped, highly expressive, or powerfully appealing or eloquent—had grasped the attention of the new and numerous ranks of city patricians, doctors and apothecaries. The garden peony—an old cross between southern European medicinal varieties and the dark Walachian *Paeonia decora* which had arrived by way of Vienna—profusely doubled and already known for quite some time as the "peasant's rose"; the immediately and avidly sought sunflower; the double Turkish poppy; the Persian and Turkish or turban buttercups of the Persian flower garden—originally

Asiatic-Iranian and African wild flowers—of which Clusius already in 1579 listed and described some twenty-one varieties, and which in the following century moved whole fortunes: all these stood—after feverish raids on Carthusians and Capuchins and on Schwabian, Frankish, and Silesian peasants—in the gardens of Catholic regions primarily, but also of Protestant Würtemberg and Switzerland, as again in those, from Nürnberg to Hamburg, of the Baroque lyric poets who exchanged correspondence on flowers. Our common pansy—which was developed with the help of contributions from the *Viola lutea* of eastern Europe's mountains (the Riesengebirge) and the *Viola altaica*, imported from Turkey and Persia—was known to German country gardens as the rightful favorite among the flowers loved by peasant girls and surely had no need to wait for the attentions of French and English florists before taking on form and size. It traveled along the eastern route, and Fuchs and Brunfels remarked on its presence in Ingolstadt already in 1554. Turkey's scarlet lightning or Maltese cross, *Lychnis chalcedonica*, from the southern shores of the Black Sea; the Greek night violet, *Hesperis matronalis*; the favorite from southeast Europe of the Carthusians and Capuchins, sweet William or *Dianthus barbatus*; the *Reseda*, or mignonette, which only in Germany preserves the Spanish name that applies to the African wild flower; and of course the "Turkish lilac," which spread from the East by way of Vienna as the Persian or common lilac; the small "cinnamon rose" to be found in Alemannian gardens, *Philadelphus coronarius*, also known as "false Jasmine," preserving the name by which it's known in its Caucasian and Armenian homeland; the hollyhock, which is perhaps the most ancient of central Asia's cultivated plants and known from China to Persia, having even been carried along by nomad peoples on account of its medicinal flowers and roots: these are the plants of the peasant and monastery gardens of eastern and southern Germany, just the same as the "peasant prune" or "domestic plum" which arriving from Persia and Turkey appeared in Hungary and Transylvania at about 1500, twenty years later to be cultivated all throughout Moravia before passing still further, by way of Brno, along the ancient route which our older variety of the plum—the *Kriechen*, a corruption of *Griechen*, for "the Greek plum"—already had arrived from Byzantium in the Middle Ages. Among them, at still very early dates, and under ingenuous names, the first flowering plants of Peru and Mexico were already to be seen in bloom, having made their entrance and finding their further route by way of Spain and Vienna: the "Indian cloves," *Tagetes patula* and *elata*; the "Hussar's button," *Spilantes oleracea*; the Mexican nasturtium, *Tropaeolum maius*, known as Capucine, or "Capuchin's cress," of which the variety from Chile and Argentina that immigrated at a later date is still called *canariense*, owing to its stop among those islands before reaching Spain and Vienna; and the *Ricinus*, or "tree of wonders," the castor oil plant, which never ceased to be admired, sketched and cultivated, having made its way from India and into doctors' gardens, and child's play to grow. Almost all of them are seed plants. The columbine and monk's hood shrubs are natives; the larkspur, in its annual form as *Delphinium aiacis* no less than as the shrub *Delphinium elatum* (southern Siberia to the Himalayas and China) comes both from the Orient and from southeastern Europe; the southern Balkans are again the home of the indispensable woundwarts, *Stachys lanata*, of which the red and blue blooms are familiarly seen in the borders of flower beds. Of the lilies, the highly sought-after red varieties, *Lilium chalcedonium* and *pomponicum*, are both of Pontic-Turkish origin; as again are the two most beautiful bellflowers, seldom seen today; and among the fleur-de-lys, the fragrant *Amberboa moschata*, from Asia Minor, is called, even today, sweet sultan. The Oriental roses, *Rosa damascena* and *lutea*, and their numerous varieties held absolute supremacy. The "peasant's rose" of the "peasant garden" was a Syrian or Persian lady, since only the unique conditions of Persia's intensive cultivation of roses for the manufacture of attar could have created the double varieties already known in antiquity, of which the first began to enter Europe already at the time of the Crusades, by way of Istanbul. The second wave came through Vienna, and was indeed so mighty that English importers regularly referred to Persia's *Rosa lutea* as the "Austrian briar." The bright clove pink or "field carnation" (*Dianthus caryophyllus*) of German peasant gardens comes directly, or by way of Prague, from Vienna, where classic cultivations of this robust, precociously flowering plant—the oldest of its species—tenaciously continue still today, whereas the potted varieties grown by loving collectors (who, as Goethe knew, included the monasteries) were developed by French and Flemish florists, as the French names of many varieties still remind us.

This seems to be only a list of names, but in fact is an image of a nascent garden: not as a geometric order, but as an order implicit in a community of plants held together by facts of botany and geography—or of three such communities, one American, one Eastern, one Middle-European. While strongly contrasting with one another, these plants nonetheless belong with one another as a unified body of choices on the part of a self-consistent human sensibility. Its driving force is the imagination, guided by a full, sensual lust for life, untouched by any notion of renunciation. The world it desires and hopes to realize is the world of fable, or, better still, of fantasy. Fantasy in the forms of native flowers, attentively encouraged; foreign flowers with strange, striking faces; fringed, piebald flowers in the roles of buffoons and jesters. Flowers that strut and preen, languish and goggle, fly into strife and graciously assuage. The pandemonium of friendly and mischievous spirits, as colorful as peasants' Sunday aprons or the paraments and banners of church processions, cannot be bright and boisterous enough. What prevents it from making itself a hell is only but always the saintly faces that there in its midst, with sounds of bells and natural modesty, remind us of the soul's salvation: "Mary's bells" and "touch-me-not." The whole world is enclosed within a fence: Moors and Indians, Magyars and Chinese, Bassas, Persians and Walloons, imperial crowns, knights' spurs, bishops' caps, hooded Capuchins and iron-helmed monks among upright Schwabians and bourgeois notables in evening dress.

The curious, the eccentric, and the cunning stand next to god-like majesty. The yellow leaves of the Matricaria, like the pale dead nettle and the "blood nettle," enchant the eye as contrasts and background patterns behind the saturated colors of the complex, towering flowers of clawed, fringed and speckled hollyhocks. Now double wild flowers—and then redoubled and overcolored thanks to the power of fertilizers—more often entered the world as miniature horrors than as tiny wonders, and degenerate dwarfs are protected, preserved, and reproduced like midgets at royal courts. All sizes and statures—large, small and medium, tall and short—live scattered among each other, all habits, and all colors. Every shape must grow extravagant; every color must be forced to segregate and revert to others, once at least, and if possible several times. All the world's peoples are to enter here, and to show themselves for what they are. So-and-so has a crimson love-lies-bleeding, and the race is on to obtain it! Or for the violet-colored cockscomb of which so-and-so else has procured the seed, from ever so far away. A notion hovers in the air: "the great wide world." This garden is its happy, self-conscious image. Taste, within this maelstrom that takes the measure of life itself, would be a crazy notion: just as it would be in a painting by Teniers or Brueghel, or in a Jesuit church, or in any other dramatic world. And like every other garden, this garden too—in no way altered or elevated, in no way endowed with more rational principles of order—spread from one nation to the next. This is England's "old-fashioned" or "cottage" garden; and again—though here its forms were of greater sobriety, and drier in their eccentricity—the Dutch garden. In Germany too it was the typical castle garden and the garden of bourgeois villas. As such, it also, fragmentarily, appropriated a number of architectural elements from Italian Baroque: there a clipped hedge, here an oddment in stone, terraces, two or three flowers, the sundial. But these features, in German gardens, were never of structural importance: transplanted Latinity merely took up a place at the side of other lands and other faces, and in the moment of being adopted was bent to its surroundings and immediately transformed. This is the German-speaking peoples' only great tradition of gardening, and indeed no other is truly their own: the Baroque garden of the old Habsburg, Holy Roman Empire. As guided and desired by Vienna, the East opened out into the West, calling cultivated flowers from Turkey and Persia to fill the vacuum of the never-broken greenery of the Western garden-theater, and resulting in a purely floral garden, which yet was hardly a garden at all, but a place into which a healthy people—peasants, burghers, friars and nuns, women and children, doctors, apothecaries, nobles and courtiers—could project themselves and their dreams, imagining a life in an ideal world which was not a world of *lost* nature, since they themselves were nature and in no way aware of any other which might have gone astray. They knew instead of preternatural, paranatural and supernatural worlds of which the natural world of reality was only a sightless mirror, and a mirror from which it might be enough suddenly to turn away, in order to discover a realm of fable and adventurous mystery, of distant lands and many peoples, of limitless astonishment and ambivalent disguise, where the soul itself is a rebus, and something stands behind it, with everything an indication of everything else.

A century later, Jean Paul was to expand this garden, his body's home, and the home of his immortal soul, into the world where his boldest and most delicate creatures live: into his *Blumenbühl*, or "flowered hill," and *Maienthal*, or "valley of May," and the flower-decked meadows of youth, in his *Flegeljahre*. Brentano then passed through it and found his choir of the dead: "There is a reaper whose name is Death." This is the ships catalogue of the German people's epic of the Baroque garden: the names of everything colorful, old, profound and melancholy come one last time in procession, one after the other. "Beware, fine flower!" Two centuries of German poetry lived in this old German flower garden, from the crude florilegiums of Baroque lyric to Eichendorff, who in its after-life, while looking back on so much by-gone glory, became its truest expression, as formulated by a new spirit, since poetry is the first and final need of the human soul, for which reality does not suffice. His *Taugenichts*, *Marmorbild* and *Schloß Durande* contain its image, intoxication and perfume, but the lyric spirit draws it back into the brief classical frame where, there on the Silesian-Austrian threshold of the poet's ancestral castle, the Turkish flora that Busbecq and Clusius had brought to Vienna—that breakthrough of the 1550s—was set to music, enchanted like Sleeping Beauty into half-Latin stonework and fountainwork against a background of "Valleys wide, and heights." "Crown imperial and red peonies, Surely they are enchanted." "A woman sits there dozing"—"And when the length of the valley darkens, she gently plucks her lyre's strings."

It was also from out of this garden, from gardens like those in which Clusius, a hundred and twenty years before, had already seen the Emperor's hyacinths in bloom, that Goethe stepped: they were the source of his scientific understanding of plants, of his botanic research, his collections, his drive to delve into nature, and again of his pique with Leipzig tailors' pranks and Lili's Park. He returned to them in the flowered couplets of "The Four Seasons," and they were the source of the nourishment on which he fed his Old-Germanic love of flowers, a love which broke again and again through the veneer of the times, always virile and always fresh, childish and amazed, plastic and exploratory, so satisfied, so healthy, so open to the new, so true, so undisturbed by aestheticism and sentimental infirmity. Because this garden desired in the higher sense to be no garden at all. Its readiness to suffer from bombast, effusion and hyperbole, from overfullness and falsity of tone, gave it enormous breadth of content and opened its future to multitudes of already ripe but as yet unexplored developments, just like the whole of its epoch. These levels of still hidden potential should indeed be examined more closely.

The German Baroque garden, which spread through all of northern Europe, is entirely at odds with the dreams of the poetry that mourns its loss: it does not belong to the past. It represents the youth of the newer and truly European garden, and till now has remained—as it doubtless will continue to remain—an inexhaustible infancy to which that European garden will always return anew. It wasn't the result of a theoretical protest that consciously played it off against the ancient formal garden of rigorously humanistic Europe, and should rather be seen as the inbreath of naturalism that had to follow that outbreath of geometry which is always necessary to the historical rhythms of form, and which then, with equal necessity, is displaced by a reacquired freedom from geometric rigor, for a return to naturalism. The driving force behind this garden was neither truly gardenly nor a question of the altered needs of the human soul; it simply reflects the historical reality around it, of which it was the immediate expression. That reality was the radically new and different geopolitical situation which had turned the Viennese throne room of Karl V into the keystone of the geographic-historical arches which so suddenly had arisen and bridged the spaces between Central America, Flanders and Persia, thus turning Austria's ancestral soil, along with its capital, into the center of exchange for new goods in the Eastern Roman world, like Paris for the Western Roman world. It was the basin that gathered the waters of newly opened streams. The central fact that Vienna had become the gate through which the East pressed west also made it the distributor of the cultural heritage of the old Near East. The other central fact that Spain, the lord of the Americas, was in Habsburg hands made Vienna's chair of botany a powerful rival of the Paris collections.

The Baroque flower garden was born as an emergency expedient for the preservation, cultivation, reproduction and further distribution of the inestimable abundance of flowers which the opening of the world on two sides at once had caused to flow into the small assortment of the old cultivated plants of the Mediterranean countries. It was marked from the start by indomitable profusion, and through it won the hearts and sensibilities of the peoples of central and northern Europe, who were overcome by a new intoxication and would never again allow themselves to be deprived of it. The abundance of the new worlds of flowers was thus to be enjoyed by vast numbers of persons to whom gardens were new, persons who before had remained outside the gates of the gardens of the princes. The revolution in the geography of botany led also to social changes in the art of gardening, in the creative evocation of natural worlds. The new flowers and the new garden belonged as well to the poor and humble, to people of thoroughly modest station, to women, to rustics, to artisans, no less than to nobles and collectors. What came so greatly to reduce the expense of gardening was the use of seed. Everyone could have it, and gardening was soon to be multiplied no less enormously than the printing press had multiplied the book and put it into even the poorest hands. It's true that lavish sums were demanded by and spent on bulbs, tubers, cuttings, variations and seedlings for as long as they were novelties; but the free and generous flower refused to allow itself to be imprisoned by human profiteering: a few years passed and plants which before had been rarities were scattered as seed near the rain barrel in the nursery beds of a modest middle class garden. Where bulbs were still unaffordable, patience was warmly kept for as many as five long years until the cycle from seed to flowering plant had run its course, and tulips and hyacinths and daffodils bloomed, repeating the wonder that occurred before the eyes of Proserpina. Contemplation and the savoring of atmospheres were supplanted by activity: a race of gardeners never seen before approached the world of flowers in equally unprecedented ways. Nature responded, and opened itself in a likewise novel way. Beneath the hundred-thousand hands of its new and vigorous guardian, the flower transformed itself.

When Clusius after years of waiting saw the blooms of the seeds of his first Hadrianople tulip, he did not stand before the mother plant, but saw instead an incredible profusion of forms: the seed had split and segregated, and he found himself looking at the whole genealogical line of an ancient, cultivated Persian variety. The age-old breeders of the Middle East and Eastern Asia already had centuries of acquaintanceship with the secrets of cultivation that the West was now to rediscover. It wasn't only that two areas of botanical geography had come into contact with one another; the new Europe had in fact acquired an inroad to the inherited wisdom of the continent that now approached it through its ancient creations. The cultivated varieties—the "breeds"—which came to be known were born on European soil. The weaver in Newcastle, the country priest in Montdidier, the doctor in Breslau took the plants which lay in their hands—wildflowers or chance mutations—only as starting points, just as the breeders of ancient China and Persia had done. Repeated planting, selection, and crossing then transformed them into creatures which were totally new, and had never existed before. This work continued in silence everywhere in Europe for the whole of a century, accompanied by a literature which is rightly called monumental: a fabulous expenditure of time and money that recorded varieties and beautifully cut their illustrations into blocks of wood. The epoch's assortment of cultivated plants was so enormous that almost nothing could be preserved of it. Today we would pay great sums for the buttercups which at the end of the seventeenth century stood in small Flemish and English gardens, and which de Heem in part so splendidly painted. The breeding of varieties brought European talents of observation to levels of absolute refinement which today have no comparison. The parti-colored profusion of the Baroque garden, if only one stopped to look, also hid the most noble and delicate creatures—immediately beside the bizarre—which scrupulous selection had managed to isolate. The perception of initially modest but finally decisive differences grew into a practice of fabulous implications and trained a generation to the tasks of research and poetry, thinking and interpretation, which the following century would continue to pursue.

Flowers were a power to be reckoned with, and as such asserted their sway over human beings. And as such, again, they took the stage of their newly conquered continent. They broke over Europe in a high roiling wave as the continent, in accordance with its innermost laws, attempted to transform them into a garden, flooding its soil for five generations and pounding on the gates of its artificial gardens where for two thousand years colored gravel, powdered coal, and yellow sand, in the guise of palmettes, dolphins and rhombuses, were the representatives of color and form. They pressed up to the edges of that small assortment—some twenty or so—of Mediterranean and central European wild flowers, mainly herbs and medicinal plants, which for two thousand years, in only slightly developed varieties, had been what Europe understood by the name of flowers: the flowers with which it had decorated its altars and plaited its wreathes, and embellished the painted ground beneath the feet of its saints from Ghent to Palermo, from Paris to Prague. The first result was here a kind of makeshift garden, and there a lingering insistence on the geometries of French and Italian gardens: both amounted to a transformation of human sensibilities as demanded by the flora of the East, which in the form, on the one hand, of the peasant garden, and on the other of the Baroque garden, with survivals from the Italian garden, had swamped the continent. Simply that.

The resolution of the conflict was long to remain impossible, owing to two circumstances. First of all, its poles, rather than two, were three: the West Roman landscape garden, which was only art; the East Roman and Oriental flower garden, which was only flowers; and, between them, the English landscape garden, which was only nature. This English garden was the creation of the transformed spirit of a new people—transformed by painting and poetry—and it furnished the space for a new poetry of endless feeling. It was imagined by poets, encouraged by thinkers and dreamers, like the garden of Eastern Asia, of which it was vaguely aware, and designed by painters; but just like the gardens of the style it opposed, it presupposed masters and vast spaces; and just as in China, it cultivated flowers beside but not within itself. Its masters were painters, and painting alone had turned them into gardeners. They belonged to neither the rich nor the poor, but to Europe's new youth.

The other rift went deeper. The Oriental and Indian flora of the Baroque garden was only an initial harbinger of the prodigy that was ready to cross the horizon: the flowering plants of everywhere in the world. Tournefort's voyage to the eastern Mediterranean—at its time, in 1700, an epoch-making achievement—was soon to pale before the scientific expeditions which the new century would send to the new continents. Capuchins and Jesuits as missionaries, envoys to the Indies and officers, voyagers of discovery and plant collectors, learned botanists and circumnavigators, all of them filled their collection bags and plant boxes in the wilds of every continent. The botanists of the colonies likewise collected and sent back plants and seeds to Europe, to institutes, to teachers and specialists, to enthusiastic ladies of high estate. Long-secluded collections of supremely developed garden flowers and the most luxuriant wild blossoms at first tentatively opened a crack in the door, and then threw it wide open. The nineteenth century marked the start of prodigious undertakings like the voyages and reports of Alexander von Humboldt, and of systematic inventories like the one which began in 1820 to gather the flora of the American West. Thousands and thousands of wild plants—not at all like the Eastern flora which human hands had already sifted and shaped—suddenly broke over the continent, filling its botanical gardens and ending up mostly in herbaries. Europe capitulated. The Baroque garden stood withering in the on-coming surge, and fell apart behind it. It was snubbed and called "the peasant garden," and its bright profusion of colors occasioned commiserating laughter. Its flowers disappeared, and soon had to be sought out by the few concerned enthusiasts who were anxious to preserve them. As the abundance of newly-arriving plants grew to uncontrollable proportions, the offerings of ordinary garden commerce—those very few classes of flowers from which it chose its stock—grew ever smaller, and by the end of the century the decline of the European garden had grown horrifying and complete. As nothing more than a cold sight worth being seen, the princely garden had turned into a monument of the past; the landscape garden a trivial, public, city park; the flower garden a caricature of old geometries and Dutch fashions, with endless flower beds, shelves of potted plants, and row after row of flowers to be cut; all of which for gardening amounted to the void.

Yet the continent learned at the turn of the century that England, just as at the turn of the previous one, had experienced a new and equally radical garden revolution, and already had begun to export it. England had resolved the conflict between the flower and the garden. Its position as the metropolitan capital of a world empire had made it the most important collector of the world's flora, and it had not shirked that post. It was fully living up to it, and in doing so had in no way belied its own tradition of landscape gardening. This new garden too, like the breeding of buttercups and daffodils in the seventeenth century, and the invention of the park in the eighteenth century, was a national concern. Like the former, it lay in the hands of everyone who had a garden; and gardens lay in the hands of all, were wanted by all, and seen by all as a human order between the flower as an order and the order of the garden. This was Europe's first step beyond the Baroque garden, while holding it within itself as a precedent. In addition to containing the Baroque garden, it also contained the great English nature parks: it dealt with flowers and flowering shrubs, garden paths and planted spaces exactly as the park made use of trees and groups of trees, of hill, lake and meadow. The park had crafted a wooded landscape; this garden now crafted a flowered landscape. Order, here as there, expressed itself artistically, through laws of composition which were also the gentlest and wisest of the laws of order. And here as there, the human being—the magician who shapes the creation—disappears: there into the whispering grove, which seems to belong to Arcadia; here into a flowering wilderness, which stands tall and sways in the air as though in lands and times of innocence. It's the realization of what Jean Paul, within his Baroque garden, could only dream, dreaming himself beyond it: the poet had thrown his goal wide out into the distance, but it found itself achieved within a century, pulled down from the heavens and given a home on earth as garden and reality. And finally—precisely again like the revolution that produced the Baroque garden—this upheaval too, which overthrew all forms and habits, wasn't provoked by aesthetic concerns, nor by attitudes, nor by fashions, nor by any lust for new sensations. It derived from history, politics and geography, society and economics and newly advanced knowledge, which became a new imperative: the soul, but as guided by the mind; feeling, but fully and finally experienced; impulse, but of the greatest depth. Equally like the Baroque garden, it was first of all a garden of seeders, and therefore of the whole of a people. But it went beyond the Baroque garden: it marked the absolute victory of the flower, which finally conquered what it could not conquer in China, Japan, or Persia: the garden as a whole. The human factor which permitted that victory could never have been an Asiatic soul. This drama of mutually opposed and yet so intimately interrelated voices could only have reached its denouement in the depth and wealth of the historical development of the soul of a free Western people—and perhaps only among those people for whom the continent's contradictions had first to be mollified by island air before landing on their shores; surely it had to be reserved to the people for whom by now four hundred years of restless, active, mystical, technical absorption in the creative and constructive forces that lie within the flower had become a common good for both their nation and society: a common, public, and almost atmospheric good. And now that wealth of experience came to the profit of the whole of the continent: to its profit, despite a woeful situation! So woeful that without its help the heritage of the Western garden—including the contribution which had reached it from the gardens of the East—would have found itself reduced to a few geranium stalks, carnation shrubs, long-stemmed roses, and forget-me-not bushes beside the twenty-five classes each of the fourteen species of flowers in retail assortments. And there it would have stood, perplexed and helpless, before the shrugging of the shoulders of its public servants and officialdom—its "specialists."

CHAPTER III

The Garden and the New Flowers

THE nineteenth century's initial response, in the course of its middle third, to the new situation of the European garden, confronted with the irruption of wild plants from all around the world, was neither passive nor unworthy. At first with hesitance and then resignedly, it relinquished the notion of the garden as an articulate expressive structure and bowed to the reality of its own historical situation. As culture in general declined, that garden, or what went by such a name, sank simply into another of the trivial musts of the new, rising class of bourgeois entrepreneurs and the commercial tradesmen who supplied them. But, in any case, it was only a bastard child of the three great centuries of gardening, and not their true son and successor. The true child, the true heir of that old tradition of passion, fascination and creative commitment went by a different name. Gardens were replaced by collections. The times had to come to terms with an overwhelming influx of new materials, and had no foreseeable prospect of treating them as anything other than raw materials, to be catalogued, described, identified and named, and archived in a herbary. Since these purposes required at least that the new plants find further cultivation beneath the observation of attentive, analytic eyes, the era provided them with suitably glazed and heated rooms—expedients—which made no claim to being anything more than containers. Or they were grown in rows in the open air, much as sixteenth-century

Flanders had done with its newly acquired Eastern bulbs. The few botanical gardens were sufficient in neither number nor size; resources had to be enormously multiplied, created and organized. The army of cataloguers, researchers and assistants required for the endless task was by no means in place from the start. The learned botanists of the university chairs were mainly theorists and classifiers, and in the best of cases highly specialized naturalists; so most of them had little preparation for meeting the overwhelming demands which attending to the flowers required; the rapidly increasing specialization of the science of botany kept them ever more frequently in the company of the microscope. The trail-blazing missionaries who had worked in distant worlds (like Camell, the Moravian Jesuit, who in the seventeenth century discovered the camellia and described the flora of the island of Luzon, or the Franciscan Charles Plumier, who discovered the fuchsia, or the Jesuit Cobe, who in addition to discovering the Cobaea was the first to explore the flora of Mexico and Peru) had in turn been only volunteers, just as with the doctors in the service of colonial governments and assigned to exotic posts, some of whose botanical accomplishments remain unexcelled. Gardeners were needed.

In the trio of countries most renowned for their traditions of gardening, the sons of the greatest gardening families—some of which for three hundred years had furnished a succession of exemplary and sometimes highly learned connoisseurs and cultivators—families with names like Haage and Reichenbach and Wendland, Zeyher, Sello and Vilmorin, Fintelmann, Lenné, Veitch, Dietrich and Loddiges, Jussieu and Benary, Verschaffelt, Rinz, Baumann and Bouché—fell into line and applied themselves to tasks which never before had been so various and changing, and so itinerant. The inquiring gardener who hoped to do something important had always known years of travel, but now no single period of residence abroad counted as sufficient. No matter what they had to offer, the famous schools of gardening where golden traditions of manual expertise were taught by eminent masters—like Jost in Tetschen, Rinz at the gardens of the Episcopal court in Würzberg and at Schöner Busch in Aschaffenburg, Carter at Forest Hill, Vilmorin in Verrières and Macoy in Lüttich, Sckell in Schwetzingen and Hayler in Schleißheim—were now no more than the lower trampolines for a younger generation that burned with ambition and the lust for the new. The Viennese gardens of Baron von Hügel or, again in Vienna, the world-famous garden where Arthaber housed his unique collection of species from New Holland and the Cape of Good Hope, or Vilmorin's Jardin Latil on the French Riviera and Bolle's magnificent compound at Scharfenberg, not far from Berlin, were surely respected seminars, but there were also heights that towered far above them, and which as true and proper wonders of the times had taken the place of antiquity's princely El Dorados: the magnificent collection of the Duke of Bedford at Woburn Abbey; the private botanical garden of the Earl of Bute in London; the Duke of Devonshire's unimaginable Chatsworth; the establishment of the Veitch family and its Knight's Royal Exotic Nursery; the personal botanical garden of a simple private German citizen, Max Leichtlin, in Baden-Baden. And, finally, as the finest commercial expression of the ever-expanding needs of the time—on a par with Vilmorin's all-inclusive Paris establishment—there were the Central Gardens in Ghent. Van Houtte, Verschaffelt and van Geert had made this place an absolute nucleus of collecting and distribution, and, in addition to countless unknown persons, explorers like Warscewicz and Wallis were traveling and at work for them in every wilderness, everywhere in the world. Germany's most important centers were Erfurt, where in the seventeenth century a modest citizen, Christian Reichart, had discovered, perfected and taught the bases of punctilious cultivation from seeds; and Quedlinburg, where the Dippes and the Grasshoffs set thousands of hectares to the commercial production of tens of thousands of varieties of seed from everywhere in the world. These were the places that attracted the attention of the youthful gardeners from Saxony and Thüringen who in cities and castle gardens everywhere in the world were soon to prove the worth of their school. The world-wide commerce of Haage and Schmidt and Benary—classical establishments of the utmost conscientiousness and the liveliest attention to the new, and advised by learned consultants—led to the presentation of their enormous assortments of seeds in catalogues and illustrated booklets. But neither commerce and practical expertise, nor the fabulously increased expanse of cultivated terrain, nor even the organizational efforts of clear-minded and energetic persons were sufficient to do justice to the task and the mounting passions it aroused.

As the flower rode tall on the chariot of its long-postponed triumphal march, its following swelled with persons still quite different from gardeners, cultivators and commercial dealers. Theologians and jurists, civil servants and doctors, merchants and young teachers and officers threw aside their professions and followed the paths it showed them. Governments were known to come to each other's aid, pooling financial resources, as the Austrian and Bavarian governments did to send Martius to Brazil; and private corporations were expressly founded, issuing stock to raise the backing for the fabulous search for new flowers. Not only Veitch and Van Houtte had traveling collectors: Prince Moritz von Nassau-Siegen financed at his personal expense a thorough exploration of the flora of Brazil; the Dukes of Bedford and Devonshire likewise outfitted their own explorers. Europe's great nobility of the castles and little Versailles of yore—which is to speak of the old architectural gardens—remained true to itself and led the century in the task which the new flowers assigned it. Prince Joseph von Salm-Reifferscheidt explored the world of the succulents; his collections were unique, and his masterfully illustrated volumes remain unsurpassed. Searching out flowers on expeditions that kept them in the midst of great privations and away from home for years, Baron von Veltheim and Baron von Hügel were worthy rivals of the great English lords. Von Hügel, in every sense a remarkable personage, also wrote classic descriptions of the flora he researched and collected: surrounded at his Viennese residence by twenty-seven expert gardeners, this was the work to which he turned while preparing to bring to conclusion the enthusiasms of his youthful years, then dedicating the rest of his life to diplomacy and foreign affairs. The man who gave his name to the mother of all crimson ramblers and Dorothy Perkins—to the *Rosa wichuraiana*—Dr. Ernst Wichura, pioneer explorer of the botany of India and Ceylon, jurist and Assessor of the Supreme Court in Berlin, Member of the House in Breslau, and then Government Counselor in the Administrative Service, was widely known to be a connoisseur and duly appointed by the Prussian government to the post of Botanist for the Royal Prussian East Asia Expedition of 1859; the final years of a life of sacrifice were thus lived out in the solitude of research and collecting in a tropical wilderness. And the daring and privation demanded by the travels of Prince Maximilian von Wied, whose work underlies our knowledge of sub-tropical and tropical American flora, present him as no less knightly than a hero of the Middle Ages in quest of a magic flower. Victims fell, spared themselves no pain, and were never counted. Consider, for example the life of Gustav Wallis, a flower hunter who was born in 1830 as the son of a State Attorney of the Lünenberg Superior Court. His story is gripping, even in the context of the passionate years in which he lived: deaf-mute until the age of six, and hard of hearing in following years as well, it's rather as though his eye had inherited the sensibility which was missing in his ear. He was off to Brazil at the age of twenty-four and spent four years in the wilderness. We find him in Panama in 1868, outfitting himself for explorations in Costa Rica, only then to fall deathly ill in Martinique. After wearily recovering his strength, he was in the Philippines in 1869, and from there traveled on to Japan. In 1872, he was working for Veitch in the still unexplored New Granada. 1875 took him to Ecuador. After three years of hardship, he returned to Central America, collapsed in Panama, again began to regain his health, but finally died all the same. These were also the years in which Ferdinand Lindheimer—who was Goethe's great nephew and physically resembled him—died in Mexico: a handsome, brilliant, eloquent man, and one of the most promising plant researchers of his generation. Karl Zeyher died at the Cape of Good Hope: along with Ecklon, he had explored the flora of Southern Africa and authored the learned *Enumeratio.*

The task at hand was highly earnest, and the honors accorded to the heroes of this European battle in conquest of nature—the honors accorded back home where the battle had been decreed—befitted it. A monument to Benedikt Roezl, the great plant collector, stands in Karlsplatz, in Prague. Eduard August Regel, the son of a school priest in Gotha and initially only an apprentice gardener at the Duke of Gotha's orangery, was one of the most brilliant and versatile figures in the whole of this remarkable process. And having proved himself as practitioner and theoretician, as traveler, collector, researcher and teacher, as an organizer of scientific investigations and an epoch-making writer and cultivator, he ended his days not only as a member of parliament but also with the title of "Excellence." He had been raised to the nobility, just like his English contemporaries Sir John Paxton, Sir John Lindley, Sir William Hooker, and Sir Joseph Banks, or again like Ferdinand Baron von Müller, from Rostock, who pioneered the study of the flora of Australia. Though Baron von Müller suffered from consumption, his capacity for work was so prodigious as to enable a single lifetime to provide posterity with a reliable outline of the entirety of the flora of a previously unexplored hemisphere.

Specific instances of enthusiasm and unrelenting tenacity often seem more like legend than truth. When in 1849 the *Victoria regia* bloomed in Chatsworth for the very first time, the colossal nymphea in the English pond house had the history of a fifty-year struggle behind it. Haenke had discovered it in 1801 in a tributary of the Amazon; Bonpland and Humboldt noted it in 1827, and Poeppig in 1832; Schomburgk saw it in 1837, and Orbigny found it in Rio La Plata in Paraguay. It was only, finally, in 1846 that attempts to ship it proved successful. Only such tenacity can explain the fact, forever to the credit of the human spirit, that Europe was able in the space of a single century, when ships still slowly crossed the ocean and travel by air was as yet unknown—and despite the terrors of previously untouched forests, deserts and wastelands, of barbarous savages and wild beasts, of tropical fevers and jungles—to obtain an initial survey of the flora of the world, which it could view, examine and grasp on its own soil. The floral reserves of eastern and southern Russia were explored by Regel and Ruprecht; Greece and the Near East were opened up by Tournefort and then by Sibthorp and Heldreich; the Caucasus, Khwarezm, Tartariya and China by Bunge; Central Asia and Persia by Michaux and then by Albert Regel; the Amur Basin, Tatariya and western China by Maximowicz; the Himalayas first by Wallich and then by Royle. After the great explorations of the eighteenth century, India was examined by Wichura, Roxburgh, Griffith, Hooker, and Wallich, and then by Gibson, in the service of the Duke of Devonshire; Japan by Siebold, Thunberg and Wallis; the whole of Central Asia and parts of Australia by Hügel, in six years of voyaging; Madeira and western Africa by van Houtte, Lehmann and Pfau; East Africa and the Canaries by Hildebrandt, in the wake of Adanson's already quite significant undertakings; Southern Africa, first by Sparman and then by Zeyher. Douglas explored the world of the flowers of Canada, the American north and northern California as early as 1823; he was one of history's most successful discoverers and apostles of plants, and his generous hand is still today essential to even the tiniest garden. Columbia, André. Mexico, Linden and Prince Wied. In Brazil—after first Plumier and the subsequent, legendary achievements of Schott, who returned from his initial voyage with seven hundred and thirty-three new varieties of seed, as well as hundreds of plant-collection boxes—we find Jacquin, Linden, Schomburgk, Wallis, Pfau, Knight, Smith, Martius, Poeppig and van Houtte, all of them following the mightiest trail which the spirit had ever ripped open in the wilderness: the trail of Alexander von Humboldt. Brazil and the whole of Central America were explored by Warscewicz; Guatemala and Costa Rica by Skinner, Wendland and Wallis; Cuba and Venezuela by

Pfeiffer and Otto; Cuba again and Chile and Peru by Poeppig, who was yet another master in the written presentation of discoveries and adventures. Santo Domingo and the Guianas fell to Poiteau; the whole of America to Benedikt Roezl, the tireless Bohemian from Horomeritz, not far from Prague, whose life has left a mark that runs through all our knowledge of American flora; the whole of Australia to Ferdinand von Müller. Germans can be justly proud to find so many of our names—in the course, moreover, of a century of no more than modest German prosperity—in these golden annals of the history of the conquest of the flower. Those who regret to find them almost all in the service of foreign nations, exerting themselves for England, Belgium, Russia, Switzerland and Holland, and receiving those countries' honors, should nonetheless be careful not to forget the names, forever inscribed into the history of plants, of those who in all the furthest places of the world—in Tovar, in Venezuela, like Fendler, in Melbourne, like Müller, in Moscow, like Regel, in the Dutch East Indies, like Ritter—were the very first to discover, teach and take the lead in the practical and theoretical procedures for the collection of flowers. The greater among them move in the resplendent air of our country's century of humanism, but even the more modest share in it; and the awareness of great ambitions, of the hereditary bond between flower and landscape, landscape and spirit, spirit and immortality, makes the writings of their spokesmen into classics of German literature. They weren't botanists; they weren't gardeners; they earned their daily bread, but weren't tradesmen. They were free and passionate natures who had come to be possessed by a dark intoxication that could only partly be understood: by a new, mighty, advancing spell that robbed all charm from sedentary pleasures, that spiced hunger and transformed pain, and which was well worth living and dying for.

The spirit lives only on enthusiasm; and it's only by way of enthusiasm that human endeavor turns itself into history. If the facts and events we have just outlined have today been thoroughly forgotten, so that once again the need exists to strip such ignorance away, this itself attests to the depth of the spiritual poverty of the feckless ways in which we toy and dawdle with gardens and flowers—a poverty which none who don't know better would imagine to possess so rich a previous history, or any continuing connection with it. But wherever the spirit expresses itself through things, things are both themselves and simultaneously the whole of their history; and those who are unaware of that history drink their wine only to quaff their thirst, and like flies have no idea of why they reel.

The collecting and classification of the still unexhausted flood of wild flowers so completely consumed the era's finest forces as to make it impossible to think of the step beyond it; but nothing, in any case, might have been done to deter the retail establishments which remained at home from obeying their inborn tendency rapidly to divert a part of the stream which was flowing by, and in any case from taking possession of the things on which retail lives: new potted flowers, new flowers to be cut. The fuchsia and chrysanthemum, which had long been available, had proved highly successful in France, Belgium and England, so the tap was likewise hammered into the still unripe *Pelargonium inquinans* and the magnificent but unruly gladioluses of the Cape of Good Hope—some fifteen to twenty plants, wild in both appearance and demands. The former yielded a class of largely misunderstood and noxious pot and bed "geraniums," whereas precipitous crossings of the latter resulted in three classes of invariably vulgar cutting gladiolas. They were bred for the florist's shop, with no thought to the garden at all, and were bastards in the very worst sense, bulky or unruly, which would have spelled a garden's ruin, if the gardens of the time had in fact had something to ruin. As the century rapidly sank from its summit to the abyss that stood at its end, the times were not yet ripe for the insight that all such attempts were premature for as long as the flowers, the demands they made, and the relationships between them were only partially understood; nor indeed for the parallel insight that the practical critique and purification of the wild flowers, for the unfolding of their form and color scales and their gradual humanization, demanded a whole new lifetime.

The temptation to supply the flower market with endless masses of easily reproducible merchandize, universally salable, was far too great. And whatever refused to meet these conditions—like the consummately beautiful fantasy Pelargoniums that England developed from *Pelargonium quinquevulnerum, grandiflorum* and other species from the Cape of Good Hope, or the magnificent *Gladiolus nanus, quartinianus* and *tristis*—was immediately deleted from the catalogues. The long and wearisome tasks of selection and acclimatization—like anything else that counseled an appeal to scrupulous rather than obtuse and lazy gardeners—were seen as unsuited to the times. Rapacious cultivation delayed the garden's proper reception of South African flowers by half a century. Though already imported, Montbretias were allowed, inconceivably, again to disappear from the nurseries, and had to be reintroduced. Few of the Tritonias, and none of the Kniphofias found their way through the thicket of commerce; and related South African species—like the magnificent Dierama, Ixia, Sparaxis and Babiana, which demand no greater attentions than the gladiolus, fewer than bulbed begonias—were, with reversed insularity, banned from the continent and immediately bequeathed to England, where countless fanciers began to develop magnificent varieties, just as before with tulips and daffodils. But the scientists in Ghent—where else?—had to face up to other tasks, at least on the premises of the storehouses where their cases of plants were unpacked, and in the midst of the tracts where the transplanted plants finally disclosed their first blooms. Rodigas recognized the possibilities which lay dormant in the Siberian larkspur bush and the phlox bush of the Pampas, no matter how small and poor and impurely colored their flowers may have been, no matter how dim and coarse the tough stalks that stood before him, badly attired and, in bearing, accustomed to privation. And for no other reason than the deeply rooted habits of the great orchard master which he was, he gave himself to the preparatory efforts for the purification of these natural forms at once so proudly planned and rigidly repressed. But Rodigas, and others like him, were still exceptions, and the torrent of new, exotic flowers streamed past them, passing through collections and into private gardens, through the hands of dealers in plants and seeds and out into the spaces of European gardening, defeating all resistance.

Hundreds of perennials, hundreds of summer flowers from the world's most distant corners stood suddenly, just as God had made them, in people's gardens, with names to which European sensibilities could as yet attach no apparent meaning. What was a *Rudbeckia*? What was a *Coreopsis*? What in the name of God was a *Gaillardia picta*? The gardener from around the corner had set them, one had just left everything up to him, one wanted something pretty, colorful, and decorative. And now it's there, and blooms. Mostly yellow, or yellowish brown; some kind of aster. They say it's partly perennial, and will sprout again in the spring, like violets. Frost shouldn't bother it. Bushes, but not your "common or garden celery bush," as the saying goes. Real bushes. Shrubs. Which after all is practical, and so much less an effort than completely replanting the beds each year. Quite "economical to use." *Helenium* is the name of another great big bush, again with yellow flowers; sort of bristly. But why aren't they known by simple German names instead of something foreign? *Solidago* is the name of a bush that's nearly as tall as I am, with little yellow bells or tassels, branching off at the ends of the stems. *Solidago*? The gardener called it "goldenrod." Oh yes, of course, "goldenrod." Which is really, isn't it, a kind of weed? But the important thing is the way it fills up space, and really it looks quite pretty. Yes, quite. The gardener said that too, it's very much admired right now. What else? An aster bush. Aha, an aster bush. Quite lovely. Nothing else? Nothing perhaps a bit more… lively? I mean something colorful, or friendly. Maybe something with colored leaves. Well, yes, surely, there are any number of striped and mottled plants, perhaps a white-leafed hibiscus, a *Perilla*, maybe a *Coleus*? No, no, thank you, thank you very much, things already look quite fine, have a nice day. But well, after all why not? That white-leafed *Persicus*—that is what it's called?—won't cost an arm and a leg. Yes, that's just what I had in mind, three-fifty is quite enough—and anything else? Ah, yes; the bright one I was looking for. Yes, rather like that; piercing colors. Oh, I see. Quite out of fashion, you say, rather like something for a peasant garden. And the other one there, is "more for the connoisseur"? Quite fine. No, no, I understand you perfectly. You have to take account of the general direction of taste. Taste comes first of all, wouldn't you say? Taste is nothing to argue about, as I'm sure you know the phrase. And, yes, of course, the bill.

Trade and commerce advanced to the fore and took the upper hand. The dealers read the lists of what the great importers in England, France and Belgium had gleaned from the flood, took note of whatever required no greenhouse, nor even winter protection in the open air. Regarding flowers that ran their course in a single year, they were content with an adequate assortment of "fine summer blossoms," in order to have offerings that suited the ambitions of gardeners from the gentry, who after all had their hotbeds and someone on their payroll to look after them. More than a third of the new flora came from so-called temperate zones, and the temperature range for the summer flora of subtropical regions was largely inclusive, or in any case was still inclusive, of our summers' greatest heat: there were flowers from the whole of North America down to Mexico's high plateaus, from the mountains of South America or from heights with southern exposures, from Southern Australia, Asia Minor, Northern Africa, the Cape of Good Hope, Central Asia, China, and Japan. But commerce was willing to take no risks. Arithmetic confirmed that the new and truly high-volume customer first appeared where the social class of hothouse owners—as well as those with only unheated greenhouses—came to an end: so commercial interests turned attention to the lower middle classes which recently had risen above proletarian origins. Commerce simply couldn't afford to take its tone from experts, fanciers, and the lords of great gardens. North American flora offered surely the safest haven. They were tough and rugged and obstinate in growth, and coarsely indifferent to types of soil; they were also untroubled by moisture, and where shrubs were concerned, by winter cold as well; in appearance, moreover, many resembled countless flowers of the German plains, and some—like the phlox, the dahlia, the zinnia and the marigold—were extremely variable when properly managed by the human hand, which was a feature that promised great rewards from new importations. All of these qualities opened their route into commercial calculations, nurseries, and assortments. The nurseries, indeed, were the most important force. The entirety of the continent's commercial cultivation of shrubs, and thus the whole of the continental idiom of the garden based on shrubs, finds its origin in the discovery of the profitability of the mass commercialization of the wild bushes of North America, and at first no room was made beside them for anything other than similar "perennials": vulgar and indestructible plants for the perfect philistine, like yarrow, Baptisia, yellow-leafed Matricaria, mouse-ear chickweed, Japanese colored grass (Eulalia), Funkia, the day lily, the Japanese anemones (which were introduced quite early by way of France, recommended by the lateness of their flowering season, as well as by resistance to anything less than chemical means of destruction), soapwort, mullein, and perhaps, with a bit of hesitation, an inferior bellflower. After all, there is no Eurasian perennial of any worth or attractiveness that one is able to divide, year in year out, into five root cuts each, and to sell some fifty times over, like an Helenium.

Frightful bushes immigrated, and took possession of the soil of Europe's gardens. Raw, gigantic prairie weeds like the mostly perennial sunflowers, indestructible scourges of the soil like the unbelievably poor and wild *Heliopsis scabra*, or the Hungarian Telekia weed, or most of the Rudbeckias and Heleniums. No effort was spared on the attempt to lessen their voluminous carriage and the unruliness of their blossoms; no effort of advertising, or invention of fanciful names, that might assure the public acceptance of the wretchedly overblown forms that began to appear on their stiff, miserable stalks. North American autumn asters—modest wild flowers that grow on the poorest terrain in the most adverse conditions—and their European sisters as well—children of the Pontic steppe which had migrated northwards along its rivers—were made to bear larger and more abundant flowers with a greater wealth of color, even in spite of a limitless rankness that contradicts the very notion of the garden; and in the company of other similar weeds, such as the Boltonias and the fleabanes with mostly villous flowers of North America and the Andes, they effectively augmented the number of species which mass commerce in flowering plants could count among its wares. Whereas the most beautiful bushes of America and Japan remained within the spaces of the botanical gardens, if not indeed of the herbaries, the simple fact of mass-scale multipliability spurred the importation of enormous, vulgar bushes like the Japanese Bocconia, with its blemished, whitish foliage: a leprous heap of leaves with hidden, button-like, dirty-white flowers. Because a flower is first of all something that requires no care; secondly, survives our winters; thirdly, gives a massive supply of cut flowers; fourthly, fills up lots of space; fifthly, suits everybody's taste; and, sixthly, the rotary presses of even the laziest commercial gardener can throw it off in unlimited numbers of new, young plants at so and so many pennies the piece. And now that the English garden has largely banned these creatures, or in any case given them the place in which alone they at best belong, the wild flower garden—style and dignity have meanwhile accrued to the autumn asters and a few Heleniums and fleabanes, thanks to the truly unmerited attentions which they stole from far more worthy plants—it's hard to grasp the crudity of the sense of color on which these vulgar yellow, brittle yellow, star-shaped flowers of the badlands, studded at times with black dots (the combination of yellow and black, in flowers no less than animals, is a signal intended to frighten the eyes of vertebrates, whereas birds and insects see colors in a different way) were able to exercise an attraction.

"Color," as we know today, is not the decisive factor of any given effect: everything finally hinges on the texture of the material that carries it. Anyone who makes the experiment of dyeing wood, paper, silk, leather, linen, cotton, oilcloth and wool with exactly the same "color" will finally encounter seven quite different visual impressions. California yellow is not the yellow of the Missouri or the Texas plains, or of the rainless high plateaus of South America. The petals of the flowers of *Heliopsis pitcheri* or *Harpalium rigidum* are the work of a plant which has used up nearly all its strength in self-defense, in its struggle against a pitiless environment, and their tissue is dry and coarse: the rough, mealy material of toneless foliage and branches extends its dullness all the way up into the plant's corolla and corrupts its colors. The sky blue or heather pink of the Novi-Belgii or Kashubian aster bushes is produced by plants that have a murderous continental summer behind them, in soil which is often stone-hard and without humus. These colors are the beggar's rags of plants that flower in great distress; they're produced—just barely so—by its final effort to attract insects to the ripe pistils and stamens that crowd within its corolla. The color scale of pale blue, heather pink, straw yellow and white which typifies this family is precisely the same, objectively observed, as that of the bellflower, Jacob's ladder, forget-me-not and stock, among others, but the tissue of the petals of the large woodland bellflower is thin, moist and silky, and makes their colors shimmer and fill with promise. The petals of North America's autumn asters, on the other hand, are the non-transparent, non-translucid, storm-fast, sun-fast, thump-resistant, permanent stuff of dried flowers. California's magnificent Leptosynes show wonderful, serrated foliage of a moist and succulent green surmounted by a beguiling star-shaped flower in pale gold and light sulphur green, with curved, gently pointed petals; the leaves' deep, luscious green continues to shine through the flowers' precious yellow. Placed in water, a few of these flowers light up a room with a moist, glowing beauty, just as a special detail in the depths of the work of a great painter may hold a gleam of particularly exquisite color. In purely chromatic terms, the "yellow" here and the "yellow" there are the "same" yellow. But we know that the final upshot when two have done the same thing may not amount to the same thing, and we should also know that this applies to plants no less than to those who plant them. The colors of flowers are an integral part of the possible scale of the colors of their landscape, since a landscape also consists of the plants that cover it. "Perennial" plants with the overall bearing and characteristics glimpsed above are typical of steppe landscapes, and are possible nowhere else. So, this period of unenlightened trade made the European garden an extension of the steppes.

There were also those who were true to new enthusiasms, and who made the attempt to acquaint the garden with the incredible number of recently discovered annual plants which ranged from the beautiful to the fully magnificent. But in just a few years such efforts were profoundly discouraged. People who had never ventured abroad dug trenches around the terrain on which they harvested commercial seed: they had no regard for the new summer flowers, and no space for them in their fields. All available space had been claimed by the need to deliver the varieties of summer plants, unbelievably over-exploited, to which "the public"—which is to speak of the small-scale gardener—was already accustomed: Lilliputian forms of summer asters with tiny little flowers, for three weeks' service as "borderings" around regularly laid out beds and then to be ripped out; lobelias in ugly hues of liver-red (only the blue ones are pretty); fleurs-de-lys in red and white; stupid weeds like the indestructible Crepis, goosefoot, the yellow "field daisy" (*Chrysanthemum leucanthemum*), the countless sizes and colors of corn poppies; absolute nonsense like the Polygonums; fripperies like the hundreds and hundreds of varieties of pansies, each cultivated for square kilometers for the production of commercial seed, and sorted according to color and number of spots. Zinnias, summer phlox, and two or three varieties of Calliopsis slowly managed to make their way through barriers of prejudice and senselessness, in the company as well of the bright Moroccan daisy, *Chrysanthemum carinatum*, various Cosmeas, the difficult Godetias, the Spanish and North African linen plants, and the North American Nemophilas with their gracious blue crowns. But it must also be said, to the everlasting honor of the only remaining enthusiasts—the poor who decked their windows and balconies with flowers—that the petunia ranked already as a potentate at the time when Stefan George not only knew nothing of the plant's existence but even declared, with a smile on his lips, to Albert Rausch, who had mentioned the flower to George and who tells this tale in his memoirs, that there was no such thing as a flower by the name which Rausch just then had so imaginatively fabricated. Schizanthus, Salpiglossis, Nemesia, Browallia, Alonsoa, and Australia's beautiful straw flowers, the numerous Ipomoeas, Mimulus and Brachycomes, Argemones, Bidens and Clarkias gradually won a place for themselves, but only very gradually. As South Africa's asters created a stir at the turn of the century with their unheard-of scale of forms and colors, other flowers which when first introduced in the seventeenth century had instantly exerted a great fascination on the popular imagination and the Baroque garden—flowers like the Dimorphotheca, Arctotis, Gazania, Venidium, and finally the Ursinias, and as well the gentian blue Heliophilas, which belong to another family—stood agape before the dealers and the experts: aghast at such new daring, it was only bit by bit that such flowers allowed their space to be usurped. The great distributors who had inherited the spirit and nourished the legacy of the heroic century of gardening, and whose clientele was everywhere throughout the world, equanimously accepted losses on three quarters of their stock for decades. If one looks at the proud assortment of summer flowers which remained in Erfurt's catalogues, year in year out—with hundreds of flowers that were never seen to bloom in any German garden (thirty-eight Calliopsis, twenty-seven Amarantus, twelve Alonsoas, ten and even later six Cupheas, jewels like the Diascia, Didiscus, Gaura, and Ximenesia, the loveliest of the small spring flowers from California and New Mexico, the Baeria, Hymenoxis, Hymenostemma, Platystemon, Loasa and Blumenbachia, the Lopezia, Manulea, Nolana and whatever else their names may be)—and then surveys the relentless decadence of only a few years later, the shrinking list of offerings, the liquidation of companies, the debacle, the thorough depletion of a wealth which had seemed inexhaustible, one need not feel ashamed of experiencing the bitterest sensations. But one must also attempt to grasp the complexity of the situation. The last word had not been spoken. The flood and the barriers erected against it showed their strength by turns. The rout was not definitive, just as victory had not been permanent. Things were won, lost, and again regained, and the battle saw ever new factors come into play.

The continental garden shut its gates against the assault of the new flowers. It made no initial step in their direction, since the following and final steps were both perfectly obvious and unforeseeable: the garden's structure would have been laid to waste by a new and threatening form, by a revolution like the one of a hundred years before. Yet the garden didn't remain confined to stances of rigid defense. Its reply to the world's wild flowers lay in lending renewed attention to Europe's cultivated flowers. In the language of a gardener, its interests lay not in classes but in breeds; in a botanist's terms, not in species but in cultivated varieties, in mutations and anomalies. The century now coming to a close had been an era of individual freedom and creativity, and had been dominated by great collectors, whether fanciers at home, or explorers abroad. The century now beginning belonged to the largely untaught masses, and to those to whom they turned for counsel and orientation: the mass-scale cultivators, planters and breeders. And in its midst stood a new, brutal and highly conditioning economic factor, unknown to previous times: cut flowers and the florist shops. Schematically put, flowers over here, gardens over there, and between them all the water-filled vases of the millions and millions of the gardenless. In England, which again, for the second time, had become the setting for the heart of the whole predicament, these interests were not seen to be at odds with one another. As remarked before, the whole of the population—like the whole of the German people in the age of the Baroque garden—was a population of gardeners, and all the problems of importation, breeding, nurseries, commerce, supply and structural change were played out harmoniously within it; and this self-assurance put commerce and its tradesman gardeners in their dryly appointed place, since the highest authority lay ever more unmistakably with the growing critical system of observation and classification (which we'll soon view more closely), with the shows, juries and prizes of the great flower and gardening societies, and with a major gardening literature that ever more prodigiously developed out of passion, knowledge, and high ambitions.

On the continent, where neither criticism nor gardening literature were able to establish an influence, things stood quite differently: rather than finding themselves beneath the surveillance of a national spirit, the commercial cultivation and distribution of flowers was a purely economic force that trampled all such spirits to the ground. So, where the old garden threatened to turn into a wasteland, into a trivial space for long since vitiated flowers and newly imported weeds, no salvation would have lain in sight if an age-old institution, transformed and preserved by the century of the collector, had not seen fit, late in the eleventh hour, to give itself a new *raison d'être.* In Holland and Germany, and to a lesser degree in France and Switzerland, the figure of the breeder inserted itself between commerce and the wider public. Though only, to be sure, a brief, passing, euphoric resurgence of the inner life of the old gardening countries, this alone can be thanked for the way in which the new English garden, when it finally took hold on the continent and drew everything beneath its sway, could be welcomed by the forces of a human activity which already again was on the rise, and not simply put up with as an empty fashion. The Haages, the Pfitzers and the Neubronners, like the Arends and the Försters—which is to speak of the whole generation that followed Belgian personalities like Rodigas and van Geert—had surely not been able, nor would even have desired, to promote the new flowers or a new garden to which they might belong; but still they had taken at least one further step along the old Dutch path, or on the path that found its source in the continent's old Baroque garden and finally in the ancient garden of the Middle East: they had bent the flower to a garden's laws, and not to the laws of any garden which might anywhere be found, but to those of an ideal garden, of a postulatory garden; and they had turned their back on wild plants in favor of endorsing the garden varieties created by the human being. They weren't concerned with new and exotic flowers that had not *yet* become available; instead, they gave their attention to those other new flowers which had never *simply* become available, since without human intervention they would never have existed at all. The ordering principle of the human garden, which always strives toward geometry, once again, before its final historical demise, stood up in opposition to naturalism and defended the prerogatives of scrutiny and planning, just as it had done a century earlier, when the continent—from Hirschfeld's beautiful classic *General Theory of the Art of Gardening* (*Allgemeiner Theorie der Gartenkunst*) up to Prince Pückler's *Letters* and his *Reflections on Landscape Gardening* (*Andeutungen über Landschaftsgärtnerei*)—had absorbed and spiritually reformulated England's new departures. The continent had something of its own to offer: a past and "an ancient glory." Though the world took them for granted—possessing the forms in which it knows them as though they had issued from the hands of God—the rose, the carnation, and the buttercup, heartsease and stock had been produced, created, and indeed fabricated by the hands of French gardeners, just as the Dutch had invented the parrot tulip, the Persians the garden hyacinth, the Chinese the mallow. The place on which one stood was defensible and honorable. England, in the course of previous centuries, had been raised to this place with the continent's help, and one wasn't now at the wave of a hand, perhaps from no more than a fashion, to abandon it.

CHAPTER IV

The Wild Flower and the Cultivated Plant

THE flowered garment that covers the earth as we know it, no matter how lavishly embroidered in distant lands, or how delightful in our own more temperate latitudes, is only the shriveled remains of a primal abundance that exceeds imagination. The aeons have not increased the beauty of this cosmic ball. The golden age is no figment of imagination; the human being can track it down.

The optimistic nineteenth century's myths of development and progress—plants too were assured their part in the ascent from humility to ever greater perfection—have ended up where scientific myths are accustomed to end: in the slogans of the semi-educated masses. Nature is a great deal deeper than imagined by the ingenuous folly of trying to get to the bottom it. Her meager advances have been purchased at the cost of enormous losses, and retained at the price of tenacious parsimony. Astronomical catastrophes have dealt out calamities, extinctions and ruptures from which she has never been able to recover. Entire geological eras of her creatures were reduced to pitiful residues which in order to mother new organisms had to sacrifice all rights to form, in favor of the features most congenial to survival and reproduction. For vast geographical regions, and vast zones of the forms and species of the world of vegetation, the plants we know today have been culled from remnants. Having now begun to develop the pink, orange and violet lily of the valley from the white one, and the scarlet, lavender and deep gold freesia from the pale yellow form, we know the archaic color scale of both these flowers to have varied endlessly: unfathomable causes determined the exclusive survival of precisely those albino forms, where color has fallen away, which in most other plants are the more unstable; all others died out. We put nothing into the flower which it doesn't already contain, waiting for us to extract it. Our European poppies, the common summer vegetation of clayey soils, are red, whereas celandine is yellow, and the perennial arctic or alpine poppies are yellow on granite, but white on chalky soil. The Gaelic *Meconopsis cambrica* on the shores of the Atlantic is likewise yellow. And the Mediterranean horned poppy ranges from yellow to yellowish red with black spots, while its western Asian variety, which takes the habit of a gigantic shrub, is again shrill red all the way up into the mountainous regions of the Caucasus, and the forms found in the Pyrenees are a bright apricot. But in Tibet and the Himalayas, the Meconopsis present themselves slate blue, sky blue, violet, orange and yellow; in China all *Papaveraceae* are white and yellow; and in America white, yellow, and orange, without a single red variety. And finally there are the two magnificent Asian plants *Papaver hookeri* and *laevigatum*, the one a silky blood red, the other a deep silky purple. This is a scale that lacks no single tone, except for very rarest of all, deep gentian. And since the time when human hands first became involved with the reddest of all varieties, the common European corn poppy, *Papaver rhoeas*, all of them, nearly without exception, have sprung from it on their own, without crossings: so all of them were originally contained and condensed within its dry, piercing scarlet. It is only recently, after many long years of care, that the slate blue tones of the Himalayan Meconopsis have appeared from it. They can also be expected to emerge quite shortly—on any tomorrow or the following day—in the Iceland poppies. The salmon tones of *Papaver pyrenaicum* and *rupifragum atlanticum* are already coming to light among poppies from the Caucasus. The purple and brownish-scarlet tones which have long since grown visible in California's Eschscholtzias begin to play with a marked proclivity for mauve shades of violet. The magnificent shrub and tree-like poppies of China and California—Eomecon, Dendromecon, Romneya—will surely one day break away from their colors in yellow and white. The Greek Roemeria exhibits scarlet and impure violet forms even in the wild. Asia's opium poppy opens out into a veritable rainbow, from which hardly a single hue is missing.

Scientific nomenclature refers to the dahlia as variable—*Dahlia variabilis*—since as soon as it came into human hands it fell apart into an unforeseeable gamut of forms and colors. The Salpiglossis is likewise known as *Salpiglossis variabilis*. In its original state, this dusky-colored gullet stays stubbornly close to the ground, and the tones it displays are brownish, greenish, blackish, ashy, yellowish. But rather than failing, these muted coals have been banked to save on fuel. In only twenty to thirty years of cultivation, this Stygian scale was to modulate into an orchid-like array of colors; height trebled; bearing slendered; the gullet opened out into a chalice. What about the buttercups, or Europe's and Asia's peonies? Did the human being "fill out" and "double" those bright, simple crowfoot shells, that semi-cupola of the "Pentecost rose"? Where would one have found the stuff with which to do so, if it didn't already belong to the plant, and hadn't been laid away for better times? The Trollius that stands beside it—its closest relative and always double—surely made no gift of it. If any single plant is "variable," then all of them are variable. The plant as such is variable. Because nature is variable. What one happily called "development" is the drive toward variation.

Alpine flowers grow from umbels or "rosettes." Their leaves lie on the ground, or are pressed to the ground, and develop in a thick radial cluster, tightly packed, so that all foliage functions as a single organ, beneath the jealous surveillance of a guardian spirit which in such a frightening environment—with the life-threatening dangers of hunger, thirst, polar cold, primal storms, and primal chaos—dare not allow the least free play to its respiratory apparatus. If the endangered creature keeps itself alive for long enough to reach maturity and thus to prepare for motherhood, a flower rises from the center of the circle with barely the minimum visibility demanded by its functions. When cultivation allows the plant to live in other circumstances, it very soon relaxes such discipline and seizes freedom. After a period of acclimatization, the length of which varies from species to species, the foliage, no longer bent to the humiliation of seeking protection on the ground, begins to climb along a central stalk and to branch away from its sides. The stalk of the flower too begins to develop leaves. And no miserly calculation of the time required for fertilization any longer restricts the plant to a single flower. It sends up ever more flowers, and grows luxuriant. But human cultivation has only supplied a situation which nature neglected to put on the path of the errant plant as it went astray. All alpine flowers, without exception, are emigrants in distress. The cliff-side cranny is an exile, not a home. Their primal relatives that remained at home sing no lament, and have known no cause to stunt themselves, no adversity to which to adapt. Our alpine primrose was once no more a plant of high-mountain elevations—an essentially arctic plant—than the Pyrenees' *Ramondia,* the dwarf gloxinia. Its Calabrian variety, *Primula palinuri,* grows on warm sea-side cliffs, and its broad umbels are surmounted by a flower nearly a meter tall. And this isn't the plant's primordial form, which grew extinct for reasons which remain no mystery to us. It didn't survive the Alluvium—the Holocene—the era when the earth was covered with marshes—since the collar of its roots, as with any number of plants, is sensitive to moisture. The original form can be imagined to have grown in the deep, loose, well-drained humus of Europe's hot, primal forests. It may perhaps, like the Belvedere primrose hybridized in England, have stood as tall as a man. Surely it shone with fabulous colors. Our mountain primrose is a lovely creature, and all who pluck it on a windy pass from the crumbling slate in which it loves to live must do so with delight, and are moved. But in botanical terms, it has to be seen as a remnant—a condensed or abbreviated form, for ears that prefer such words—which only survived where it found protection in the drier regions to which it fled. Like other high-mountain plants, it is sometimes carried downhill by melting snows. In the Bavarian moors, in the Isar valley, it's seen as "rare." But a rare plant is always a plant which has gone astray, or which hasn't yet grown fully extinct in a place where otherwise it would be at home. Nature knows no rare plants. She produces plants only in simultaneous tens of thousands. Where she doesn't appear to do so, the heavens and the earth have ripped her magic nets, and she turns to mending their strings.

When a man plants half an acre of land with zinnias, or with the small South African shrub *Lobelia erinus*, and then stands at flowering time before a vast expanse of the surface of the earth in dull red or fleur-de-lys blue—such as one sees in Quedlinburg—he hasn't created, as bogus sentimentality insists, an artificial or unnatural scene that can only send a shudder through refined aesthetic sensibilities. Quite the contrary! He has reproduced a primal landscape. It's in the very same way, looking down from the hills of western California, that the endless, uninterrupted expanse of the glowing yellow of Eschscholtzia fills all hollows and covers the valley floor, as though spread by a giant roller of orange paint. Prodigious expansiveness, prodigious density, prodigious powers of endurance and germination on the part of minuscule seeds—all of which are inadequate and only partial terms for overwhelming fertility—are the norm demanded by nature's drive to self-variation. Six years ago, the writer planted and raised the seeds of *Nicotiana silvestris* in his garden—that tall, lovely species of decorative tobacco with abundant, white, long-stemmed flowers—but then, for technical reasons, decided to eliminate the plants. That garden today contains no handful of topsoil from which its seeds don't bothersomely sprout anew, year in year out, and have to be removed. Ten years ago, in a previous garden, he sowed the Mexican chamois-horn flower, *Martynia fragrans*, and again immediately removed the plants. This spring, it suddenly sprouted in the soil of a potted plant in his current garden. One of its large, hard seeds, in appearance like a lump of coal, had been transported with his shrubs across many miles from one garden to the next, slept dry for a decade in a storeroom's dust, then slipped into the compost in the course of sweeping up and preparing soil for potted plants, and now the unmistakable hammer shape of its rigid gray cotyledons stood stubbornly on tiny roots in a new location. It is quite well known that precisely the seed of the so-called "fine seed" plants—where a single gram contains over a hundred thousand potential descendents—begonias, gloxinias, Mimulus, lobelias, Calceolarias, petunias—and with the single exception of oily seed—remains capable of germination for great lengths of time, up to twenty-five years. Begonia seed, if left to its own devices, covers all available soil with a thick, protective moss from which the strongest individuals rise up tall and mature to flowering, whereas the surrounding earth is felt-like, its surface shot through with the roots of the brood, and allows no other plant to sprout and find nourishment in the ground moisture, which the tiny begonia shoots hoard in common for themselves. Plants do not live "socially." Their most elementary drive is to cover the earth entirely with themselves alone, creating a forest, a jungle, a meadow, in the very same way that fire reaches out and burns whatever it can touch.

What was once the primal violence of the massive proliferation of single sorts of plants remains surely no more than partly visible in the winterless forests we know today. It was previously remarked that individual plants and species of plants have been forced to retreat to the places in which they currently live. But that doesn't yet say enough. The realm of plants as a whole has been forced to retreat, since the solid earth we know today is no longer what it used to be. There is much more water and much less land than before. And of the land which now remains, only a modest belt of latitudes has soil conditions of constant warmth in nearly every season, such as once stretched north throughout the whole of Europe. The Mediterranean sea which recently invaded the space between southern Europe and northern Africa surges over a buried realm of vegetation. The waterless, plantless deserts of Asia are likewise of recent formation. Much of the newer land which has lifted itself from the ocean floor consists of arid high plateaus and arid mountains. Limestone peaks like those most recently formed also prove to be largely inimical to vegetation, and vast orders of plants avoid them, as though they were plagued or poisoned. The advance, finally, of the conifer forests and their occupation of enormous spaces drives away all flowering life by depriving it of light, as has recently grown clear, and by poisoning the soil with tannin. From this point of view, the flower is hemmed quite tightly in, and is everywhere in a deadly struggle for space with its peers. It finds its energies overtaxed and must nearly exhaust them. Ways in which plants can be forced to show extreme frugality have already been discussed. The ways in which they adapt their habit to the tasks of simple survival are clear to see. The unilateral use of their powers for the development of merciless battle techniques can hardly be surprising. Mexico's *Tithonia speciosa*, an annual shrub as tall as a man, and magnificently charged with red flowers, is equipped with powerful shoots reaching out for over a meter from its foot and sides: within a circle of a meter and a half, they strangle all other plants—regardless of their strength or size—and prevent them from maturing their seeds. As well, it sends out its blossoms on shafts which not only are a half-meter long, but which also are covered with a silky hair that aids their penetration through alien, neighboring thickets so as then to cast their seeds as far abroad as possible. The *Hibiscus diversifolius*, an annual plant that's barely a half-meter tall, has a shaft that bears its flower, but it also covers the whole surrounding area with creeping, densely-flowered shoots, covering the ground as though with a carpet: an enchanting sight when the broad, ivory-colored, cup-shaped flowers with a central crimson eye and a tassel of golden pistils lie in masses that seem to have fallen to the earth; but the other plants which still this year have managed to sprout from the carpet can enjoy no prospect of holding their own against the beautiful strangler and its profligate scattering of seed.[†] And no mention has yet been made of the most ferocious stranglers—the subterranean stranglers—like fall asters, bellflowers, dragonhead, *Verbena venosa*, alkekengi and countless others. One might keenly argue that, basically speaking, there are no such things as individual plants. There are only communities: the wood, not the fir; the cluster, rather than the individual; the stand of flowers that forms a unit, or attempts to form a unit. Where stands appear, they do so surely as a necessary act of self defense—just as herds of animals protect the lives of the single individuals that make them up—but the stand of plants is also an original, irrepressible, hereditary tendency; an expression of the impulse to return to conditions of primal abundance; an acceptance and expression of the will of nature. Because nature's longing for unfettered variation can find its satisfaction only by way of her own unsurveyable abundance. Seen ideally, as well as specifically, two fully identical plants never occur; every plant is a variation, a variety all its own; type is a purely theoretical assumption. Yet the level of variation which we consider to be perceptually significant, the mutation, is a natural phenomenon that only takes place among masses of individuals, and only, indeed, among very large masses of individuals. Stinginess and envy are sterile. Only waste and lavishness can manage new departures. It was profligate waste that allowed primeval nature to vary the forms, colors, and dimensions of plants, raising mutations to the status of mothers of whole new breeds, mutating them again and finally promoting lawless, incestuous nuptials. Primeval mutations were followed by primeval crossings, robust bastards, anomalies. Anyone today who rears ten species of columbine in the same garden will allow no seedling to grow unless he is willing to face a legion of blurred and befuddled forms. On farms where seed is produced, squash, cucumbers and melons—and, in America, cassava and citrus fruits—are first of all to be grown with distances of miles between them; and individual varieties must likewise be

†The plant which appears in botanical literature as *Hibiscus diversifolius* (the swamp Hibiscus) shows little if any resemblance to the one to which Borchardt ascribes this name. The name of the plant to which Borchardt refers remains unclear. The description here is also slighty at variance with the description offered in the Catalogue, p. 254-55. — H.M.

kept in strict isolation from one another. Because nature's aims are different from those of the human being. Nature wants always to come up with something new. Nature does not view the cucumber, the squash, the melon, the cassava or *Aquilegia glandulosa* as a given or a goal, but as a wave in the sea of forms. The human being builds dams, nature wants to flow. Everything nature has created has flowed forward, flowed together, then set itself apart, was again transformed, and again resmelted. Each of her creatures is a concentrate and compendium of its whole previous history, as well as the premise and harbinger of its unforeseeable future. Nietzsche remarked, from the depths of his loathing of history, that the human being is only a moment of transition. That's surely true where the human being is most related to the plant; since that, precisely, is the nature of the plant, utterly and entirely.

This enormous torrent of forms is no disorder; but even a vague intuition of the co-ordinates of the order that frames it is reserved to the superhuman and the supernatural; and human notions of order must rest content with their own particular deductions. The first premise we have to establish is that the wild plant is neither an absolute, nor a canon, nor a superlative; it is a stage of development. The second understands this stage to be intertwined with all the conditions in which it naturally occurs: climate, soil, levels of moisture, free or cramped positions, sunlight, nourishment, the temper of the seasons, altitude. If one or more of these conditions is lost, abandoned, or altered, the stage of expression to which it belongs disintegrates, or can disintegrate, if not immediately, soon enough, bit by bit. When we say that years of care have led a plant to cultivated forms, we simply deceive ourselves. It should only be said that the plant which the human hand has freed from a particular stage of existence has begun to explore a return to its greatest perfection, and to wander through the realm of its natural freedom.

There was a moment when so-called dwarf forms appeared among Mexico's enormous, bulky Cosmeas, since the cultivated plants stand much more freely than those in the wild, and no longer need to stretch up giraffe-like necks in order to lift their flowers out over the pampas and into the light. Eschscholtzia and verbena likewise found their way to tall (*erecta*) and "compact" (*compacta*) varieties: regular watering and fertilization had led to the appearance of mutant or exuberant (hybrid) forms with a wealth of foliage and a great profusion of large-blossomed flowers; the range of possible colors unfolded; species-specific traits grew indistinct in apparent imitation of those of other related species, and even veered toward features of species to which they are unrelated, or which perhaps are extinct, and in any case unknown. The semi-creeper *Tropaeolum lobbianum* has given birth to non-climbing forms, to small flowered bushes. Or, conversely, a bush like *Bidens dahlioides* has developed flowers with stems that start to wind the one around the other, bringing the plant, to a certain degree, into the neighborhood of *Bidens tereticaulis.* And umbrella-like clusters of flowers are now to be found atop the stems of asters and balsaminas. The human being did not add or append such qualities to plants: he unleashed them. He unleashed them by destroying the natural conditions which framed the appearance of the plants in the wild—an act of destruction already implicit in his first unnatural intervention, the planting of seeds in protected places—by setting the plants apart in unnatural isolation, and then by the process—surely not unnatural, and indeed imitative of nature, but artificially repetitive—of enormous plantations of isolated species on uniform terrain, cared for in uniform ways. Such disruptions of the complex, organic fabric of natural environmental conditions at first provokes complete disorder. Nature's forms lapse into states of unprecedented regression; locked doors spring open, revealing the secrets behind them. Adam's sons will find no more than small-minded triumph in seeing themselves as masters—or in savoring future profits—on the basis of any such plaything as the first example of a double *Dahlia variabilis,* the first white carnation, the first *Tagetes patula* to reach the height of a tree, the first prodigiously deviant *Begonia tuberosa,* or whatever else the case may be. But even if he didn't create that wondrous thing, man has the power to stabilize it. The will of nature has placed itself in his hands, and from this point forward he can guide it. Again and again he will only call forth what would have lain free to appear on its own from out of nature's original store of possibilities—what in fact lay free. Even where he crosses—choosing parents for offspring in which he intends to blend those parents' characteristics—he sets his will, in Schiller's words, to doing something that will-less nature might have done without him. But all this work, if endlessly continued, will nonetheless result in something it's proper to call a cultivated plant: a plant no longer simply derived from nature, and instead entirely alien to it. The oldest of Europe's cultivated plants—heartsease, the carnation, the rose, stock, and already as well, today, the dahlia, the Chinese aster, and many others—have truly ceased to have any other homeland than the human hand. They are as human, and no less masterpieces, than a festive face, a bejeweled hand, a precious painting, a splendid dress. Their landscape, their skies, their characteristic setting, their original habitus are things from which breeding has freed them, and have vanished. They can never again be imagined in the wild; there was no primeval time in which they looked as they do; nature would never have designed them as they are. The exaggerated characteristics, one-sidedly developed, which humans have decided they're to bear—the long, rigid stems of carnations and roses bred to be cut, or the fluted buds of America's hybrid remontant rose, those buds no longer suited to their flowers, which in fact bloom badly—have ceased to be natural forms. Nature's resistance to the sabotage of her own established course is overcome through further, persistent bastardization, and something in the depths of the plant is broken, and will never heal. Cultivation becomes only a question of always coming away with more of something which is always the same. These rampant creatures are no longer plants, but an idle, extravagant game. The spring has snapped, the apex has been driven beyond itself, nature has been misused, the harvest is dead. But since human beings are finally not to be fooled, hybris and superfluity run aground. Indolence may lead one to purchase such products from the merchants, but one does not raise them. The enormous American carnations which grow so double as to split their crowns are found in no one's garden. They issue in thousands of uniform copies of themselves from the commercial greenhouses of entrepreneurs. It's only exceptionally that the connoisseur decides, for once, to try his hand at the new roses—when a wonder like the President Hoover or the talisman succeeds in wringing from nature a creature of the stature of the Maréchal Niel—but he all the more avidly returns to the fine, healthy, antique species which run the risk of going lost. Yes, he turns back to wild roses from abroad. None of America's Wichura ramblers—which were further developed from the crimson rambler and the Dorothy Perkins—have so profoundly influenced the garden as the splendid Chinese bushes *Rosa moyesii* and *fargesii*: the spring is overwound, the pendulum jumps its track. If the cultivation of pansies continues out into senselessness, beyond the recent, giant Swiss varieties, in order to force a plant which can only achieve its effect in groups to disproportionate individual size, then the first large, exotic violet on the order of the Engadine's picture pretty *Viola calcarata*—no one who has seen it bloom on the slopes overlooking Silvaplana, where it spreads across whole fields, can forget its bobbing silk-blue faces—will drive them from every flower bed.

A discourse on the flowers which human beings have created by working in opposition to nature reaches such conclusions even when it doesn't focus on the garden for which such plants were created. Yet it is only when the garden is its starting point that it finds a proper standard on which to base its judgments. Because the order of the garden is a human, humane and finally ethical principle. And as such it will always tend to grow anti-natural and geometric, banning the flower from its precincts, unless the flower too adheres to its order, and likewise undergoes humanization. The garden is anti-naturalistic, and detests and combats wild plants. We have seen this conflict again and again, and must also see it to reveal the value of the cultivated plant.

Breeders exercised the right to strive not for a flower's most characteristic form, but for those of its forms most suited to the garden. Their final products were shaped by notions of the flower's best integration in the garden. Bearing and structure, the height of the plant and the abundance of its blossoms, the size of those blossoms and the various factors that increase their effect, such as the degree to which they're doubled, their purity of color, their singleness of color, or some striking form of mutation—the star phlox, the Calliopsis with twisting petals, the cactus-like forms of the "sunshine" class of asters—have been especially influenced by such ideas. Where the one controlling image is the image of the garden as a whole, each of its individual parts must be compatible with every other, and content with its own particular place. Things that spill out from their appointed place will feel the snip of the shears. Dwarf forms, which allow the largest possible number of flowers on limited areas of space, are especially sought after. The dwarf lobelia has driven out of the garden the tall and wonderfully beautiful species from which it derives; and the recent appearance of pulvinate, cushion-like forms of the marvelous sapphire blue *Browallia viscosa* will have a similar effect on its taller forms, despite their incomparable grace; the tall forms of the magnificent Ageratum, a shrub with an inexhaustible wealth of flowers, are hardly to be seen any more, except in England, having ceded their place to the dwarf forms used in borders, where they reign supreme. There's also the question of adapting plants to the climactic challenges of wet and windy lands, where strong stems and compact construction are sure to be preferred. But such a direction of breeding contrasts with nature. The plant wants quite the opposite: the plant's desire to "kip over," and thus to scatter its ripe seed as far as possible away from the mother, is the most primordial form of movement on the part of an earthbound creature that nonetheless craves locomotion. Rudbeckia bushes, like *Rudbeckia hirta*, and Coreopsis on the order of *Coreopsis maritima* remain close to the ground and in the form of a cupola for as long as the plants are entirely green, and only preparing to bloom; but once in flower they fall apart, spreading out radially and away from their centers, and bending toward the ground, with a great gaping hole in the midst of them, if one doesn't tie them up. One hears, of course, that as little as possible ought to be bound. American breeders grow dahlias on shafts so strong as to require no further support, even to the point of having created a kind of dahlia tree, such as could never appear in nature. The creation of shrub varieties exasperates the notion of compact construction while ever more narrowing the species with which the breeder works, all in the name of defending the goal of a shrub garden, which, once planted, will be thoroughly undemanding, and then will have nothing other to do than year by year to grow more beautiful. With ever more stringently cultivated flowers, the garden would be sure of becoming their master, if indeed the garden were only the expression of a principle of order, and the flower no more than raw material. But there's a threshold where it comes up short, and finds itself forced to retreat: at the threshold where the garden itself is a dream and the flower a living thing. The garden, the flower and the human being are each a pole of the other, and therefore eternal. They find their renewal through reciprocal contradiction.

The flower is a living thing. While surely bending to the hand of the human being, it also escapes him, since it grows. A healthy bed of shrubs can remain untouched for only three years. Then the human being must mediate between the weak and the strong, save the oppressed, divide the exuberant, eliminate the suffering, renew depleted soil, refresh spent vigor. His assumption that plants, simply by virtue of having been bred into bed plants, love to blossom while crowded into the near vicinity of other alien growths in a flat tract of flower bed is no less unnatural than false. They abhor it. They want to flower among themselves, and to tolerate nothing alien beside or among them. Stronger roots infiltrate the ground beneath weaker ones; rapacious roots steal nourishment from everything around them. Different species, moreover, must be manured in fundamentally different ways. Larkspur shoots grow sterile in the vicinity of a large sea holly that is just beginning to bloom, and for half a meter in every direction absorbs all nitrogen and phosphorus from the garden's soil. The battle takes place beneath the ground. The garden's master—who essentially wants flowers to pluck—shakes his head, and stands before a fluid situation: fluid because it's alive, and refuses to be called to a standstill; in constant transformation since it's made of organisms, not mechanisms. No feat of breeding can give the sunflower's collar of dry roots to a midsummer blossom that tolerates no moisture. Schizanthus, the butterfly flower, and Salpiglossis—simply to name two favorites—can be effortlessly raised on upper Bavaria's thin layer of humus, since the morenic gravel of the subsoil drinks up every gush of rain. But in normal garden soil, part sand, part clay, as demanded by most summer flowers, no artificial drainage is of any avail. These flowers are the children of rainless summers. They grow green and luxuriant in the rainy spring, in order then to hold their nuptials in cloudless heat and develop their seed, and finally in drought to wither into straw. So, is one to keep them in pots, if one wants to run no risk and to see them bloom? Not really. There are also other means. But they exclude the flower bed, and the blank, dead order of the regularly ordered garden. Ah, yes, we know; but surely you'll never get the best from profusely blossoming cultivated forms—the Imperial Salpiglossis, the *Schizanthus wisentonensis*—without the kind of scrupulous care that can only be managed in a proper garden, with proper preparation of the soil, and hoeing, manuring and watering. Really, only there? And are you truly willing to deny yourself such gorgeous new flowers simply because they refuse to live in your "properly" laid out flower beds? How will you manage to plant—and only a fool would neglect to plant it—the magnificent new *Venidium fastuosum* from southern Africa, that orange, star-shaped flower with the form of a double crown, and a central disk that slowly fades from bluish-brown to gold, all in the midst of luxuriant, serrated, gray-green foliage, as heraldic as the leaves of any Acanthus. Planted in a bed, it will send its roots throughout a circle of soil nearly a meter across—where will you find such space, and what will you deprive of it? If you want to make this plant's acquaintance, you must plant it like a melon, forcing its roots to descend into the earth, and you must know how one goes about that. That's too much bother for you? So, let cobblers stick to cobbling. Content yourself with the small assortment of the undemanding designed for the undemanding. Quite a pretty garden can in fact be made with plants that make no special demands, and indeed put up with anything; and there's even a bit of room for avoiding a couple of things you hold to be just too common. White snapdragons are no less shy of moisture than Salpiglossis and die in all heavy terrain, no matter how well drained, unless you work the soil quite deeply, year in year out, and give it abundant lime. Snapdragons are flora of the loose gravel and cliff-side fissures of the Mediterranean countries, and live wild in extremely arid places: they sink their fleshy, woolly roots to astounding depths to tap the moisture below, and then remain unfazed even by heavy frost. What kills them in the north is the soil's moisture, not its cold—and it's a great shame to lose them, since old, woody bushes are true showpieces. The white varieties are the most delicate. And if you don't want to lose them after only a few years, plant no lilies, crown imperial, or columbine in beds. That's why columbine doesn't deserve its reputation as a short-lived plant. Properly planted, it has quite a normal life span. Of the lilies, only *Lilium regale* tolerates being planted in beds. All others wither. *Lilium speciosum,* the splendid Japanese lily with gold streaks, blossoms for more than a single season only in thick grass. In the naked terrain of a flower bed, kept always free of weeds, its bulb can no longer be found after three years. In other words: stick to the proven garden forms. Since what they have proved is the good humor with which they'll put up with you: force fed when sated, watered while wanting to remain dry, planted in places where they do not want to grow, thrown into the society of bad neighbors, isolated where they want to live in groups, they gratefully blossom all the same, serenely hold their ground, cause no disturbance around them, and give you pleasure. This garden too expresses your relationship to nature, and its sense of order is an image of your own: an order free from tension, since what do you include within it, what do you exclude from it? Surely not nature, since you seek her out and love her in places outside of your garden, and in a certain sense she constitutes its other half, its correlative. Her meadow and mountain flowers, her sprays of heather are as dear to you as your vase of asters. You do not fear her; she causes you no anxiety; you do not banish her beyond your gates. The order you create in your garden holds no longing to see nature repeated at your own home, humanly recreated and creatively transformed. Your order, in a certain sense, is only a large, perennial, prettily arranged bouquet, culled from a nature which does not exist—a nature of garden flowers from seed packets and commercial exchange. You exclude nothing but the difficult. And you create no realization of what you dream, not even a normal caprice.

But where the order of the garden encounters dream and longing and situates itself between the wild magnificence of nature and the closed precincts of human activity as an act of imagination that equally participates in both, the garden's geometry falls away along with the monopoly of cultivated plants, and both are perceived as the will-of-the-wisps which they are, finally, to the eyes of the garden itself. The regularly constructed garden with nothing but highly cultivated plants is a house of cards which can only be kept from falling down by constant shifting, mending and tinkering: a strenuous and only apparent order that speaks exclusively of the gardener's expertise; an artificious mosaic with an exiguous choice of materials. A push and it all falls down. And that's what makes it the favorite and most protected child of all the branches of commerce that live on making the garden an occult science: the professional gardeners and garden specialists and garden architects and all the commercial interests which use them as conduits through which to reach out to customers. There is a difference between this apparent order which presents itself as an order, and that other apparent order, that greater apparent order, which presents itself as a lack of order and conceals itself behind it. That too is a human and cultural fact; that too belongs to the human being whose hand transforms the flower. It too sees the garden as a fixed point which it will not sacrifice to the flower, but that's not the garden from which it derives and which it imagines itself to know; that's the garden it has yet to encounter, and toward which it strives. It too will include the flower within its order; but rather than alien to the flower, that order relates to it. It must therefore know the flower. And those to whom it only serves as raw material for the crafting of images of their own invention do not know it. This order, again, won't find its canon in the wild flower, but the wild flower is endowed with features which it will not want to undo through any art of breeding and hybridization—its habitus, its physiognomy, its character, which accord with its landscape. And finally it will close its door to the intrusive beggar, meanwhile grown quite bothersome, who inserts himself between the flower and the garden and makes demands on our time: the flower bred to be cut, its privileges, and its florist shops. While making no attempt to grow flowers in the wilderness, it will grow them in freedom. It won't from the very start gainsay the natural conditions in which they appear, and instead will attempt to recreate them. It will lend close attention to every change in form that controlled cultivation, different soil, and an altered climate necessarily provoke, but it won't stand guard against every adultery in the greenhouse. And in never a moment of the plan of the garden and its planting scheme will it forget that it's a child of its times: of the century not yet and no longer of the garden, but instead of the new flower, of which thousands of varieties stand before the fence, begging for a private conversation that makes no room for the specialized tradesmen and designated professional experts. The real bloom and the dream of a world in flower want to come together, and even, if need be, at the cost of dispensing with the cultivated plant, just as Lili's suitor and the English park came together by dispensing with the laurel hedge and the slender yew tree pyramid at the side of the statue of the Oread.

CHAPTER V

The Flower and Its Landscape

WE ARE accustomed to think of the palm, the cypress and the oak as characteristic features of clearly definable landscapes, and the image of such a landscape appears before our eyes as soon as the name of the plant is mentioned. Germans speak of the "Brandenburg pine," the English of the "English hawthorn," and notions such as "a German forest," "an English country lane," or "a Tuscan olive grove" belong to common language. They assume that plant cover and landscape are closely, physiognomically related; that each is explained by the other; that each contains the other. Many will find it effortless to associate the flowered stalk of the red digitalis, or the Turk's cap lily, or the great bellflower (Canterbury bells) with the half-sunny woodland clearing in which one has seen them grow; or wild columbine with steep meadows; mullein with arid, rocky hills; lily of the valley, garden balsam, Solomon's seal, red helleborine, corydalis with dense woods; the wild primrose with open pastures. The feeling that these particular plants uniquely grow in these particular places, as expressions of their physiognomy, is more than imagination, and correctly intuits a truth. The habit of a plant in its natural setting is shaped and determined by the specific conditions in which it lives; but these same specific conditions also shape its natural surroundings as a whole, compelling their adherence to a local scale of forms and colors that the flower reflects and epitomizes. The result is a natural order which we perceive to be organic and harmonious: the impression is aesthetic, yet appears at the conclusion of an orderly chain of phenomena. The further step of regarding each of these just named plants—individually, and as groups—to be confined to certain "wholes" is something that some of us will hesitate to do. Doing so, one indeed would go too far: without exception these plants are common to all of Europe, of central Europe, on out into Asia. And this, precisely, is this sense in which the returning expatriate who meanwhile has grown accustomed to exotic plants will greet them as those of his own continent. He will see them to wear a European face, quite unmistakably. He will find a European quality in their fine and tenuous color scale, in their delicate structure, their modest faces, the concealment with which they bloom, their fragile forms that ask to be sought out. These impressions too are right and proper, since beautiful necessities stand behind them. Though civilization has made our climates drier, the habit and bearing of the European plant continues to speak of the stormy, rainy lands of primeval times, such as the Romans encountered, and of forests that knew little sun. This is the source of these lightless, hovering, half-toned colors; the explanation of these pendulous crowns, umbrellas over pollen dust. Vividly colored flowers are beacons that work at a distance; damp woods are no place in which to find them. Nothing here can blossom in geranium red, gentian blue, snapdragon purple, shimmering violet or fiery orange. The same holds true for these flowers' forms. They have been designed to work from up close, for eyes that observe them carefully; they demand to be sought out, like forget-me-nots, violets and columbine. They have a secret grace, and no pageantry. Some of Browning's most famous verses—"Oh, to be in England now!"—reveal that the poet was also an attentive gardener: he compares the flowers of England's spring with the melon blossoms he saw in the south, and his homesick longing for their chaste, timid grace prompted a stern rebuke of the sumptuous, alluring Indian plant: "that gaudy melon flower." That's how things stand. The flower contains its landscape, incontrovertibly.

This, too, is why gardens never hold those flowers that grow freely just beyond their fences, turning instead to those of unaccustomed landscapes: landscapes of otherness, dream, or longing. The fence sets apart two worlds, and otherwise why would it be there? Even the garden's best loved flowers speak of distant loves, and make them real. Of all the trite and peevish objections to unknown flowers, the most senseless is the one most frequently heard: that the well-known garden flowers are "familiar" to us. Such a view bears witness only against itself, since these flowers by nature are not at all familiar to us, but have only gradually and very slowly *become* familiar; and in order to do so they had first of all to be welcomed to our soil by those of our ancestors who felt the attraction of precisely what made them most alien. "Garden flowers," as one protectively calls them, are the wild flowers of other lands, now cultivated; and no matter how highly altered by cultivation, as they doubtless are, they always maintain an intimate blood relationship with the wild forms from which they spring, and with the characteristics of the landscape in which those wild forms grow. And they are always fundamentally at odds with our own wild flowers and the physiognomic traits that typify their surroundings. Anyone who plants Reseda (North Africa) and buttercups (Asia Minor), summer asters (China) and day lily (Japan), summer phlox (Southern Texas) and straw flowers (Australia), gladiolas (the Cape of Good Hope) and zinnias (Mexico), garden balsam (eastern India), dahlias (Chimborazo), verbena (Argentina) and sun flowers (Peru) within a single small garden has already unwittingly drawn together all the latitudes of all the earth's continents. He walks through a color scale of strong unbroken tones, dry or glassy, hefty or deeply fired, reflecting the hues of always sunny skies and scorching earth, such as here in our native latitudes could show in no bird's feather, no butterfly's wing, no pebble. The lymph of the stem he cuts is thick and viscous; oddly shaped tubers and clumps of rhizomes, fortresses charged with stored vitality, lie in the soil beneath the upper shoots of the plants; verbena covers the ground with a felt-like carpet of fiery umbels; day lily flowers only for hours, as tropical creatures typically do, and not like our own lilies for days.

And the door-yard garden of the priggish, suspicious personality whose liking for plants is confined to those with which he's already acquainted will be flanked by the garden of his neighbor, who, quite the opposite, will only grow what no one else has planted. And since spatial extremes are always leveled by time, stubbornness only slightly arrests the flood. There more slowly, here more swiftly, ever new flowers automatically press their way into the garden. One of them sets the tone, the others follow. What a few years back was exceptional soon grows common. In England, the Schizanthus of Chile and Argentina is already known as "the poor man's orchid." And the best Salpiglossis seeds (another Chilean plant) come from Scottish gardens. This slow seepage is the end result of enormous pressures that lie in the distance behind it. While gradually running its course, the nineteenth century's flood of exotic wild flowers had revealed and defined a number of reserves from which European gardens could draw new flowers that demanded no more than modest protective measures, or even none at all: the reserves of regions like Asia Minor, China, Chile and Argentina, California and Mexico, continuing on as well into the high plateaus of Central America; or again, South Africa, New Zealand, Australia. Other regions of flora, once less conspicuous, began to assume importance: the southern, or Patagonian reaches of South America which Elliott explored; the region of the Li-Kiang Mountains in western China, discovered by Farrer, and gifted with apparently boundless treasures of plants which before had been entirely unknown; the so-called Islands of the Blessed, as the Canaries and Azores were known; the area which at first quite gradually expanded from Arizona to Florida; or the northeast Himalayas and Tibet. And to make it clear that this lengthy list proposes no confusion between the interests of gardening and botany, one can briefly remark on the outposts to which these latter-day paradises have managed already to advance: one finds their flowers not only in sophisticated gardens, but also in those which have no inkling of the history and origins of cultivated plants. The bush-like slipper flowers (*Calceolaria rugosa* and related species) come from Chile and Patagonia, like all other members of their family. The salmon-colored Namaqua daisies (*Dimorphotheca*) and orange gazanias, already quite widespread as easily cultivated summer plants, find their natural range from the Cape of Good Hope to Natal. The sulphur-yellow larkspur (*Delphinium sulphureum* or *zalil*) comes from Abyssinia and Palestine; the giant poppy (*Papaver orientale*) from the Caucasus; the blue Meconopsis poppy, which has risen to the heights of a fashionable flower, from the Himalayas and Tibet. Godetias, Eschscholtzias and Clarkias, now highly common summer flowers, all hail from California; the common yellow cutting flower *Chrysanthemum nivelli*, the "yellow daisy," is native to the Canaries (like ragwort, *Senecio cruentus*). Cosmeas, which already have turned into barnyard flowers, are Mexican. *Cynoglossum amabile*, a bright, sky-blue flower that's commonly planted in beds and resembles the forget-me-not, is a recent arrival from China. All Gaillardias come from Mexico; all garden lupines from the region that stretches from California to Central America, which again is the home of all the varieties of Mimulus. All Nemesias come from the Cape of Good Hope; just as all the most popular strawflowers—Helichrysum, Helipterum, Polycolymina, Rhodanthe—are Australian. Turning to shrubs, the indispensable Aubrietias are from Greece or Asia Minor; the Astilbes are Chilean; the orange-red and now ubiquitous *Cheiranthus allionii* comes from Siberia and western Asia; all the species of Eremurus from the Caucasus, on to as far as Taurus and the Himalayas. All freesias are South African; all Incarvilleas Chinese; and nearly all the new lilies (*regale*, *sargentiae*, and so forth) either again Chinese or from North America; all Pentstemons from California, Oregon, and the American mountains down to Arizona and Florida; almost all the new and fashionable primroses in stunning colors (*beesiana*, *bulleyana*, and so forth) from China; the pin cushion shrubs from the Caucasus. The *Thalictrum dipterocarpum*, already fully domesticated, comes from Tibet, like the pale lilac pagoda variety of bellflowers over fine columbine foliage; all tall speedwells from America, Australia and the Caucasus.

All of this, moreover, makes mention of only the most commonly cultivated names and species which no eye has found surprising for the last twenty years. One also might have listed an equal number of flowers of similar origin which still today can count as "rarities," but which a few years time will render as familiar as the previous group. The tide can no longer be turned. The current revolution in the range of available flowers is no less total and general than the one which took place in the sixteenth century. Back then, the invasion from Asia and America came by way of Vienna, and was one of the expressions of the world-wide Habsburg empire. Today it comes by way of London from all the corners of the earth, and is one of the expressions of the world-wide British empire. Yet further back, as an expression of the world-wide empire of Alexander the Great and the plants he sent to Aristotle, one can still make out the shadow of the movements which surely brought Europe its first cultivations of the spices and delicacies of tropical Asia—the pepper plant, the pumpkin, colocynth, the cucumber, the melon, taro, ginger—while also revolutionizing the Greeks' stock of plants for unguents, and of foliage to be worked into wreaths. We would also recognize its transformation of the Greeks' patrimony of flowers, if only a bridge could ever be built between that moment and the literary heritage that followed it—the writings on plants from Theophrastus to the sources cited by Pliny, and the little we're able to glean from Athenaeus—or if ever we could learn the names of the plants that grew and bloomed in Antioch, the Syrian city that stood at the center of what was then the replenished abundance of the Greek garden. The world's gardens lie beneath the sway of the laws of world history.

In the final decades of the nineteenth century, the distribution of wild flowers from all the parts of the great wide world passed out of the hands of the Belgians, French and Dutch and entered those of the English. This isn't, moreover, to speak of English trade and commerce, but of the whole English people, just as before in the Baroque period. In truth, these hands had never lain idle, even in quieter times, and at numerous decisive moments had also been the hands of women. A woman's hands brought the dahlia to Kent. The hands of another woman produced the first true seed of the brightly colored sweet pea, and this purely English creation thus began its triumph across the globe. The influx of flowers from all the corners of the world had been experienced on the continent as a brief flood tide which then had been diverted by the dikes of gardening's economic powers, and only retrieved through tiny apertures for entirely commercial purposes; that wave in England had fallen against a series of sieves: the large-mesh sieves of the people, and the ever finer sieves of a grandiose system of inquiry and study which the people themselves produced. Commerce and trade, as they ought to do, followed suit and obeyed. In furnishing the continent with the results of these studies which remain unique in the history of gardening, the commercial dealers in seeds and plants functioned simply as organs of distribution. The new garden plants which were mentioned above—plants which everywhere in Germany and all across the continent have grown quite common today—are all of English origin. The newer generation of scholarly, self-sacrificing explorers and discoverers was quite exclusively English, and in the service of the new English garden. They were also active in America, and America's flower collectors were soon won over to England's criteria and guidelines. Such forms of collecting are exhaustive, whereas those of the nineteenth century had remained in many ways desultory, with their sights set mainly on showpieces. This characteristic of the new collecting can be thanked for the fact that notions of South African flora, or the flora of Asia Minor, or Chinese flora, and so forth, were forced to abandon their status as learned concepts of botanic geography, and automatically found themselves transformed into the human and humanistic terms of fanciers and connoisseurs: the flower was released from confinement and fired the imagination of a new community.

As cultivators increasingly turned their attention to creating selections from specific botanical regions, it grew ever less possible for plants from the Canaries to be flanked by others from the Cape of Good Hope, or for Tibetan and Patagonian plants to stand together. Feelings spoke against it, and conditions of cultivation forbade it. The grouping of plants of similar habit and physiognomy established itself as a practical reality before becoming a principle and the expression of an attitude. The great geographic surveys to be found at the botanical gardens also trained the public's eye. At London's Hyde Park—a popular institution, and no strictly scientific garden—the English were able from as early as the 1880s to view a living map of the world's flora divided into botanical areas in full bloom, and they began to look askance at their flower beds. But collecting too was a passionate interest at all the various social levels of this people that ruled the world, exchanging plants and seeds all across the earth, discussing them, comparing them, corresponding about and pursuing them. An inconceivable number of private gardens, smaller gardens, fancier's gardens specialized and experimented. By the end of the century, the new flower had become an English *agon*: a competition for prizes and championships. The actual nature of the contest will best be seen while noting the role these specializations and experiments played in the creation of a whole new type of garden. Here and now it's sufficient to note their inevitable contribution to the new appreciation of the flowering plant as a sensual image of its landscape.

American flora, as found on its continent's luxuriant prairies, is typified by a coarse, rigid, powerful structure. It branches always at the same angles and is therefore of great geometric poverty, but this is also a source of concentrated power in terms of efficiency of growth. Star-shaped Compositae are nearly everywhere dominant and rise up over their neighbors to more than the height of a man, thus making far too excessive demands on what were originally the plant's interior reserves of strength; so the tall construction begins to collapse almost in concomitance with the flowering of the plant and the final formation of seed. Calyces often reduce to empty globes and tend to snap, just as lateral shoots are woody and break at the slightest contact, accustomed as they are to supporting one another in the flowering thicket. The color scale glows hard and somber; the yellows are those of the pelts of prairie animals, with flecks in black and brown; the warmer and more fecund the sky and the soil, the stronger the dusky rosy pinks, the deep cloudy reds. The fact that these various tones appear nearly all at once in nearly all families—orange tones in flowers that blossom pink (*Cosmos aurantiacus*), dark rosy reds in yellow flowers (*Zinnia linearis* and *mexicana*; *Echinacea*, which is also known as *Rudbeckia purpurea*)—points to a common, original source of coloration, as reflected in yellow forms with darker, originally reddish zones among some species (Gaillardias, for example) where the color scale still cleanly splits into red and yellow, and again among others where cultivation immediately tends to make this split appear. The tendency to elongation impoverishes corollas in favor of erect, cone-shaped seed pods, to the point of reaching monstrous forms (such as *Obeliscaria*) where nothing more than a gaggle of small, tortured petals hangs sadly down from the summit of a column-like calyx. The parsimony of sequential, parallel branchings is one of the laws of the landscape's physiognomy, and is also found among other families of the continent's plants as soon as their representatives advance toward the flowering prairies (as with *Gaura lindheimeri*). Whether coarse and from dusky to blackish green, or smooth but unpleasant in smell, or indeed repulsive, their foliage is a form of self-defense, protecting the plant from being eaten. It may even, indeed, be poisonous. Magnificent plants (*Martynias*, or chamois-horn flowers, for example) are covered with a slime that stinks of animal hide; their flowers resemble gloxinias, but with lips that show six rigid, yellow, parallel stripes. The shape of the plant as a whole can tend at best to grow elliptical, but most show rhomboid forms, or are crude and angular. As they rise up the slopes toward higher elevations and turn into mountain flowers, they take the form of bushes that grow from tubers. In the glare of powerful sunlight, their costume softens and grows more lively, the color of their flowers grows more pure and takes on a fiery glaze, though always remaining entrapped in orange forms that economize on energy. Corollas recede toward yellow. The nightshade plants (*Browallia*), the Scrophulariaceae (*Alonsoa*), and the Oenotheraceae (*Cuphea*) are built just as stoutly and their flowers show grimacing, mischievous faces while heaping up—in ashy pale and deep dark blues, in vermilion reds and dusky plum-like tones—into thick masses of color, all individual flowers staring like the stalks of a broom in the same direction, as tough and bristly as shrubs, as fragile as herbs. The structural principle is everywhere the same, monotonous and primitive; vitality exuberant; the scales of forms and colors closed and hard and lonely; the mien silent and brooding. The flora here is Indian, like the people and the landscape. The plants of the mallow family (*Anoda*), with compact shoots raying upward on a slant around them, grow up into simple bundles of shafts, charged with abundant quantities of bluish and pale pink chalices. They too round out more placidly as shrubs (*Sidalcea*) and purge themselves of their bluish tones, but still remain always damped and fesseled.

California has deserts, mountains, forests and wetlands, and a limitless wealth of forms that perfectly correspond to them. Poppies creep along the ground as herbs in delicate cream-white dwarf forms; or in sand are armed like thistles, with large white and resoundingly yellow shells; as shrubs they rise to classic, tulip-like beauty with solid gold-green crowns on wondrous grayish-silver foliage; as bushes they take on great sweet-scented corollas, in delicate snowy white. Among them, in all tones of yellow and orange, the Eschscholtzias, as the plants that most define the landscape: as small, delicate, retiring herbs; as vigorous shrubs; as woody dwarf bushes; mile upon mile. The Compositae tend again to grow graceful and delicate, in a color scale that turns from yellow and black to yellow and white (*Layia*). Tubers are supplanted by bulbs, surmounted by fascinating butterflies (*Calochortus*, or the lantern flower) formed only of three spotted, over-blown petals; or often by compound blossoms (*Brodiae*) like those of our leeks, in violet to white and deep yellow. The stone of the land strengthens, coerces and educates, insists on style and proper form, controls the scale of colors. Rainless summers encourage the growth of thickened, club-shaped stems (*Leptosyne, Hunnemania*) which unlike those of the Canary Islands remain quite vigorous and nourish luxuriant foliage. In periods after rain, the deserts lie decked in the multicolor magic of the grayish leaves and shimmering blossoms of sage, semi-mallows and sand verbena, in colors that play through delicate flesh-like tones to pale violet and dry vermilion, each fresh and clear in its own particular way. Dwarf lupines with leaves from gray to bright are blue, white, red, and yellow, and in various mixtures of them all. The phlox and its various relatives, always erect, but with a sometimes quivering, sometimes rigid bearing, rise up into prickly bushes with needle-like leaves and flowers in a range from vibrant lilac to brick red, or all throughout the color scale of the lantern flower's butterflies, whereas true Polemoniums grow noble deep blue panicles in cooler mountain air, while turning on dryer hotter cliffs into splendid bushes with flowers the color of straw.

The realm of European plants here reappears with wondrous variations. Columbine blooms glass green, like shimmering drops of water, or wine red, or at times shows woolly down, and its various forms are nearly always sweet-smelling. Delphiniums develop tubers, like those of Ethiopia, with blossoms on a scale from scarlet to yellow and brick red, or take the form of low shrubs with deep blue flowers and leaves which run from needle-like to thick, stiff, and deeply serrated. The lilies, showing yellow calyces with blood-red spots, adhere again to the same scale. California's true and proper alpine flora is also inclusive of dry, brick-red pseudo-fuchsias (*Zauschneria*), and of equally magnificent tall red campions. A horn of plenty here first begins to spill in our direction. The Phacelias, which insofar as they make their way into higher elevations are redder than their bluish siblings, make their own contribution to the characterization of the mountain landscape through maculations, no less than with stamens that explode and ray out from clusters of flowers; the Godetias known as *Oenothera* through fine red blots on white petals. Pentstemons, too, reach up to these heights; but on leaving zones which are free of frost, this flower that blooms bright red in the deserts, where it covers brittle bushes with pliant runners, here rises tall and deep blue from the thin soil, like all the other Jacob's-ladders. The land is a mammoth, stony hamper of forms and colors, which bending toward the sea spills out its content, ablaze with splendid flowers that seem to spring like marvels from a box of magic tricks, all alive with the festive spirit of the children of a blessed climate and pure soil. But there are also extremes where this flora turns magic into ghostly visitation. Those who have seen the desert sage (*Salvia carduacea*) display its headlong growth—a downy-silver, glassy-glittering phantom with blossoms of open, silvery-lilac gullets that spew out rays of red stamens—have also seen it dry and crinkle and disappear after only a matter of days: to have seen this sight and still seriously to hope to wed this apparition with a flower bed would surely require an incorrigible dreamer. Those who want to know it must follow it back to its home. Nothing could be thought more recalcitrant to the regularly ordered garden than the mad caprice of California's flowering plants: plants that crawl, infest, hang loosely down, stand tall and stiff, go gray instead of green, turn flecked and make themselves conspicuous. Decked with cream-yellow flowers, that poppy creeps along the ground. What use might a flower bed find for it? And what might a flower bed do with California's lobelias, as beautiful as jewels; with the blue-white-yellow Clintonias where the fascinating faces of the flowers hide in grass-like foliage? Where will one find a place for the so-called Ipomopsis (*Gilia coronopifolia*), a tall, stiff, widely-spreading bush with a rigid, central inflorescence, from vermilion pink to yellowish red? Will it be given pride of place as one of the "solitary plants" of the castle gardener of "the good old days," thanks to its "difficult biennial cultivation"? These are plants that feed on ambrosia, and with few exceptions will show no liking for the fat, bourgeois diet to which we refer as "garden soil." They want to sup on drier, more spiritual stuff. And who will give them satisfaction?

The botanical wealth of California finds its twin in the southwest portions of the paradise of Chile and Argentina, with its mountains, forests, rivers, and prairies, just as northern Chile's slopes and mountains stand parallel to the heavenly garden of the temperate regions of Mexico. Verbena and fuchsia here discover their realm of unconditional freedom and fully unfold their array of forms. In arid soil, verbena abandons its colorful carpet of creeping, flowering tendrils and rises into flexible steles that, meters tall, repeatedly branch in accord with the regular American pattern. It turns woody in the form of lantana and emits its glows through dark foliage. Fuchsia descends from the imposing heights of Chile's mountains and enters the southern rain forests as a giant, blossom-laden bush. The slipper flower (*Calceolaria*) shares its range, in a number of different forms: as small, resplendent, yellowish-reddish bushes that grow on rock debris; as vigorous summer plants with yellow, button-like flowers; as tall, woody shrubs with myriad, colorful pouches. The nightshade plants likewise appear in all their forms. As tiny, delicate bushes, they have blossoms that resemble bellflowers, with wide calyces ranging in color from crystal to dusky violet (*Nierembergia hippomaniflora*); as Salpiglossis they create an alien realm of dark, magnificent netherworld flowers; as Schizanthus they exhibit serrated and sometimes bright, crinkled foliage and terrifying crews of cobold faces that surpass the limits of even the American bizarre. It is here that we first encounter the typical visage of the Chilean flower, with narrow eyes and mouth, and a sharply rising roof petal which bears an eye that beckons or puts to flight, here in a dark, purple pink with sharp, golden-yellow highlights, or in rusty pink with orange lights; or dark purple with flashes of grassy-green among the tuberous

Alstroemeria, in the family of the Amaryllidaceae (this is the true Alstroemeria, and much more easily kept and cultivated than the bulbed begonias) or, again, among the related, creeping Bomareas, where the contrasting colors are inconceivably surprising, but nonetheless convincing. On the continent too they were once the pride of lordly gardeners, but now grow only in England. They live among magical snakes and enchanted birds, and resemble them in appearance. The Schizanthus are residual shrub forms, and grow like California's Leptosynes and Hunnemannias on thickened club-shaped stems, reaching up in deep loose earth to more than a meter tall: the breeding of their European garden varieties has run counter to the will of nature, and the future will be sure to reshape them entirely.

The power of the laws of the landscape unhinges every human rule. The Cruciferae too (cabbage, radish, and stock) tend like Schizanthus (the butterfly flower) to defend themselves with monstrous little faces, in their case white and tattered (*Schizopetalum*), just as those faces are yellow among the region's Tropaeolums. As everywhere in South America, the Liliaceae that flower in the dense primal wilderness refuse to lie low, and develop winding stalks or adhesive leaves with which to get the better of oppressive neighbors and to bring themselves and their deep pink pendulous blossoms (in the case, here, of the Lapageria) upwards into the light. (The appearance of the non-climbing Maurandias—*Maurandia purpusii*—has allowed us to conclude that such climbing forms can only be classed as ancient adaptations.) The Amaryllidaceae—represented in Europe by daffodils and the several varieties of crocus—rise here from damper soils in festive, godly forms. The narcissus here is an enormous trumpet with a richly fringed corolla, its white blending over toward cream yellow, or yellowish green, in departure from the flower's primordial sulphur yellow—cultivated varieties (*Ismene*) are again an exquisite sulphur yellow; or according to the nature of the terrain, the petals of the perianth draw themselves out in fantastic spirals (*Elisena*). The gentian blue pseudo-crocus (*Tecophilaea*) has the odor of the violet; and in its shy and modest carriage it's again more violet- than crocus-like, and at an uncertain level of formal development. Max Leichtlin in Baden-Baden began their selection and purification and sent magnificent varieties to England, where they continue to be seen in the new gardens; in Germany this wonder has again disappeared. Blue—true blue, and not the pseudo-blue of the scale of blue-red-white—is in Chile, as in California, an inflection of the will of the landscape, and crafts the deep blue carpet of the beautiful creeping Nolanaceae, which pile their abundant foliage into low mounds on the ground; the Commelinas, which in Mexico are sky blue, here turn cobalt. The magnificent Leucocorynes—bulbs that rise into odorous cups at the summit of tall, wiry, quivering stems—seem to strive to reach this color which elsewhere the members of the lily family have almost entirely lost, and the hue of the variety now cultivated will grow even deeper very soon. The region's characteristic withdrawal of the plant's vital energies into restful depositories (tubers) is also shared by nasturtiums, fuchsias, and even verbenas; and while remaining still stiff and uncultivated, the lovely, sweet-scented *Verbena priva laevis*, of a mild sea-shell pink like the pseudo-verbenas (*Abronia*, or sand verbena) of California, awaits no more than the hand which will know how to open it.

The great plateaus that stretch from north to south, a flowered flight of steps on the flank of America's second western coast, as inexhaustible in majesty as the first, thus drop down from divine heights toward already cooling seas. Since England here has fewer interests, the region remains still largely unexploited. The Leucocoryne, the alpine slipper flower, the perennial fuchsia remain the most recent imports. The seeds of the wonderfully beautiful shrub *Verbena bonariensis* become first available only as these lines are being written: this plant of the heaths of Chile and Argentina has been grown in thick stands and quite one-sidedly developed, but its reddish lilac, like that of its sister *Verbena venosa*, will soon give rise as well to varieties in impure white and lavender; its primordial color is deep pink to yellow, and is hardly likely ever again to be split into its separate parts; no one yet has managed to pry apart these sacred colors of poverty (scabious, thistles, Centaureas).

The bearing of American flora, regardless of its species or stage of development, always includes the possible reversal of the petals of the flowers: the blooming corolla folds rearward toward its stem. Asters, fuchsias, poppies, and members of the nightshade, primrose, and lily families throw back their petals and perianths at a double right angle—as here in Europe only occurs with alpine violets and a few species of narcissus—thus thrusting forward the lap of the desire for fertilization, finally to the point of grotesquerie with the *Romneya trichocarpa*, a golden clump of stamens in the midst of a white, drooping, poppy-like shell, or the Obeliscarias and Echinaceas, where the brownish-yellow or rose-red petals remain half stunted at the sides of column-like pistils.

The continent and landscape pursue fertility with a special, demonic lust that reaches even these extremes. American seed outbids all other in vigor and abundance of germination, and the absolute vitality of American flora can hardly be imagined. A garden left at the mercy of American species of plants will in moderate climatic conditions grow wild in only a very few years and turn into a kind of flowered American wilderness, in which all non-American plants have been strangled and suppressed. Plants like the beautiful, ash-blue *Lobelia syphilitica*, the *Nicandra physaloides*, the tobacco plants, headed by the bulbed *Nicotiana silvestris*, the herbaceous slipper flowers, and the Mimulus can be dissuaded from their powerful inclination to build extensive populations—this alone is the meaning of "going rank"—only by tenacious battle. No Asian, African, or Australian species can equal *Physalis francheti*, the Novi-Belgii asters, *Verbena venosa*, or *Dracocephalum virginianum* in transforming itself from single plant to marauding army, first by way of thickly scattered seed, and later through meter-long stolons that run beneath the ground, sending up shoots that everywhere break through. This American exuberance doesn't repudiate the garden, but it does repudiate the flower bed and all alien rules of order, which stand powerless before it. It presents itself, indeed, as one of our times' most potent forces in the transformation of the garden, just as the tulip once was, with its peremptory demand for terrain, or as also is true, in a different sense, of South African flora.

The regions of southern Africa which experience and remain unacquainted with frost don't follow one another as a question of latitude. They intermix with one another according to conditions of coastal or continental climate, rainfall and irrigation, clayey or granitic soil, veldt or mountain, and they share and cross their flora in the richest and most curious ways. In the interior regions where Africa's clayey or sandy soils lie scorched and turned to rock by heat for two thirds of the year and then are subjected to freezing winter nights, asters and Iridaceae are nearly alone in their victory over adversity, and thus are the plants that dominate and determine the landscape's character. They lie beneath the earth in durable, concentrated forms that have proved resistant to frost and heat (rhizomes, tubers, bulbs); and above the ground their leaves and stems are rich in lymph, and prone to deviant configurations that offer sure protection from evaporation. Whole classes of plants even seem no longer to resemble vegetation, and have taken on a habitus which, just as with the cactuses of Mexico, is a résumé of the frightful environments in which they live. At the other extreme lie opulent, bulbed plants which range from the lily to attenuated forms of aloe: plants which thanks to harmonious conditions are purely built, and which give full expression to a world of their own in the woody growths of a garden of the Hesperides. For a few brief months, the Karoo is a single, unbroken meadow of flowers where tough, thick grasses cede a place to members of the iris family which in order to be able to compete with them have themselves assumed a grassy form. Leaf sheaths grow tall and thin, one-sided, one-dimensional, one-stemmed growths as flat as the blade of a knife; the stem of the flower is supported by the thicket of grass, and thereby enabled to do no harm to its tiny bulb in the ground, which is far too weak. When gladiolas, freesias, and numberless others issue from their housings, the stems of their flowers immediately develop struts with which to rest on shorter, neighboring plants and take the weight off their bulbs, which even when they grow into a complex thicket would otherwise have too much to bear. Montbretias and Tritonias rise up from whole networks of exuberant, subterranean rhizomes that remain concealed beneath the sward; the plants themselves build wide expanses of grass-like brush. Ranging far above them stand enormous irises in the form of canes, which, tall as a man, sprout clusters of branching stalks that might be bright, bronze nests of snakes, hissing their tongues at one another; or shafts like giant grasses, with pendant, sky-blue bellflowers; or colossal Watsonia gladiolas with rose-red panicles; or the Aristeas, where the color is blue; or the Galtonia and Albuca snowbell trees. Shorter grasses are instead the home of foot-tall species of gladiolus with large flame-like blossoms on more anemic panicles; and again of a countless legion of always new and varying plants that retrieve their clusters, spicules, bells, shells, chalices, cups, and cushions from tiny bulbs. This is the landscape's springtime face, with the purity and splendor that mark spring flora everywhere on earth. But owing to the shortness of the flowering period, there is also the shock of a conflagration of courtship colors which in heat and passion remain elsewhere unmatched. The characteristic feature of southern African flora and its influence over its landscape lies first of all in a level of chromatic splendor with which no other part of the world is acquainted, combined moreover with the most exquisite tissues: resistant without being coarse, delicate without the ephemeral quality found in other regions. These tissues hold their pigments in much the same way that flickering lights seem captured within a stone. This image is no exaggeration. One has only to look at the most recently imported of southern Africa's Iridaceae, the *Schizostylis*, or "Bantu lily," and the similarly colored Nerine lily—a deep damask red—which is found nowhere else: their metallic flash would seem to come from a crimson shot with gold. Any number of typically African plants are in fiery yellow to fiery brownish tones, which are also the basic colors of the Kniphofia (which is aloe-like, aside from the freshness of its greenery); here, however, as elsewhere, these colors strive already to deepen toward sulphur saffron and to brighten toward fiery orange, just as in the related Veltheimias they shimmer in fairy-tale enchantment toward Reseda green and rosy violet tones. But Tritonias and Montbretias also soften to a pink and a transparent rose (like the wonderful *Tritonia hyalina*) that challenge the limits of credibility. More humid soils develop succulent, sap-rich stands of giant-leafed Amaryllidaceae on bulbs as large as children's heads, and half above the ground. White, red, and pinkish lilies stand a meter tall, rising from bulbs which month after month in humid soil allow their incessant self-renewal. Plants that flower like snowbells develop to the size of smallish trees, covered with whitish green or pinkish blossoms. The Musaceae give birth to the fabulous Strelitzias: nearly as tall as a man, these griffon-headed creatures set purest orange and cobalt sharply against each other, and possess a muscularity that allows them to summon the honey bird—rather than any insect—for the purposes of pollination. Veldt and cliff are dominated by the heavenly asters which are always at home in this dry, noble land. Grouped for minimum evaporation, but as well with maximum upward exposure of their gaze to the light of the sun, this race of plants is thinkable only here, with abundant leaves, from leathery to succulent, from rounded to roughly dentellated and with silvery, felt-like undersides, on herbs no less than bushes. The flowers' central disks, which in other lands are yellow—the eye is astonished on first taking them in—are here sky blue, or pale violet to bluish brown, to deeply burnished bronze; their surrounding petals from soft azure to deep blue, and then to violet, from fiery yellow to full-fruited orange, from ardent to blackish brown. The carnelian red Gerbera with a yellow disk has torn itself away from this color scale in one direction; in the other, again with a yellow disk, we find the small and perfectly unbelievable *Felicia bergeriana*, with petals in the blue of the fisher martin. The *Felicia bergeriana* is one of those masterfully colored jewels for which nature would seem to have exceeded her own resources, and to have plundered the realm of fantasy. All of these wonders have adapted their habit to the surrounding environment and take the pulvinate form of mounds or cushions charged with an incredible abundance of blossoms. From a crack in the rocks, *Arctotis aspera* sends up a woody stem, and the plant spreads out around it—overladen with giant white-gold stars and noble, dusky, serrated foliage—for two square meters. In dry, semi-desert terrain, the silver-toned *Arctotis grandis*, a suffrutex with silvery-lilac petals that start out white from a deep lilac disk, hangs moon-like over the umbel half a meter below it. The round, frightening gold-black figures that look like eyes and that serve as a defense for American flora have here become quite different: in the gazania, a black and white zone like a peacock-eye around the disk; and again the same with the mammoth aster *Venidium fastuosum*—a staring, orange sun of ardent beauty—which seeks out places of moisture and produces a luxuriant growth that stifles the frugal economies of its stiff and noble sisters.

A comparison of the Ursinias of southern Africa and the various Calliopsis that live in Texas—two groups that share the yellow-red to yellow-reddish-brownish-purple scale of colors—offers a drastic example of how the continents veer ever more widely apart from one another after moments of extreme approach. Both are short-lived herbs; both show foliage which runs from serrated to dentellated, and which even at times is filiform; both have yellow, star-shaped flowers, for conspicuous areas of frightening, defensive coloration. But the tissue of the old-world plants is fine and resilient stuff; and as children of endless light, they feed on drier foods; elegant in stature and with beautifully balanced structures, the flowers they develop are preciously equipped, silky rather than velvety, and with moist rather than molten colors. The American plants, on the other hand, are rudely built and massively available on endless, flowering prairies; with blossoms like piebald signs hung out in advertisement for pollination; coarse in fabric; invasive in behavior; degenerate in the bearing of their petals; addicted to variation; playful, wild, bizarre, formless, willfully ephemeral. And the Ursinia stands in a splendid orange combined with the cobalt blue and transparent glazes of the dwarf lobelia and the Heliophila. Only southern Africa produces such dual color schemes. Asters and other daisies develop into woody bushes, creating star-decked shrubs and bushes, deep-lilac as well as golden yellow (Chrysocoma, Euryops, Felicia), with prickly or broomlike foliage. And October and November, finally, bring to light from the light soils of Namaqualand—which in no way implies that they always offer meager nourishment—the vernal magnificence of the Nemesia's tiny gorge-shaped flowers in all the colors of heaven and fire: South African versions of the South American slipper flowers, but glowing, as this land requires, like blood, fruit, sky, gold, snow, and fire (with even, in the related shrub-like Diascia, a wondrous salmon tone, which also seems to belong to the palette of the Dimorphothecas)...ardent and glowing but nonetheless fresh, like everything found in southern Africa, strong and yet highly selected: a wonder. These regions are not the antipodes of Egypt, Carthage, or Numidia, but of the great, sunken paradise now flooded by the Mediterranean: that paradise of which the Azores and Canaries—those Islands of the Blessed—and the middle elevations of the Atlas Mountains are only a remnant or a pale reflection. Yet it was only with the appearance of explorers from Europe that the land encountered men who thought possession of the wonder worth fighting for, thus beginning as well to give its flowers a history. Because of all living creatures, only the hapless human being is debased by gazing toward Antarctis; and before the arrival of the first Western ships, he had stood among these paradisiacal flowers in conditions more damned and humiliated than jackals and hyenas.

The habitus of the plants of the Canary Islands shares the tendency for woody development which is found in southern Africa; the dwarf bush strives to turn into the dwarf tree, with flowers and foliage organized into a clear and well-defined crown. But more than might be found at the antipodes, it also insists on solid, compact construction, for a shape that can hold its own against the wind: life finds ways to protect itself from the heat and storms of these highly exposed islands. The shrubs and herbs of southern Europe and northern Africa—bellflowers, viper's bugloss, digitalis, asters, forget-me-not and the lupine—grow tougher here, and purer, and don more quiet costumes. Varieties of plants with rich foliage and abundant sap here take on the qualities of gorse and broom. Stone, sky, the flaming sun, the stormy sea and the heavenly strife between the sisters Europa and Africa all have an effect on the natural forms which arise in response to their whole, general constellation. Digitalis, here, is a glowing, bronze-gold candle; viper's bugloss a monstrous porcupine, with countless panicles half a meter tall; or it turns, above the rough palmettes of a ground-hugging umbel the size of a wagon wheel, into a rose-colored, flowered tree, twice the height of a man, which rises and dies in the space of two years. Bellflower trees see bulbed sisters clamber up beside them, with yellow, red-striped bells. Forget-me-nots are small-sized shrubs, full of deep velvet-blue eyes. Fabulous daisy bushes take the form of enormous, star-studded spheres that issue from a crack in the rocks, free of all sign of a stem. On the cliffs at the edge of the sea, the Odontospermum is a wonderful, woody, leafy bush in light, silk green and canary yellow, next to low, non-woody, ground-creeping sisters of the same species, decked with the same flowers. Higher up on the rocks stand the silver-green bushes of the island's magnificent Pyrethrum, of which the thick, exquisite foliage is itself an ornament, with every curve, every indentation a delight for the eye such as elsewhere might be found only in a Greek rendition of a motif drawn from nature. The color scale is as rich and proud as in the stained glass windows of churches; the splendor of the princely blue of the viper's bugloss centers itself against these skies and seas. Potent, unbroken tones hold sway—blue, bright pink, white, yellow, bronze—preserved by the stony terrain and shielded from caprice and degeneration; yet even the most powerful still reflect the simple, basic hues of nearby Europe. They are fit for temples, but still for temples of our own gods. The horn of plenty is only just beginning to tilt in our direction and overflow. The flowering herbs, the bulbs, the high alpine plants still have much to offer. The red varieties of Senecio—pretty bushes with bright, colorful star-like blooms—have been made to yield the ragworts, in a widened range of colors that entirely transforms their bearing. It's only now that promising relatives begin to press forward and to follow them.

To the east of the Mediterranean's irruption into what was once a flowered plain, the high plateaus of Asia Minor form the complement of the westward pillars of the Island of Tenerife. Their continental climate of scorching summers and frightful winter cold ascends from shelf to shelf and to ever higher mountain ranges, and we finally peer off into the distance at the stony, snow-charged heart of Central Asia and the ancient world beyond it. The flora has risen from the warm sea coasts and entered rocky heights, entrenching itself within them: impoverished, large, and of noble structure, and always in possession of a proud, steady and disdainful gaze, it finds its composure interrupted only by the brief spring flame, released from its bulbs and tubers, of restrained, short-lived passion. Individual plants stand free and alone, exemplifying the Eastern no less than Western notion of the dignity of a life that withdraws to within itself. Woolly, gray-green foliage, from leathery to thorny, or widely dentellated, testifies to the need for defense against climatic extremes. A barely flexible if not quite rigid stance speaks of the pure and astringent lap of the stone which gave it birth. Such plants are emblematic images of an unmistakably reserved and solitary world. They move in spiritual no less than atmospheric winds. Their character makes their simple color scale partly inconspicuous, partly becoming. The threshold that lies between the Mediterranean and the Central Eurasian hinterland expresses itself through astonishing exchanges of bearing and form between species of plants that are highly distant from one another. All blossoms strive toward lily forms; all central axes to robust stems. The magnificent Michauxia bellflowers, as well as a whole group of the region's tulips, are pseudo-lilies; the Michauxia stands some two meters tall, erect, rude and eccentrically constructed, covered with palely reddening, flatly opened lily bells—an unforgettable sight. Others as much as three meters tall, like the rose, yellow and violet, and entirely yellow cousins of our own Eremostachys, with flowers shaped like lips: they stand on the arid cliffs as though in memory of the giant Eremurus of the Caucasus and the Himalayas. The great sage-like plants are hardly less remarkable, with widely yawning gullets in silver blue and deep lilac, or with delicately contrasting bracts, their bitter foliage deeply ruffled, thick-skinned and creased, their odor from spicy to strongly aromatic. The higher elevations of the rocky terrain are inhabited by an at first almost invisible flora of cushions and umbels, luminous blue pseudo-forget-me-nots (*Omphalodes*), deep pink-red campions arising from whitish gray rosettes, yellow and deep pink carnations, blue primroses, ornaments fit for mountain nymphs. Shady slopes and meadows are dominated by the Fritillaria, in varieties no less numerous than the gladiolas of southern Africa, with its singularly spare and dark, capricious color scale, between swarthy plum and dusky olive, pinkish and blackish, yellow-toned and tile red, and mixtures of all together, blended and woven into patterns—which is one of the laws of this territory, where the carpet knotter was born. These colors are locked secrets. We don't yet know if cultivation will be able to break the seal, for example, of the colors of such a large, haggard Cinderella as the *Fritillaria armenica.* On the other hand, the various species of tulips and the deep blue Ixiolirions branch off from one another in the purest of colors; and these too all stand alone, just as they're seen in Persian miniatures: a triumph of the soil in blood scarlet, egg yellow, and the lily's trinity of white, red and yellow; villous, with abundant blossoms; serrated; luxurious delights of a short, fleetly returning season. But in this area of heavy soils tormented by frost and burning heat, the last word—just as in southern Africa—belongs to the irises, with bulbs or tubers, whenever they're able to reach maturity in the clayey soils that the mid-summer heat transforms into stone, and securely to protect their splendor from the winter's arctic cold.

The entirety of Asia Minor stands full of irises and tulips. Their crazily colored jester's hats and pertly red or reddish-green or yellow-green or pinkish-golden turbans are the decorations which the soil has spawned around images of peoples on horseback, in tiaras, cowls and turbans, brightly colored and solitary against the endless brown land. The Orient's fairy-tale color scheme here shows itself in accents which directly oppose the scale of the Fritillarias: tones of roses and violets on black or felt-gray backgrounds; striations of blue or yellow on felt-like whites; the improbable *Iris iberica*, with a range from the Caucasus to Persia, shows patterns in black and dark purple on a dark red ground. These are princely, old-world splendors, in front of which all unsung tropical wonders stare agape, despite their audacity and air of challenge, their agitation and ostentation of difficult color schemes. Small, bright varieties of blue and yellow iris wonderfully pursue dwarf tulips into crevices between the rocks: these minor peoples in gaily colored costumes are diminutive departures from the large, despondent, imperial blossoms of the realm near Susa and Babel. There among the ruins stands the Persian yellow rose, and all its pinkish sisters of the region from Syria to Iran. And with pink or yellow clusters of pea-like flowering grapes among grayish leaves and a cloak of thorns stands the Tartar acacia, the *Caragana*, high above the continent's deserts and summer herding trails, twisted, short and densely crowned, and in winter the naked thorn bush recorded in the sagas; yet, there at its side in the great colorless expanse of the land, the *Parrotia*—what Persians call "the blood bush"—defends its scarlet autumn mantle against all the storms of the high plateaus.

Ward's every new voyage has demonstrated that we have only just begun to open the gates that lead to the flowers of Asia Minor, even if half of Europe's garden flowers have already flowed through it in the course of the centuries. There's the desert flora which magically conjures up the whole prismatic spectrum from the ground as a sequel to the very first rains, then falling apart like a colorful mirage after the hastiest flurry of pollination; or the mountain flora of medium to high, to highest alpine elevations. Such plants still barely begin to appear in herbariums. Even as these lines are being written, ever more beautiful Caucasian varieties increasingly flank the magnificent summer poppies—long well-known—of Persia, Armenia and the Caucasus; this fact alone might make it clear that the plants of these regions remain to be fully studied. This also holds for the measureless stretches of the landmass to which it connects in the east, for the Himalayas and their foothills, above all for China, and for the mountainous regions of Japan, which only now are beginning to be discovered as an endless source of wild flowers.

In the eastern half of the Himalayas, both north and south, in stretches from Tibet to Nepal, this last decade has seen the appearance of the new flower which truly is most its own, just as earlier epochs found their flower in the Karoo gladiolas or the Chimborazo dahlias. Meconopsis formerly had been no more than the name of a pseudo-poppy of Europe's Atlantic coasts: an enchanting, poppy-like growth with gray leaves and abundant blossoms with medium-sized orange petals. But then things changed, when it was suddenly flanked by relatives from India and Tibet: by poppy-like plants as tall as a man, and from altitudes which in Europe know only seas of ice. And even though some were yellow, most of them, to the horror of occidental eyes, were sky blue, deep violet and peacock blue, slate blue, wine purple and midnight blue. In addition to the taller varieties, there were also others of medium size, and some no taller than a foot or so; in a very few years the number of species had grown to more than twenty, and the plants had been introduced into English and Scottish gardens: the floral wonder our times might never have hoped for, and which still remains to be explored. In the 1840s, the fine collection of illustrated cards published by Ghent's Central Gardens had already included an illustration of *Meconopsis wallichii*, but it had gone unnoticed in the epoch's flood of novelties. Its acclimatization was difficult work, its cultivation complicated and only to be guessed at; only now does it begin to be appreciated.

The characteristic feature of the plants that live on the roof of the world in the midst of a landscape of Titans is the form of the powerful, upright pillar. It is found among these new, gigantic plants, just as it's found among lilies and the Primulaceae. Their central axis strives always upwards, taking the form of a pillar, and is covered along the whole of its length by blossoming shoots which are driven by a similar tendency. In winter time, like all the region's plants, they lie dry and protected beneath deep mounds of snow, and in spring they drink its melt-off water, rising toward the skies from well-washed sands and mountain humus while still sheathed from above to below in a gray, plush-like pelt; even their calyces are warmly covered in down, much like our alpine anemones, *Anemone pulsatilla* and *Anemone halleri.* The plant's thick leaves protect their innards from penetrating cold by step by step elimination of the fringes and dentellations which are typical of poppy foliage; they finally show a single, continuous edge and assume the form of a heavy, hairy spoon, like those of the Olympian mullein. No one knows what slumbers in its scale of colors. The annual *Meconopsis heterophylla* has a brown poppy ring in its chalice of orange petals, like the horned poppy; a variety that flowers in white has split away from the magnificent *Meconopsis wallichii*; and a wild variety in purple-lilac has also made its appearance. So, it's clearly acquainted with all the tones of the primrose color scale, as well as with the pinks and the full, true red which belong to a poppy's birthright. Everything else that might be found in the larder of these fairy-tale creatures remains unexplored. Shrubs and bi-annual grasses appear to grow right next to one another, but the difference may in fact be determined only by exposure and location. The whole species may be basically perennial. Its habitat extends into China, and this oldest of Asia's poppy lands almost yearly provides new information that redefines the limits of what we see as these plants' natural possibilities. In addition to the Meconopsis, there are also other pseudo-poppies, annual as well as bi-annual, which stand nearly as tall as a man, but of somewhat attenuated pillar form: the Dicranostigma, with thick, gray, leathery foliage, and a shaft that rises in shimmering bluish reflections and then turns violet as it reaches its summit, where it ends with a cup-shaped crown of four bright yellow petals that tend to throw themselves backwards, for an overall appearance that might be a blend of the Meconopsis, the horned poppies and the prickly poppies. How the chain develops further while extending east is something we do not know; we are, however, acquainted with the last, till now, of its demonstrable links, the wonderfully beautiful, pale lilac poppy of the mountains of Japan: a pseudo-horned-poppy hardly as much as a foot tall, and with abundant foliage. Though subject here to the laws of another soil, it has made no shift in its color scale, and likewise preserves its pillar-like bearing.

But the most amazing development of the column-like habitus is found in the Himalayas among those plants of which the reductive forms in our own particular latitudes are the Ornithogalum and the *Anthericum liliastrum*: gracious, agreeable flowers that grow from bulbs as cones of spherical blossoms over soft, earthbound palmettes; in southern Europe, already taller, the asphodels; in southern Africa, the giant snowbells. The giant Eremurus of the Himalayas, overtowering their shorter brothers in the Caucasus, are shafts with clusters of pink, cup-shaped bells, and rise in their tallest forms (*elwesianus* and *robustus*) to more than one and a half times the height of a man. In the light, damp forest soils of the foothills of the mountains of northern India, lilies feed on rich humus watered by eternally melting snows and develop into thickets where the plants are as much as three meters tall, with giant, nodding, whitish-greenish blossoms, their interior tinged with violet. Primroses grow with tier on tier of blossoms, inflorescence following inflorescence, to the height of more than a meter, and, knowing no further bounds in cultivation, nearly to a meter and a half in the case of the Scottish garden wonder, the *Belvedere hybrides.* Here, of course, the human hand has intervened and busied itself with crossings and selections, in order even more richly to develop the color scale found in nature; but here, for once, the great mother herself has cast aside restraint. In the midst of a nearly mythic world of towering heights and monstrous gullies, abundant water, blazing sun and incredible depth of the soil, all of it bordered on one side by a world of colossal ice, but close to the tropics on the other, she for once has indulged in the satisfaction of endlessly playing with one of her forms and left no tone untested, from white to pink to rose red, to white and red, to scarlet brown, orange, deep yellow and cream yellow, to celeste, azure and lilac blue, full blue and the deepest velvet blues. Rainy lands create umbrella-like corollas and pendulous blossoms. Lilies, Meconopsis and primroses drip with water and nod their heads; with the finest of the Himalayas' pseudo-bellflowers (the Codonopsis), one must lift up a corner of its belly-shaped, Mongol bells in porcelain blue in order to peek at the gracious design of gold-black eyes that decorate its throat. Kashmir's variety of the larkspur wears a smoke-blue raincap and looks from a distance like an enormous Campanula, or like so many of these mountain creatures is covered with heavy down (*Delphinium vestitum*). Primulas send up shafts with spherically shaped flowers that serve as rain spouts: a dense inflorescence of rigid corollas. The meadow-rue (*Thalictrum dipterocarpum* and *Thalictrum delavayi*) which grows in our own humid soils, and also in those of America, and which otherwise, though in any case at considerable elevations, sprawls out into a broad cushion or pseudo-umbel of whitish-green, yellowish, pale lilac stamens, without corollas, here turns exuberant and builds magic, pagoda-like towers, as much as a meter tall, of countless clear violet bells. It's also, now, accompanied by an enchanting white variety (harbingered by North America's *Thalictrum anemonoides*) and forms in both yellow and pink are sure to appear in the near future. They extend all the way out into China. The study of the vast floral resources which are native to north and northeast India has barely even entered that initial period which always directs its attention to rarities and great showpieces. Enormous lacunae still gape open. The range of the larkspur has been seen to stretch from the mountains of Kenya on the south and Portugal on the north all across Europe, Siberia, northern India, and China, and on to California. The two ranges of the columbine—from the Pyrenees to the Pontic steppes and on to Kashmir, and from Japan across the Pacific and uninterruptedly to Guatemala—are well defined, but the bridge between them remains incomplete. The Campanulae break off in Asia Minor, and first reappear, in countless varieties, in America. The coming century will find its tasks in India, continuing the efforts which the current century has begun in China.

The exploration of the immense new floral resources of China's western mountains—which have never been covered with glaciers, and allow a vision of the plenitude of the whole Eurasian land mass in the period preceding the ice age—will stand on a par—as soon as its results appear in gardens—with Europe's introduction to American flora, which crowned the middle of the nineteenth century. Where Europe and Asia have managed the rescue of two or three species of a particular plant from the age of cosmic ice, western China displays some twenty, thirty, fifty of them. Looking up over the rim of these formerly untrod mountain regions which now however hold a place for the human being, we cast a living gaze into the otherwise everywhere frozen lap of form-creating nature. This is why China's flora can't be seen—not even theoretically—in terms of any dominant habitus among any given species. Other lands are divisible into continents or portions of continents; China is a unified world of its own, and no power can reduce it to a series of component parts. Aside from its bush-like and semi-arborescent poppies with white and yellow flowers that throw their petals backward (Eomecon, Dendromecon), or its incomparable primroses, violets and Jacob's-ladders, which are lipped and gullet-shaped blossoms that grow on stony soil and the faces of cliffs, the lilies alone present themselves as a great, new and hardly imaginable realm, in which the pseudo-lilies too play a part that remains to be entirely defined. Since our gardens' introduction to the dazzling royal lily (*Lilium regale*), with its noble scale of dark, stiff leaves and chaste bitterly scented flowers, Chinese lilies from dry, stony places have been followed by relatives that grow to the height of a man. Lilies of the type of the Turk's cap lily, likewise as tall as a man, from orange to yellow in color, and at home in fresher soils, have swelled into an army. In the wake of the "gold-striped lily" and the "Chinese lily" with pink, gold, and brownish spots, bands, flecks and stripes on a great, claw-like calyx—both of which have been long well-known as magnificent garden plants—our gardens have also seen the appearance of the fairy-tale Nomocharis, already planted in four or more varieties: a butterfly, its carriage reversed and stance askew, modestly sized, with a flat, inverted calyx, pinkish, scarlet, white, flecked with brown, or carmine. Of similar bearing, on tall stems with coarse hair and a thick growth of leaves, the Tricyrtis pseudo-lilies unfold a stand of stiff, white, short, upwards-looking blossoms, their faces daringly flecked and spotted with reddish-brown or pinkish-violet decorations. These, in turn, lead over to China's pseudo-irises, to which the daring of their bearing links them: to the orange- and red-eyed leopard and Belamcanda sword lilies which assured the dreamer's bliss in the age of the German Baroque garden, and which then became lost in the garden's period of decadence in the nineteenth century. They stood beside the bleeding hearts from China's leafy forests, that crown of all the world's fumitories, that lovely plant that wings imagination, and which no child's eyes have ever been known to tire of. The Campanulae which have made these lands their home have likewise grown anomalous; in the case of the Adenophora, pale, flat, blue bells hang in rainy forests from pliant stems; the Platycodon has a tuber, and the flowers rise on rigid stems with leathery leaves like those of periwinkles, finally dangling down in the form of large, deep blue cups, again like the periwinkle. Submitting to the laws and history of the soil, all relations are not so much reversed as restored to primordial completeness, and tend toward both its poles. Trumpet creepers—which everywhere else are woody, developing into powerful vines or great, magnificent trees with stone-hard trunks—have soft stems in China, and range in height from hardly a handspan to a foot and a half, rising from tubers and decked with scarlet-pink trumpet flowers which are disproportionately large (Incarvillea), as though already turned into dwarfs by nature and readied for a dwarf garden. But farther to the north they take the form of true and proper woodland shrubs (*Incarvillea olgae*) that resemble the foxglove; and there are also intermediate forms (*Incarvillea variabilis*) with a cryptic, anemic, freesia color scale of Streptocarpus-like blossoms, from which the future will retrieve whatever forms and colors it desires. Here, the wonderful plants of the Rehmannia family of snapdragons likewise resemble the trumpet creeper, with colors entirely in the pinkish scale of the Incarvilleas, and blossoms in the form of great, fantastically draughted gullets. These are children of the light woodland soils in which, by way of underground migrations, they strive to expand into imposing thickets. On the other hand, Eurasia's mighty peonies, of the family Ranunculaceae, which already in the Caucasus begin to exchange their pinkish-scarlet tones for yellow hues, tend in China, just like the poppies, to flee the ground, and rise half-woody in yellow and deep red forms; in the taller varieties, as tall as a man, oddly angled structures of branches bear giant blossoms in their original carmine-pink beside tall semi-arborescent poppies and magnolias: lignification and shrubification have lifted the latter almost entirely off the ground, but the very low shrubs that belong to the family—and which appear nowhere but here, barely a meter and a half in height—still show stamens of a residual scarlet-pink, thus pointing toward more ancient plants with rose-red blossoms that may still stand undiscovered on some Chinese mountain range. The sage plants cede their territory to the two-lipped dragonheads, and here form fluffy, hemispherical cushions in a deep, velvet violet hue, lavishly seductive, and year to year in an ever greater wealth of varieties.

With these and other species of plants, Central Asia is a watershed. No narcissus makes its way to east of the Mediterranean; no hyacinth crosses the Taurus, no tulip the Indus; no true bellflower or sage, no true carnation crosses the mountains of Central Asia. Chinese carnations, dragonheads and pseudo-bellflowers replace them. The asters of the Pontic steppes go no further; eastern Asia's propensity for individuation and isolation leads instead to shrub-like summer plants with a large, solitary star-shaped blossom, on the order again of its great, flat-faced, paper-like, solitary, lavishly colored pseudo-carnations. Everything that on the soil of the steppes was subtracted from the single-flowered calyx in order to promote the countless blossoms of tough, aggressive shrubs here finds expression in the great solitary star at the summit of the plant's tallest stem: dark violet petals ray out around its black or dark orange center, or with a truly Chinese physiognomy split apart and crinkle into a great eccentric mass of ruffled filaments, (*Aster farreri*) and a strange, strong, wildly-featured face. On the other hand, the point where aster bushes stop marks the appearance, with similar bearing, of chrysanthemum bushes, which in the region between India and Japan, and northwards to Korea, have strongly scented and richly serrated foliage and great masses of small flowers, or solitary calyces halfway up the stem and a scale of forms and colors which, even if their own, resemble those of the Compositae that live in poorer soils, they too in the form of dense, compact bushes with partly woody stems. Here again, the two oldest forms—the "China chrysanthemum," which is the mother of all the giant varieties, and the "Chou-san aster bush," imported since 1862 and the mother of all the pom-pom chrysanthemums—are joined by a constant flow of new varieties, from the lovely Korean chrysanthemum to the small, abundantly flowering Japanese mountain chrysanthemums, and the end is not yet in sight. All share the same, compact color scale—so fundamentally different from asters' scale of blue, red, white—of yellow-yellow and whitish-yellow, in which a slumbering range of primordial colors lies waiting for release and rediscovery by the human being. But the ruffled, Baroque forms which ancient Japan, ancient China, southern France, and England have coaxed from the hardly even slightly straggling petals of the wild flowers are no breeder's flight of fancy. These are old East Asian faces, like the one that's latent in all the Chinese asters and which finds unsullied expression as a fundamental feature of its landscape only with the *Aster farreri.* The same can be said of the bizarrely tattered and needle-like petals of the Chinese carnation, which was once a naïve delight of the old German flower garden, but which today an era of philistinism, with its gardeners enamored of obtuse notions of order, has blithely made once again impossible to find in commerce.

On the other side of the territory, tropical southern China and southeast Asia send emissaries and harbingers of the most extraordinary kinds northwards from out of its lands of orchids and into the zones of chilly Chinese winters. It is here that one finds the finest terrestrial orchid of any temperate zone, and the size of its flower, no less than its delicate, magnificent colors can rival those of many of its exquisite and difficult greenhouse cousins. Its colors are those of the Cattleyas or, better, the Sobralias. Indeed, we are dealing here with the little sister, barely as much as a foot tall, of the latter, which is the largest and most impressive of all the terrestrial orchids: both are a lively violet pink and show a protruding, crinkly, undulated lip, beautifully fringed and scarlet in color, but brighter on its inner side; both have stems with an abundant foliage of nerved and folded leaves, as well as a cylindrical bearing, on respectively smaller and larger scales; and both, in the course of the years, form dense thickets. This can't be said to be China's only beautiful terrestrial orchid, but it's the only one that's imported and widely known; it, in fact, has lived in our gardens for hundreds of years, but has ever and again been ripped up out of the earth and transplanted into glasshouse pots by gardeners who incorrigibly harbor the feeling that their effortless cultivation can be no source of fame, and therefore consign them to neglect. Yet, there's hardly a more tenacious, more patient, unconditionally generous plant, or a plant that offers a more rewarding beauty than this singularly lovely blossom which wants no more than to drink in light and to be given a minimum of protection from complete frosting, and which then will be ready to shame Solomon in all his glory (*Bletilla hyacinthina*). Here, where Japan stands at the threshold between the old and new worlds, our own part of the earth reaches its end.

But beyond all other shoals that rise up out of the seas, presenting itself as a navel of the earth of primordial times, lies the group of islands which form New Zealand, hardly with any true link even to the strange, prehistoric world of Australia. A mountainous land, half-tropical in the north, in the south sub-arctic, New Zealand everywhere discloses a stiff, heavy eccentricity of forms and creatures that cannot be compared with any other. We have to think back to the abstract plants retrieved from our coal deposits, and then attempt to complete and decipher them if we want to find anything similar to a world of plants which here has remained at a standstill at the point from which the flora of the rest of the earth first departed and began to develop its shape. The laws of this soil and environment remain to be deciphered. Only the fewest of the plants imported from New Zealand have been able to be kept alive in our parts of the world. Tubers of the magnificent New Zealand buttercup—its leaves and stems metallic-green, ending with large, metallic-white flowers—die when replanted in Europe. The plant will be impossible to acclimatize, if not by growing it from seed, which again is quite reluctant to germinate in our soils. We turn to peat, heath soil, and various acidic additives in the attempt to offer the plants a substitute for what their land seems to give them easily: nourishing soils rich with fermented vegetable matter. New Zealand's herbs remain almost unknown; its shrubs only slowly take solid root; its typically woody regional forms of perennials also known in Europe just begin to allow us to make their acquaintance. We stand in amazement before such sisters of our blue speedwells as New Zealand's woody, cypress-shaped Ericaceae, of which the flowers seem to have been stuck in artificially; or the dwarf bushes, no more than inches tall, with thick, fleshy, grayish and greenish leaves, and white speedwell blossoms; or the plants with leathery periwinkle leaves unfolding two by two, violet on their undersides, and with violet, reddish, whitish-bluish panicles developing in pairs from the junctures of always further ramifications; scaly, wiry, bristly gnomes that belong to a primordial world. Its logic is wholly archaic, and creeping plants with fleshy leaves are one of its most forlorn expressions. New Zealand's flora lives a colorful life only in desert zones. It reaches deep beneath their sands to hidden waters, which also nourish the hollow, tubular roots of acacias (mimosas), mainly Australian, as well as certain stupendous varieties of *immortelle,* of which the thickly-leafed and pale gray or greenish stems rise up into scaly, armadillo-like, straw-colored calyces around a yellow center. There's also the odd, hellishly scarlet desert or lobster claw pea, with three or four almost finger-long beaks jammed one against the other. Marked as well by a rigid coal black gaze, at times completed by the surrounding white of an eye, it reaches the height of a meter, or snakes and climbs as a gray vine for meters along the ground. The dull red parrot's bill pea (*Clianthus dampieri* and *puniceus*), with smaller flowers, is its hardly less frightening sister. The plants that live in humus, heath, and the moors, where the soil has components of clay, show metallic, glossy leaves, and dead, otherworldly colors. The tree ferns, which are as tall as trees, press forward nearly into the temperate zones, as they did in Europe in the Carboniferous Period; New Zealand's Cyathea and Dicksonia tree ferns survive without winter protection in Riviera gardens. Star-shaped flowers stand zinc-white on the spherical, motionless, evergreen or, even more strangely, ever-yellow Olearia and Pachystegia bushes; or even metallic white, covered by a glossy, lifeless glaze, on low mountain shrubs (Celmisia) with dark green, leathery umbels lying flat against the earth. Mallows take on the look of Plagianthus and Hoheria, of which the branches at blossoming time are covered for the whole of their length by calyces that might be made of glassy tissue paper: the picture they present so little resembles flowers as the new, lifeless, glassy wings of pairs of ants in nuptial flight resemble those of butterflies. Aside from this whitish non-color, the scale here is slate red and slate blue; the flowers have not yet reached a flower form, or have lost it along the way, or allowed it to be petrified. The dwarf, climbing Acaena, a member of the rose family, terminates, over half-hidden sexual organs, in small chains. The giant Phormium reeds, members of the lily family, terminate in mighty clumps of a murky, reddish-green or reddish-yellow semi-grass: formless, faceless, and aeons removed from a free-standing floral crown. Myrtles press their branches forward in the form of scale-like growths, as though the plants were crawling on constantly budding organs up into the empty air; and then—when the respiration of the final, advancing segment, covered with scale-like leaves, has been assured—all further progress comes to a halt while the plant peppers its woody growth with thick red brushes of interwoven pollen strands (Callistemon), or with spheres of them (Melaleuca); it then creeps further, with a further outgrowth of blackish scales, until reaching the point for another brush or sphere. In crippled, primordial bondage, fertilization dares not distance from the woody stem; its only hopes, inside this deathly dark and featureless, scaly foliage, lie in passionate shifts in hue, which strive, after leaf-green, greenish-yellow, whitish-yellow captivities, toward the slate-colored tones that again belong to the leaves and play across their undersides, yet nonetheless break out into pure, blushing crimson. So, the flower reflects the banks of love and form even here in the ferruginous waters of its Acheron. In its travels in pursuit of flowers, humanity would have abandoned its path before reaching its goal if it had not taken this final step to a place beyond the flower, or to back before the flower: a place where the human being is able to see it not as we usually do—in terms of pleasure, possession, or, in imagination, as the key to our own secret past—but with the eyes of God and of history, as a hope.

These are the terms on which it is possible to understand the ways in which the habitus of the flowering plant, its character and mien, helps to determine the nature of the face of its landscape, and bears that face within itself: its style and demeanor must finally be seen as a given that derives from manifold relationships, from which they remain inseparable, and which also offer the only basis that makes them fully comprehensible—not only intellectually, but also in terms of sense perception. We have shown that this habitus in many cases—and at least some few of its parts in all cases, if it's not too rash to insist on such a premise—constitutes a form to which the flower has been forced to retreat, an emergency form, in the course of its life and death battle to hold its own against adverse conditions. And it follows that the flower which the human being rescues, sets free and nurtures will sooner or later vary, and abandon the mien it was formerly constrained to wear, so as then to run backwards through its whole compendium of forms.

The limits of this human activation of natural forms—limits concerned, on the one hand, with accepting the ways they play and, on the other, with playing with them pure and simple—can by now be seen more clearly. The limit lies at the line where a style, in the sense indicated above, would be destroyed. Or in the rejection of the style-less creation of style-less simulacra, and of the false rather than true humanization of wild, untamed forms. Because we're speaking simply of an insight into the ways in which the flower's habitus is specifically conditioned by the landscape, and by geological history; and of an empathetic, sympathetic, intuitive respect for all such circumstances; and finally of the contemplation, resulting from it all, of precisely this creature that looks like this and not like that. And none of these things are natural science, botany, or the learned discrimination of "the dissector of his own delights." They are the consummate reflection of the image of nature in the free human spirit. Biology, physiology, and even, in part, the study of the morphology of nature and her children belong to those research methods for the acquisition of natural-scientific fact for which the lily can hold no greater status than pond plankton or the plant louse. The physiognomy of plants—and plant morphology to whatever degree it includes and collaborates with physiognomy—is a very different method: it belongs to the humanities. Those former methods make no presuppositions. This latter always presupposes—both consciously and not—that the human being is the only being—the exclusive medium—whose organs of perception turn things into phenomena; and it plucks its flowers from within the view of the creative human gaze. Biogeography is more than the study of the distribution of plants; it is also the study of the landscape in the light of its characteristic vegetation; and landscape is that phenomenon in which a specific, restricted portion of the surface of the earth is grasped by the physical, sensual eye of the human being and then transformed, through the soul's experience and the light of the spiritual eye, into history. Surely, yes, there is a natural-scientific way—and we are all familiar with it—of reducing the *Gestalt* of the blossoming flower to the concourse of the physical, chemical, organo-centric factors inside the creature's every cell, but this is not the only road one might pursue. The history of nature as known on the earth is the historical path of the flower as a being in becoming. And in the sense in which the flower is a determined and determining process of form which reflects and shapes the total image of the landscape, its observation surpasses the threshold of natural science and its claim on everything mortal, and enters instead the unsurveyable and inexhaustible realm of immortality. This is the space of which the human sprit is the active force, and the place to which it leads whatever it mentally perceives, juxtaposing and comparing it to itself. This one-day child of wood pulp, water, and pigment, this empty snatch of brightly colored hay, this children's toy for garlands and rapidly discarded nosegays, this cheerful ornament that stands before our houses would be truly only all of that, and less than all of that, if it weren't inhabited by human thoughts, and thus transformed from nature into history. This is why the study of the physiognomy of plants—the science of the plant as phenomenic appearance—could only have been created at that single juncture of world history where, thanks to the creative mediation of poetry, history and nature exchanged their rights, and the human being—who in theory falls apart into an historical and a natural man—was able, as creator and creature in eternal oneness, to make himself the measure of all things. Alexander von Humboldt, who was the first to marshal this grandiose approach to things, and who left it orphaned behind him, was led to the task by the precursory example of Goethe: not Goethe the natural scientist—who as such was a speculative morphologist—nor Goethe the man, who rejected history, but Goethe the poet, who *was* history, since the poet *is* history. It thus became possible in the thinking of Goethe's friend, the greatest natural scientist since Aristotle, for *physis* and *humanitas* to be united and balanced against one another—"They appear to flee each other, Yet quicker than one might think have found each other"—in a new science, just as they likewise met, contemporaneously, in the work of his brother, Schiller's friend, and the greatest of all Platonists in the use of the world of Ideas in relation to the historical conditioning of the human being. Alexander von Humboldt's *Aspects of Nature* and the great work of Wilhelm von Humboldt's old age encounter each other's insights, once compared, at precisely the point which the German mind—if it has such a point at all—must call its Archimedean place to stand, from which to move the world.

CHAPTER VI

The Flower and the New Garden

THE European garden of the closing years of the nineteenth century and the beginning of the twentieth, on the continent and partly in England as well, was of bourgeois origins even where in fact it belonged to kings and great lords, and where large sums of money were spent on it. Those sums were spent in bourgeois ways, out of pockets of sufficient or considerable depth, and delivered straight into the purview—with no personal spirit or demands—of the customs and traditions preserved and served by the professional gardener, the specialist, who was one of the institutions which bourgeois principle saw fit to respect. The garden was the work and realm of the "gardener," and the garden's proprietor almost always remained content with simply being an onlooker, and of course with taking pride in his able man. And the spaces the garden was to occupy—when new houses were built for the well-to-do—were already fixed and measured out before being passed along to the gardener. Such measurements were the work of the architect who had drawn up the plans for a client's house and garden; and though surely those plans had not been made without due heed to the proprietor's desires, those desires in turn were usually readjusted in the light of the superior insights of this second institutional expert. The continent, in the great majority of cases, thus witnessed the construction of a large house with a small garden, whereas English custom generally led to a large garden and a relatively smaller house. Here too, however, nearly all the period's homes attempted to achieve the essentially architectural ideal of a unity of house and garden: in terms of image, both were to work for an overall effect; and in structural terms, the architectural principles that governed the house were also expected to control the garden's outdoor spaces. It followed necessarily that the garden was subordinate to the house. The period's garden was an instrumental addition to the house, the ornamental frame that surrounds it. Though dispensing with the compass and the ruler, its *intentions* were guided by notions of geometric order, even if now of the flattest, palest, most soulless kind: little else might indeed have been managed by the geometric thinking of an age of bourgeois entrepreneurs which had lost all connection with the heritage of the centuries of creative style, and which thus no longer possessed, nor even missed, an orderly image of nature, just as it lacked an orderly image of art.

The garden, like the ground on which the house was built, was flattened and leveled. Gardens on hilly terrain were warned against, owing to the high cost of leveling it. In places, as in England, where precisely such locations, for reasons extraneous to gardening, were preferred as sites for homes—places with a love for houses on heights that dominate the surrounding environment—the space for the garden was won from the slope, or adjusted to fit it, by terraces with proportions and lines of sight that harmonically related—again a geometric relationship—with the articulation of the home's facade. Landscape photography, as it grew always more adept and sophisticated, also began to exert an influence—here above all—on the image which the garden aimed for, and was finally no less powerful than Dutch landscape painting had proved to be, a hundred or two hundred years earlier, with respect to the model for the English park. The design, construction and planting of gardens lent strong consideration, whether consciously or not, to the illustrated publishability of an imposing overall house and garden complex. The period's magazines had begun to publish such pictures, and pride and the love of competition felt powerfully drawn to the possibilities for an always better showing.

The leveling of the garden's terrain, and especially so on the continent, had to be accompanied by the drainage of the soils which leveling, in areas of abundant and never entirely absent atmospheric precipitation, had deprived of natural drainage. The professional gardener had no particular love for light and porous soils. A nice sandy loam, a soil of medium weight which allows the planting of nearly whatever you like right next to nearly anything else, a loose, rich humus—"garden soil"—that's where he felt at ease. As well, he didn't much care to wield the spade. At the time when the garden is first laid out, before initial planting, it's clear, of course, that the soil will be turned once and for all down to three spades' depth, and that the furrows will be thoroughly manured. But afterwards, when the ground is covered with permanent beds, how will one be able ever again to dig it up so deeply? Yet, a thorough loosening of the soil is the only means of natural drainage, at least without turning to the costliest system of all, which is a network of pipes. So the garden's terrain was first leveled and afterwards drained, with the result of a healthy layer of soil for planting. Then came beds and paths: beds and paths which were suitably arranged in pleasant, decorative relationships for the eye's appreciation. The very name of the beds of perennials, which are known as "borders"—the custom spread from England to the continent—refers to their relation to the edges of paths. Next to the "borders" ran similar "annual borders" of more demanding summer plants; these were also the tracts where bulbs blossomed in the spring; and, here again, as the summer flowers withered, plants that would bloom in the fall germinated around them, or room was made for fine, flowering grasses, previously cultivated elsewhere but then transplanted. But the general rule, outside of England (and there as well the custom persisted, thanks to the professional gardeners who always so tenaciously defended it), foresaw rigid configurations of circular, oval, quadrilateral, multilateral and even star-shaped "flower beds" in the midst of expanses of lawn. Such ornamental installations also went harmoniously hand in hand with the other great need of the epoch, as expressed through the absolute primacy of color. The creation of great masses of color, as vast and as uniform as possible, and as saturated as possible, was frenetically pursued and counted as the one great goal. An age of Impressionist painting had led the eyes of peoples with a genius for draughtsmanship—eyes which before had seen their own reflection in the pungent chastity of the motionless columbine, in the solitary majesty of the shaft of the lily—to a new theology of pigments dissolved in light, and the gaze which in England was weary of the dusky, the tonal, the gloomy and the dark, thirsted now for a beaker of fire and light. It found its motto in "sheets of color." The continent didn't lag behind, and in its own way developed the impulse received from abroad into the motor of a systematic machine. Just as the garden had been turned into a pendant of the house, and thereby made subservient to it, the flower now became a tool for the production of color: not only destined to serve, it was understood to serve *en masse.* Yellow gardens, blue gardens, red gardens were wagered, proclaimed and attempted. Everything "blue" was bunched together. The fact that this "blue," even in the best of cases, remained an empty abstraction, and that all this appalling rhymelessness pastiched together for the briefest common blooming season was a parti-colored medley of a hundred different hues, but a far cry from "blue," as yet occurred to no one. Even when arranged into carpet-like beds—which garden plans, in persistent obtusity, had always continued to prefer, despite all laments and objections—never had the flower been so debased as in this degradation to pure and simple pigment, with tracts of colors sharply defined, as geometry demanded, by paving brick or low, picketed, wrought-iron fencings. Beside them—since all the forms and levels of bourgeois soullessness continued their existence beside and thanks to one another—stood the enormous reserve of potted plants and flowers set out into beds, a practice still today the rule in the continent's public gardens, and even in the private gardens of French *rentiers*: fuchsias, geraniums, heliotropes, lantanas and the like with brightly colored displays of leaves arranged around Musa, Gunnera and giant tobacco, or other similar plants, for the greater delight of the nurse maids, and the pride of the man of note whom the period had turned into a garden aficionado.

Such installations had treated the new arrivals much as they considered correct for the old; the newer species found a more or less friendly reception and just as much space in which to develop as was given to the novel colors of the new varieties of the older species—and why not? Whatever appeared on the market was duly planted on these leveled and nicely drained terrains, in this standard, uniform garden soil conceived to do justice to all demands: a solid mixture, not too light, not too heavy, loam with a measure of sand, soil from deciduous woodland and proper stable manure, well-seasoned. Any caprice that refused to flourish in it must surely have been very strange. In other words, whatever found no satisfaction in such a kind of nourishment and with such a group of neighbors "doesn't do well in our part of the world." Such things, to be sure, were bound to happen from time to time. This or that would die, the collar of its roots would rot, it would suffer and languish, would flower disappointingly. So it was "difficult," and quickly eliminated. England, however, was also to invent the rock garden—it surfaced from the depths of the imagination of a people of flower lovers—and it was something quite different from the "rock parterres," "grottos" and "rockeries" with which earlier times had toyed. The rock garden was first of all the place for the rebels that spurned the bourgeois flower bed, for the proud mountain children which enchant the climber in any and every latitude; the climber, indeed, had collected them, taking them back to his home as seed, plant or root stock so as better and fresher to hold them in his memory of them; but in beds they dumbly and contemptuously went to rot, just as animals trapped in the wilderness refuse the food pushed into their cage. And next to the English rock garden, there was also its contrary pole: the English water garden. The one was the space that welcomed plants with a love for arid terrain, the other the place of assembly for those that drink to the full: both were for fugitives from the decorative swath immediately around the house. The rock garden clambered upwards, the water garden sank downwards. A vertical co-ordinate had broken up into the horizontality of the leveled garden, and this mutinous new dimension destroyed its flatness: no longer a plane, the garden rose up around it as a three-dimensional space.

But the rock garden and the water garden, even if perhaps the most decisive, were not the only levers that made the upheaval possible. The eternally unchanging problem of what is to be done, while creating garden paths, with the excavated, excess earth had led to the creation of "banks" along one or both sides of wandering paths, and then to planting them with something. At a single stroke, enchanting little nature gardens were born. It was then automatically discovered that certain plants—you know the reasons why—grow best and bloom most healthily on slopes: the gardeners' fable that all columbines are "short-lived" perennials (the very best drained of loamy soils are incapable of hosting them in permanent beds for very long) didn't survive their planting on slopes. With only the slightest external aid, slopes are self-draining, and unacquainted with the soggy winter soils in which that notorious circle of rot inexorably destroys the heart of stands of noble plants. Banks also demanded retaining walls: mortarless, dry-stone walls constructed slightly on a slant, for a firmer hold. Whoever at home or abroad had seen wild flowers on the walls of country lanes—plush pillows and pyramids of blossoms which had made him wonder how they might find nurture in the meagerest cracks for so much splendor—set to work and began to experiment: his walls blossomed, those gorgeous plants had been no vulgar gluttons, but lived on spare, exquisite stuff, on calcium and a few fresh crumbs of daily filtering earth for which they carefully searched, from one fissure to the next. As well, dry-stone walls and blossoming banks had shown the new space the additional dimension of the slope. The old, flat surface of garden plants had been cracked and warped, and bent in every direction. The garden had come into movement, could tumble down declivities and rise toward heights, scale its way along byways in order to encounter itself, become a ladder, and flights of steps. Small gardens on modestly-sized terrains spread up and down and sidewards into the air. Both smaller and larger gardens freed themselves entirely from the level surface and the house, at first still unsuspectingly, and simply driven from one experiment to the next. Only when already victorious did the revolution grow gradually aware of itself and its goal, which lay in making the garden a mirror of a landscape.

In accord with the English national spirit, the process was not noisy, and felt no need to be introduced by literary fanfare. It was a practical, calm, and patient process, as conducted by a people who found it customary for each to go his own way, to allow others to go their own, and to reserve the conduct of private life, endeavor and activity, even to the point of whim and eccentricity, entirely to one's own guidance, free from any need of anyone's authorization; and as well by a people to whom it could not suffice—unlike the Germans—only to dream of a deviance from convention, roaming in fantasy to construct some light creation, and then again dispelling it. The tenacity and moment of what by now was a century-old practice of true connoisseurship and creativity had to give pursuit to what it imagined and to bring it to realization—had to see what it finally looked like, to reach it, to experience it. And since the final thing itself was what had to be kept in mind, there was no such thing as theory, no method, no historical or stylistic prejudice involved, no overly hasty systems or precocious principles of uniformity, no models, no foregone conclusions. Each started out as though he were Adam once again, from something fresh, with the utter naiveté of a stubborn, childlike, womanly empiricism; and women, from the very start, were very much involved in the process. In fact, it was the work of whole classes of people who knew exactly what they did and did not love, and who seriously intended to obtain the things they loved. This straight, sound, and energetic path had to shape the form that would give it self-expression, like a foot by way of a footprint. It was finally and exclusively the path of the passionate *amateur*, of a multitude of amateurs, the path of the individual, of a society grounded on the individual, the path of the man on his own terrain, no matter if the most unassuming citizen on the half hectare of a garden at the edges of a town, or the grand lord on the vast expanses of a tranquil country seat. Profession and commerce had nothing whatever to do with it. The gardener, if seen at all, was the carefully instructed assistant in the service of the garden's master, and of the garden's master's experiments: an assistant instructed in the arts of observation, and asked for expert technical aid, for understanding and support, nothing more. It now again went no differently than a hundred years before; the creation of the new garden no differently than that by poets and painters, Pope, Addison and Kent, of the reinvented park.

But even if the amateur had become the active force of the process through which the English garden was destined again to rank itself as a creation of the English people, he had not been the drive initially behind it. The initial impulse which had burst the old garden out of its seams was the flower, and only the flower: the new flowers. The century had introduced them, had plucked them from their homelands, brought their seeds and seedlings to commerce, or, where commerce had not yet taken them up, to an inestimable number of individual aficionados: their hands overflowed with the booty of a people accustomed to dominate and travel across the world, and to write reports that spanned its continents. They made no secret of what they planted and cultivated. The national passion created its national voice. With tens of thousands of members of every station and all across the globe, the Royal Horticultural Society embraced the whole situation and turned it into a single body, of which the size, means and ambitions were uniformly imposing; and it furnished the flood of plants, which now for more than a century had unabatedly flowed—but as well unbridled and uncontrolled—with what it most pressingly needed: an indisputable critical authority which had nothing to do with tradesmen or their interests or their self-promotion, nor with commerce and its goals, and which instead was exclusively guided by the finest connoisseurship and a steadfast spirit. No such thing had ever existed before, in any place or in any previous century. But there had likewise been no previous century with a similar need to protect itself from a threat of total submersion: minds and spirits were called upon, as never before, to confront an untamed demon—which the blossoms from the wild might well have become—in ways that might subdue the new and multicolored monster, and finally force it to take on a human dimension, just as its various predecessors had all been forced to do. All who thought themselves to have come into possession of something special, or to have managed some new development, thus began to make a habit of submitting it to the scales of this highly respected panel of judges. Whoever in fact had something special exhibited it. Whoever was able to do so made further experiments with the exhibits of those before them. General assemblies turned into sittings of evaluation committees. And evaluations were organized and guided by the great general principles of isolation and selectivity. Examples of plants which were fascinating but largely unexplored were afforded the dignity of trial cultivation and observation in the experimental gardens at Wisley, the largest and most rigorous in the world, and the West's first model of an institution that might supersede the botanical garden, which it had created many years before. But more than anything else, the Royal Horticultural Society gave the English people the one great thing they can never truly do without when their souls are fully engaged: a place of competition. The Chelsea flower shows, the largest of which take place in the spring, became a floral Olympiad, a national feast, and also an arena. Awards and prizes, medals and trophies and announcements of the names of winners established world-wide opinion. What merited victory in Chelsea—where selection and judgment were highly exacting, and competitors included the finest talents—was certain, sooner or later, to find itself firmly established. The Society's official organ, the *Journal of the Royal Horticultural Society*, recorded the competitions, the lists of the winners and the names of the plants, and invited the country's foremost connoisseurs and specialists to describe their work in the greatest possible detail. The world could see the developing new garden to be permeated and elucidated by the judgments of a corps of observers which had never stood at the service of the pure and simple flower, and it heard them spoken in the calm, clear language of that highest level of cultivation for which simplicity is never self-indulgent and always to the point. And the driving force of the great central competition led the rest of the country as well to deck itself with contests, both large and small. Daffodils and gladiolas, dahlias and flowering shrubs and the sweet pea developed national societies all their own, with competitions and examining boards. Every provincial city, every county, every village had its annual flower show, replete with awards and prizes; and with a view to such shows and prizes, all of their gardens all year long pursued and perfected ambitious achievements. Indeed, whole years of work could be sacrificed to a single, extreme accomplishment: maturing it for exhibition and bringing it to the height of an honorable mention demanded and created the highest levels of expertise and sensibility.

A naïve spirit of empiricism and an adventurous sense of the total environment had allowed the private amateur to take on the task of creatively extending the garden out into the dimension of space, yet the garden would never have entered a whole new epoch without the aid of the enormous range of critical activity which exerted an influence on the growing population of plants, preventing it from fully taking root before first decanting and reordering itself. England's critical study of flowers in the years around 1900 influenced the form of the Western garden more greatly than might be said of any other historical event. Neither scientific botany, nor the efforts of breeders, nor the passion that inspired collectors were of equally pervasive effect. Its selections and discriminations prove to be of no less weight than the great systems of the classifiers, just as its research gardens stand on a par with the renowned botanical gardens of the past. It beautifully embodies procedures that were only slowly to assert and vindicate demands that a need experienced by a whole free people—one of its dominant and most passionate drives, its feeling for nature as expressed through relations with flowering plants—be regarded with absolute seriousness, and purified and ennobled through rigorous work. Botanical sophistication is beside the point to the attraction that draws human beings to plants. Yet the human soul could find no peace or sense of fulfillment in a relationship of purely sensual *gourmandise.* The human soul needs order, and all of its raptures are in need of order; they attempt to preserve or respect an order, and this need is true of even the subtlest of human feelings. Centuries marked by critical thinking precede world history's epochs of great creative thought as though according to the dictates of a sacred law; they likewise come in their wake, radically questioning established certainties and breaking soil that will then receive new seed. Despite the extraordinary level of its gardeners' practical expertise, Germany never found access to incisive, critical attitudes to the flower and the garden. During the years in which the English were performing this work, critical intelligence and critical courage lay fallow in Germany, without exception, in all fields of endeavor; and in the realm of gardening this shortcoming pinned the country's contribution down against the ground. Criticism is the life blood of all free peoples. To subject a thing to criticism is to take the first step toward respecting it. The things we have judged are the only things we in fact have taken seriously. Things we allow to slide have slipped already into places regarded with indifference. Enthusiasm is a deathless, driving force, but its strength first comes to be gauged by the opposing force that delimits it. We consist not of song, but of drama. Wherever we discover the human spirit, we will surely hear two voices. It is not true that criticism lames creativity; criticism is the most impelling of the forces that lead it to surpass itself. And nothing, conversely, could be more false or more unjust than to ridicule the English love of gardens by calling it a national hobby horse, a psychosis, an eccentricity, or a fashion-driven craze. To say such a thing is to show one's ignorance of the cold and sober laws which a dark and elementary passion on the part of a vast community of people has given itself so as better to strive for the highest level that a passion can achieve, through the spirit of intelligent work. One would also show no lesser ignorance of the forms to which this work has led.

The trial cultivation of the new flowers from the wilderness demanded situations that had little to do with gardening, as traditionally understood. Those who desired to exhibit in Chelsea a new Canary Island Echium, a new Chilean Nierembergia, or a new South African Arctotis had not brought them up in any colorfully miscellaneous bed. Watchful eyes had carefully studied their needs, in order to guide them to exemplary form and habit. Such breeders had dispensed with the old, standard garden soil in which everything worth cultivating was supposed or forced to grow. They had created beds of sandy soil for flora that demanded dry conditions, of sour and moor-like soils for this particular specialty, or deep, light and rich for others. There were stony soils, and clayey soils mixed with coarse gravel; pure humus, and soils free of limestone. Shadow, half shadow, full sunlight, soils perpetually moist and others painstakingly drained played well-calculated roles. And of course there were zones of transition, and others where borders went unrespected. Many plants that flourish most beautifully in a given set of ideal conditions will also somehow manage in relatively similar circumstances; they often adapt to something other than their favorite soil and favorite conditions of light, making do, but tolerably satisfying. Yet English criteria were basically opposed to approximation or imprecision, insisting instead on absolute perfection and tolerating no compromise. This strictness of principles promoted intransigence and effectively established the flower's autonomy with respect to the garden and the gardener. The experimental gardens of all the researchers and amateurs who intended to exhibit their achievements took the placement of plants with utmost seriousness. Rock gardens and small stony hillocks had their sunny and shadowy sides, their sandy pockets and fissured crags, their areas of granitic and others of calcareous soils, their small moraines with a constant trickle of water; dry stone walls hosted enormous festoons of South African asters; the children of California deserts and the bulbs of those of southern Africa were given sand; Mimulus native to America grew rank while drinking the waters of moist, half sunny plots. The periwinkles of New Zealand and North American stood in moor-like ground beside the grimacing faces of tall blue and scarlet lobelias; deeply rooting plants were supplied with elevated beds; and so on and so forth, endlessly. Such arrangements were as little like gardens—or more than a garden, already a garden—as had been the tracts of land where Holland in the sixteenth and seventeenth centuries had developed the bulbs that now belong to the Western world. Here as there, once again, the flower had dissolved the garden and reigned unchecked on subjugated earth, where all previous principles of order had collapsed. These installations found none of their conscious goals in any thought of creating a form that a new kind of garden might assume. Just as continental breeders ever more thoroughly took their cue not from the garden but from florist's shops for cut flowers and potted plants, the English raised flowers not for gardens but for flower shows, or for prizes and competitions. Finally, however, the new flowers were by no means only those supplied by nature, as new arrivals and new species. Amateurs were breeding plants in much the same ways as experimental botanists, cultivating ever more perfect hybrids at the expense of great tenacity, and thanks to a similar immersion into the will and potential left dormant in the plants by nature. Broad fields were decked, in hundreds, by the delphiniums, bellflowers, iris, lilies and Eremurus of sharp-eyed gentlemen connoisseurs, of lady breeders whose ambitions were never stilled. The mighty spikes of the towering Campanulae produced by the Jekyll and Willmoth sisters, the wondrous colors of Major Stern's Eremurus, the hybridized Martagon lilies developed by Bath, and the larkspurs which every year grew more fantastic transformed the gardens of breeders starved for space—and how many later world-famous English country priests raised their plants in parish-house gardens—into densely crowded nurseries.

Now classic strains of plants, some of them modest and others quite sumptuous, found their way from quarters which were hardly believably cramped to honorary diplomas in Wisley and Chelsea, but the price for that lay in sweeping away the garden with a broom. The amateur who was blessed with land was able to leave his neighboring decorative gardens undisturbed. Up until very recent times, the most radical negations of the garden in the name of pursuing the flower have continued in fact to be flanked by the blossoming of the same old flower beds, four rows wide and charged with Rudbeckias, Heleniums and goldenrod, larkspur and Caucasus poppies and asters, Galliardias, gladiolas, and foxglove as single-stemmed plants; then Geum and scarlet lightning, buttercups, anemones and primroses, Ageratum and cushions of Arabis—gorgeous, enormous heaps of color, a hundred meters long, why not?—why not a hundred and twenty, why not two hundred? Because the space has run out. Space? Space never runs out. That's something we have learned by now. Because the grounds have run out, you mean. When the grounds run out, the creation of space begins. When space runs out, you create new space.

Come take a look at that dry stone wall. Blooms rise for meters along its sloping face, whereas the area of ground it covers measures one and a half square meters, not even enough for a couple of hardy bushes. Come up with me here to the right, along the path that goes steeply to the top, with the rock garden to the left of it, the flowering banks, bordered with stones, on its right. Calculate the amount of flat ground it covers; and calculate the number of plants you could plant on a plot that size, one right next to the other. And look at what's blooming here on a slant, up on the heights, steeply sloped, next to one another, on top of one another, dangling down, in spaces between one another. The flatter your ground, the less you can grow on it; the more broken it is, the more up and down, the more you can make it hold. Now, I don't mean of course to take your flower beds away from you; you'll recreate them again and again, reshaped and transformed. It's never so much a question of the thing itself, as of the spirit in which it's done. This here, my friend, no matter how lush and wild and riotous it seems, was all artificially created. You can see that right away. But there's also the look of it, and how it's supposed to look: as though it had happened on its own!

The sober, functional spaces of precisely such research gardens led the eye to dwell, again and again, on perceptions never known before: flowers were observed as they developed and bloomed under natural conditions of growth, freely and undisturbed, at one with their immediate environments. The rock garden conjured up the wonderful spectacle of blossoming cushions and dangling growths in riot over stone, festoons springing from fissures, tall thin panicles rising from outcrops of tuffstone, organically fused with the cliffs and the air and standing free on natural terraces in the company of natural neighbors: how different a sight from the running borders, meter after meter, of feather carnations at the edges of geranium beds, or Iberis encircling groups of shrubs. But what's to be said of that sandy bed where the creeping gray-green desert verbena of southern California (*Abronia*) sends up countless flesh-pink tendrils that peek from between the bright, stiff cups and chalices, hairy and smooth, of Mariposa tulips and lantern flowers (*Calochortus*), Babianas and Homerias? Now that was a heavenly plot of earth, a heavenly corner from a distant clime, but where? Variegated Mimulus runs rank at the edges of the pond, but giant flowering Dierama grasses, from the marshes of southern Africa, have likewise found accommodation and dangle bell-shaped blossoms, pale blue or pale pink, from quivering hair-thin stems. Water, here, is rare, so all the world's various continents have come together to drink at the trough where a dip in the ground holds the garden's pool, an almost natural community of plants such as nature herself might create, no matter how few of them would ever have met without the help of the human hand, which while calling them together with no particular effect in mind has given rise to a tiny, wild paradise. The opposite spirit came into play with the "island" gardens which in regions warmed by the Gulf Stream specialized in plants from the Canaries: flowers here construed the whole of a landscape, with all its characteristic features; whole square meters covered by tall, luxuriant, nearly monstrous towers of flowering viper's bugloss; compact bushes of wild, blood-red ragwort; chrysanthemum bushes as tall as a man, veritable trees with spherical crowns, decked with star-shaped flowers; the statuesque Canary Island foxglove, as though cast in bronze, rising tall from among the rocks; the stiff, round Odontospermum bush, silk-green, tightly clamped into fissures in sea-side cliffs, and studded with chrome-yellow stars. The garden, here—which did not want to be a garden, but to sacrifice itself to the greater perfection of the flower—has turned into a free and open landscape. The flower, liberated, and provided out of human goodness with a soil entirely its own, showed thanks for the gift and fully revised the sight of its appointed piece of cliff, beach and slope. A divine island had been conjured up from which nothing was missing but more beautifully feathered birds and the Hesperides, beside golden fruit in the morning dew. People who had been there and seen it dreamed the potent dream of those who had fallen to its spell, and who henceforth wanted nothing more than to express as much as they had taken in. The research gardens were simply the letters of a new and unknown alphabet, poured out at random and without any view to combining them into words, to shaping a meaning by way of words. Yet that further step was not to be held back, since the flowers of the new paradises—studied, approved and identified, precisely researched and annotated in terms of their particular demands, and familiar by now to appreciative eyes—no longer wanted to be crowned with prizes and recommendations, and demanded instead to be planted. Study and observation at some point had to reach an end. The immense new stock of flowers had entered imaginations like new wine; and its always fresh and still untried abundance led it out into the reality of real gardens. What was to be done? How could it all be managed? How was one to hope to do it justice?

Justice could be done only by spaces that fully developed in all directions. That alone could accommodate—in purely quantitative terms—its enormous mass, its great variety of species, and still leave space for new arrivals, just as a properly thought out library leaves room for new volumes. The second essential factor—and it gave the epoch its own particular face—was the elementary principle of raising plants from seed: pure seed-bed gardening. It was unthinkable to postpone acquaintance even only with the newly arriving perennial plants until such time as commercial nurseries had provided themselves with sufficient quantities of an unsurveyable assortment as to be able to distribute them. Just as at the time of the Baroque garden, seed was planted by one and all; seed was within the reach of modest purses too; and the enormous joy in the cultivation of flowers from all around the world showed that face—just like the cultivation of those of the Western world—which God loves most, of equally industrious pleasure on the part of both rich and poor. The new garden—like the Baroque garden—saw the passionate involvement of a whole people. Its highest development came about in the hardest times of the Western world. English nurseries of great renown were forced to close by a lack of heating fuel. Stately properties with famous gardens fell to ruin, or were sold at a loss and parceled. Personnel had to be let go. The yearly expenditure of the English people for gardening activities sank in statistical relevance, and wavered for years between short sudden surges and renewed collapse. The garden proudly accepted the pressure of hard times, and deftly threw it in the dust bin. What the nurseries lost went to the profit of the powerfully developing establishments for the commercial distribution of seed. What check books no longer could afford grew possible instead for savings books, as imaginations in difficult times strove to outdo themselves. The earthly pains, on an ever more gruesome scale, of countless victims robbed of all they'd owned, of widows, orphans, and the mutilated, of people left half lame, embittered, rescued, longing for forgetfulness, fled toward the haven of the making of gardens with the full spiritual power of loving, human solitude, deciding once again, as a thousand times before, to see the garden as everything the heart most misses, and to make it the image of its longing. As a shaken solution releases a crystal, these woeful times released at their edges a reversed and different image of themselves, there free from woe. While not belonging to England's poetry, but an English poetry nonetheless, the verses of a great American poetess attired themselves in Sappho's veils and sang her savage dirge to the weeds and multicolored herbs, to the mullein and the flowering bliss of mountain pastures. The oneness of the world of flowers, from the plants that typically pine and wither in the dark of untrod woodlands, to the Alyssum on the sands of the Riviera, from the characteristic flora of dry, chalky slopes to the exuberant explosion of springtime garden shrubs, from the blue iris that will not burn in the fire that consumes the universe, to the *Iris chrysographes*, which the first Japanese, no sooner than having been saved it from the first primeval earthquake, once again planted on their roofs—this oneness, guaranteed by the oneness of the human heart, makes the poetry of Edna St. Vincent Millay contemporary to the new English garden. As she stares half thoughtless from the window of a slowing train, the gaze with which she quickly and surely takes in the cedars of the mountainside village churchyard—not planted trees, but natural, self-seeded on the sheets of slate of the mountain promontory—this contemplative, imaginative gaze in an eye charged with burning tears is the gaze of the garden of the time. The maturity of knowledge that immediately builds the bridge between wild plants and the planted landscape, against a background of quiet spiritual participation, and the assumption that such an allusion will be immediately and generally understood are things which had never existed, nor could have existed, before.

So the first step taken by the new garden as it turned toward becoming a landscape of flowers was the same, on a different level, as the one with which the new park had begun to become a woodland landscape: it set itself completely and unconditionally free from the house: from links to architecture and preoccupations with inhabitability, from orientations with respect to facades and from concerns for the view of the whole. It became self-contained and entirely revolved on its own center of gravity. Its organization was henceforth prescribed only by the will of the flower: wherever the flower saw her chance for the purest possible development, the garden was ready to follow her, along paths which it prepared for her. The new gardener knew no other paths than these, or such that bonded paths like these each with one another. For flowers that demanded protection he planted shadow and shrubs, or indulged their love of trees; he channeled waters and made them flow, or lie in marshes, or collect in pools. The landscapes to which flowers belong had become a part of his senses, and making them arise from those landscapes was what he knew to be his only goal. The aged Miss Jekyll recounts how she managed to make the giant lilies of the pre-Himalayan forests take root and grow in a clearing in Munstead: a pit as deep as a man is tall was filled all year and stamped tight with all the vegetable waste from her farm; the half-rotted mulch was then again covered with a further mound of fresh waste, of which the decomposition was also encouraged; the bulbs of the plants were then sunk deep into the midst of it. She had no other way to provide the fabulous creatures with a replacement for the accumulated humus, centuries deep, of their jungle homeland. But it's at similar depths that nature's largest and most wondrous bellflower, the Ostrowskya, wants to ramify its glassy, brittle, fragile, rope-like rhizomes. No matter at how great a distance its forests lie from those of the giant lilies, the garden recreates no Himalayas and no replica of Turkestan, but dream landscapes that only obliquely refer to real ones, allowing related scenes to flow together and form a third, which will be new. The garden is no reconstruction of bio-geographical realities, but a free creation in which the knowledge of the botany of a particular kind of landscape, and the understanding of the characteristic habit of its flowers have appointed themselves no purpose of self-display: their goal, instead, is to summon a spirit, transmuting into spirit, and as learned knowledge to disappear.

There are no fixed schemes; there are no recipes. The garden architect's blueprints, which for twenty years had furnished every capacious purse with the conventional originality of the same commercial pattern of rock garden, beds of shrubs, flowered parterres, cozy corners with a sundial, pairs of steps with tiny flowers in pulvinate cascades, and then the small mosaic garden all pasted into the plot, found nothing they might copy and coin into tradable ware. Grounds were developed imaginatively, unfolding in all directions and at every height, turned back to before the time of the flattenings and levelings of human cultivation: the terrain was once again allowed to result from primitive natural process, from the natural ways in which the earth's surface has split, lifted, sunk, and weathered. Rock cropped up through the hillside where precipitation had washed it free; and lay as scree and debris where shattering frost had broken it apart and allowed it to flow down the hill. Retaining walls were erected where the clay of the otherwise washed-out slope appeared unable to disadvise them. The stones that edged the paths were not held in place by cement, and made it possible for vegetation to grow between them: the path had thrown them to its sides and left them there, and a wealth of plants had rooted among them, with their protection and nourished by their chalks. Steep slopes at the flanks of the paths were terraced naturally, and the jump in the terrain presented itself as an elevated, deep-soiled bed, which is what it was. This was the place for the delicate, deeply rooted plants of subtropical forests: an innocent community of cupolas, pyramids, and rising and falling cascades of blossoms. Here the hill faces southwest, and shows various hollows and niches. There perhaps a tree may have fallen, springing open the ground with its roots; the hollow now has been filled with stones that offer protection to a great profusion of exotic climbers, some of them woody, others with pliant stems, small colorful gorges, tiny scarlet gullets, delicate ewers, noble cups. Beneath them, ever lower down where the slope dropped ever more dry, draining itself of water and basking in the sun, grass was allowed to grow. But how many flowers bloomed within this grass! How many different blossoms! Flowered meadows from all across the world here found their synthesis. The deranged conviction that flowers blossom well only on crumbly naked earth, kept rigorously "free of weeds"—this idiocy in the mouths of gardeners, despite the way it's made to pale by every flowering mountain meadow, with its primroses, orchids and buttercups, its corydalis and globeflowers—had seen its day. Grasses and bushes, grasses and rhizomes are natural communities of flowers that protect and invigorate one another, peaceably sharing the nourishment provided by the earth—not so much to each his own, as to each a something different. This can't, of course, be said of all grasses; and blossoms won't appear on every plot that's overrun with greedy quitch. And where the grasses stopped, South African flowering bush could begin: the pseudo-gladiolus and pseudo-tritonia irises whose stems no superficial eye can tell apart from Carex. The grassland prairies bloomed, here again as a synthesis, even if in this case the characteristic plants of the various different continents were held apart, since their wrangling color scales if they had all been thrown together would have cancelled each other out. The thick green grass was also the home—since this is the only place in which it truly blooms—of the gold-striped Japanese *Lilium auratum*: and it bloomed year in, year out, its scepters of flowers growing ever more numerous and ever more heavily laden, whereas when planted in rigorously weeded beds the imported bulbs shrivel to nothing in three years time and must once again be purchased from Asian merchants with enigmatic smiles and shipped across the sea. There, toward the west, came shade and wooded copses—light shade—pierced and dappled by sunlight. For the various flora, beside one another, of the leafy forests of China, Persia and Mexico: fumitory, crown imperial, Incarvillea, bizarre varieties of dog's tooth violets with fluttering swirls of petals, carpets of curious cyclamens, columbines that might be blown from shimmering green glass, and there, in bobbing solitude at the top of a wiry stem, Guatamala's scarlet columbine with a lemon yellow gorge. The springtime creepers that wind around young tree trunks, the cherry-tree clematis, cede their place to those that take on color in the summer: stone-blue morning glories in the heights; at middle heights a chalky cream; and then in the fall, above flaming, blood-red Persian bushes (*Parrotia*), the South American Mina drops wondrous, forking clusters of blossoms down against the blue of the sky through yellows and rusty browns, their scarlet buds subsiding to a range of pink, pale yellow and pure white flowers.

Because the clearing is a hollow, still and slightly sunken. Rising deep blue from out of the ground—an army in celestial armor—a giant stand of larkspur, in massive, natural profusion; clusters of the smaller, Chinese variety in ultramarine and gentian blue might be heralds sent to announce it. Dark clumps of orange Japanese globeflowers see fit instead to hold their distance. The different blue of patches of monk's hood relieves it as the season advances. The carpet of sky-blue Apennine anemones, shot through with the checkerboard patterns of egg-shaped fritillaries and multitudes of wild dwarf lilies, begin the spring around these colossal shrubs, up until the fall when the Palestinian savior's lily, the *Sternbergia*, everywhere unfolds its deep yellow calyces and the autumn crocus holds the places where throughout the summer the South American pseudo-crocus, *Zephyranthes*, white, rose red and delicate yellow, rose from bright tufts of grass. In the next patch of protective half shadow, at the edges of the clearing, the flashing blue of cushions of lobelia; the dark purple of a dwarf poppy, shy and exotic; the glow of crocuses and violets, peering half-hidden from the green. The path rises through sparse woods, past tall bushes of wild roses with deep red and dull pink petals around old-gold tufts of stamens, past great plants of mallow with yellow and bluish chalices; scattered here and there between them, the blossoming shafts of solitary flowers, a foxglove, a Jacob's ladder, the tower of tiny bells of a foreign meadow-rue, a luxuriant staff of tall, milk-white bellflowers with spotted throats; and from higher up, creeping fuchsias heavy with large-belled blossoms hang along the face of the steep embankment, and down into the path, whereas briar fuchsias with miniscule blossoms numbering into hundreds stand man tall and hold its upper edge, as sentinels from Antarctic America, and accustomed to winter cold. The stream that flowed beside us has now carved deeper and lies between meter tall banks at the foot of another declivity, where light, airy, clayey walls are covered with the white crepe-petaled flowers of the silvery bushes of the California poppy shrubs, and higher up above them the yellow arboreal poppies of China. The course turns off to the north. Shy of the sun, but in tower after tower of all the colors of deep, glowing velvet, the tall primroses of eastern Asia (*Primula nirvalis*) press forward to the edge of the water, and there on the right, where the banks have given way, it overflows, and the half marsh glows with the rose-like magnificence of the Himalayan primrose. Over there, higher up, the slope is dry and rocky. Limestone breaks through thin grass, and further toward the top assumes the shape of a low bluff-like wall. April, here, is aflame with the blood-red flecks of dwarf tulips, and miniature irises with violet faces and short gray stems continue upward toward the summit. Now, in summer, powerful growths of sage are content to feed on arid earth and strong sun, showing colorful upper leaves or lavish gullets, as shelves or rising into cupolas, in tones from lilac to yellow, pink to white; late in the fall comes the raw brick red of the splendid Leonotis. The lily-like Michauxia bellflower and the stately *Campanula laciniata* build unforgettable stands, and woolly plants become numerous; plants of mullein in the various colors revealed by cultivation crowd taller than a man into an excavated crevice in the flank of the hill, with gravel up to their lower leaves; tangles of deep blue dragonhead lean against a stretch of cliff face, and bolsters of aromatic blossoms make a place for themselves among the first of the mountain carnations, the toadflax, and the succulents. Here, in the spring, in the midst of an expanse of hundreds of colors of stone primroses, the enormous Eremurus sprang up in the shelter of the wall, rising like a shot from the earth still sodden with the waters of melting snow, and thrusting its single flowered shaft at the sky. Thanks to the shade, blue Soldanellas likewise sprouted in the last puddles of snow water, while further down the slope, where the ground was damp but sunny, spring asters from Cilicia and California (*Limnanthes*) threw their initial gold into the year. Then, as it rose, the naked cliff began to flower. This was no longer the common rock garden known to previous decades: to be sure, its cracks and fissures, gravel deposits and dips and hollows all had their own populations, but here on the healthiest of all terrains, educated eyes and mature experience had gathered together all those plants, from no matter where in the world, that refuse to be overfed and overwatered on dense alluvial—and the "garden earth" of "garden beds" is nothing else. No one had ever seen the Hunnemannia, the world's noblest poppy, bloom healthily and flourish among miscellaneous similar species on grounds maintained meticulously damp. Up there, in deep, open soil shot through with chalk, on a sheet of morainic debris, this magnificent creature that insists on germination in the very same place in which it grows readily develops the enormous shock of dentellated gray-green foliage which then supports its solid, exquisite, lemon-yellow flowers, shaped like tulips; this is the place where its stem swelled out into a pestle shape, it's here that it was covered and protected by the simplest of all precautions, a pennyworth sheet of glass on four supports of simple galvanized zinc wire, as a shield against winter moisture, topped by a bundle of loose straw for defense against hard frost. Where does the wallflower, where does the snapdragon flourish and grow most beautifully? This is flora of the gravel and eroded cliffs of the Mediterranean countries, which as well includes the whole Cheiranthus family, insofar as it doesn't consist of plants that grow on the even more meager sands of seaside beaches; Alyssum too, and Jonopsidium, and all the other bright, sweet-smelling Cruciferae; and again the magnificent, orange-colored Siberian wallflower (*Cheiranthus allionii*). But what about the stony places of the subtropics; don't they have flowers too? Do their snapdragons, as shrubs or suffrutexes, behave very differently from those of Europe? The new gardens allow vermilion Cupheas with black and white beaks, the *Verbena venosa* with its heather-blue buds and rampant underground roots, the gracious, grassy Eschscholzias (*Eschscholzia caespitosa*), and the spherical clusters in gentian blue of the sticky *Browallia viscosa* all to work their magic together. In a protected hollow all its own in a space between faces of rock, the invasive rhizomes of southern Mexico's *Lobelia cavanillesii*—whose only contribution to any bed has never been other than to ruin it—can develop to the full: the plant can spread its fresh, green luxuriance as soft and tender as it will over blocks of stone, and its countless rust-red blossoms with vibrant yellow throats, three times larger than ever seen in any normal garden, will reward the wisdom of the gardener who decided to plant them there. No tuber, aside from those of Composites (dahlias, and Helianthus), desires to be packed into compact soil. Even the potato is less than content to be planted deep or in earth that's firmly stamped: every farmer is well aware of what gardeners still have to learn. The tuberous California larkspurs—the scarlet *Delphinium cardinale*, the tile-red *Delphinium nudicaule*—here build thick stands in aerated soils baked dry by hot rock; and here alone does the fabulous Abyssinian larkspur—sulphur yellow, with orange spots—along with its blue Kenyan cousin, achieve the fullness of the form of its exquisite candelabrum.

And now we've rounded the crest of the bluff and reached its other side—facing again to the southwest—which has been allowed to drop off more sharply, as though its feet were planted on the sands at the edge of the sea, and this is the place of purely cliff-side flora: no plant more imposing than perhaps a taller variety of saxifrage disturbs the purity of the illusion of a world of vegetation that place, position, and exposure to light press down close against the surface of the earth, and which then springs away from it in a brief moment of violent flower. Yet the mountains of South America, southern Africa and the Canary Islands have wed their jewels with those of Europe's and Asia's peaks; the dwarf gazanias and dwarf Odontospermums, the jewel-like slipper flowers of southern Chile and Patagonia stand in the company of rock-jasmine and gentians, for as long as their color scales don't disturb one another, or their physiognomies threaten to cancel each other out, which then requires that some inconspicuous separation—a low stone ledge, a shallow ditch—be slipped between them, to hold them apart. And there, finally, at the bottom of the slope, is the shimmer of white sand. Beyond it a stand of foreign and native pines, and bald cypress still further off, which allows one an intuition of the shift from sand to bog. And no, we will listen to no complaints! When you wanted to eat asparagus, you arranged for sufficient sand to be carried to fill up the long deep troughs; you wanted sea kale, and created a section of beach in your vegetable garden: so those here who aim not to flatter the palette but to please the eye and the soul must be allowed to play with the earth's possibilities as freely as you have done. Here a beach is in flower; over there a desert bloomed; reeds and canes form a natural shield that cuts them off from the realms of humus, clay and limestone; and mighty growths of sea holly, with leaves like screw-pine or agave, stand guard between different expanses. Yet the palest color of soil does not everywhere hold sway. Where the addition of decomposed organic materials has darkened it, the goddess swirls her apron with the jewels of Namaqualand: a field of Nemesia glows with lapis and gold and blood and snow; like snapdragons, these solitary blossoms of the great English varieties, which the continent barely knows. The golden California poppies roll out their luxuriant carpet, shot through with mauve, pink, and fire brown, to its edges; still other California jewels, *Aster gracilis*, with the light of the face of a child, *Salvia carduacea*, the phantom sage, sand phlox and lily bushes build flickering groups and lead the way to white and yellow prickly poppies, to the yellow horned poppy, to the horned poppy in dark ochre, the sand thistle which ripens blue, the ragwort that ripens white, the watery white Euphorbia—the wolfsmilk bush—from Mexico. But California's serrated desert lily here stands next to the sea-side lilies of Italy and Dalmatia, which are our local relatives of the splendid Pancratium of the tropics; and, see, these too, even if not at their greatest vigor, stand there as a group in the shelter of rigid, thorny Solanum bushes, the fine thread-like petals of their perianth surrounding a snow-white calyx. And here, finally, an array of desert bulbs. Who knows their names? To whom would their names be of any help? But the small Sisyrinchion canes, with their iris-like blossoms in blue, yellow and brown, this people of beaches from Bermuda to California has long since ceased to be nameless. Not only the rosy Abronia spreads its creeping carpet between these canes and the following stand of pines; the uniquely lovely species of Mimulus which thrives in sand (*Mimulus fremontii*) shows deep rose-red chalices over thick, ground-hugging foliage. Then there are rhododendrons beneath the conifers. These exotic, ligneous, leather-leafed bushes have spread out everywhere, already catching the wind of the nearby bog, but meanwhile standing in sandy peat-ish soil in the neighborhood of such wonderful species of flowers as the stiff, checkered Tricyrtis lilies, the rust-brown Wachendorfias, the Trillium pseudo-lilies which could almost be called too pale, the nearly black Kamchatka lilies.

A new landscape of now melancholy dreams opens out before us, but melancholy too is made of countless flowers. England's new breeds of lobelias here advance a foot halfway into the swamp: enormous crossings of *Lobelia fulgens* and *Lobelia cardinalis*, with shafts five feet tall, richly decked with the red of the hunting jacket and the purple of the bishop's mantle on bizarre, broadly splayed out flowers with white, projecting stamens. Beside them, only slightly shorter, the magnificent, pure blue *Lobelia sessilifolia*; the bronze-brown *Lobelia tupa*; the glowingly blue *Lobelia glandulosa*, a foot in height and perhaps the most beautiful of all. Behind them, filling the background, a scarlet wall of countless true-to-type cardinal lobelias, as though marking the moral of a blood-drenched fairy tale. In other directions—there among the flattened orange crests of the tall, peat-loving butterfly weed (*Asclepias tuberosa*)—one sees the advance of the semi-aquatic plants: Canna; Hedychium with its tattered corollas in colors of sometimes humble, sometimes triumphant magnificence; Tradescantias and Commelinas, rising lilac and cobalt-blue from felt-like greenery at the edge of the bog. Drier, but nonetheless still moor-like places magically bloom with what might seem to be transfigured pansies: these are the Torenias of the Nam Ky region of Vietnam, pale blue with velvet lilac eyes, or golden yellow with eyes of a velvet brown, the ones thick bushes of medium height, the others a creeper that carpets the ground.

Here is a path. Beside it the drainage of the overflowing water from the moor. And here once again are the shade trees from which we started out. What we have seen isn't everything, nor even the most. Corners and smaller lanes, short cuts and minor rises here and there have been ignored. The great beds of cutting flowers, hidden behind the sidelines, where dahlias stand in simple alleys, pyramids of sweet peas in long rows, summer asters in small garden beds, and so much else besides, have been given no consideration. The difference between the fabulous blossoms created for shows—dahlias, chrysanthemums, carnations, roses, and so forth—which are flowers of which the production essentially demands the sacrifice of the plants on which they grow, and the flowers which live in flower gardens—which are living things and blooming creations—this difference has been sharply and consciously observed. The garden in which today's dahlias—or today's carnations—might be garden plants is no longer a garden that our longings and imaginations would care to inhabit. The wonderfully developed vases that stand within our houses—and indeed our houses themselves—are the vessels and spaces these plants must have in order to be able to express the forces with which we have charged them. Open air, scattered light, chaotic backgrounds destroy their lineaments. They belong among polished woods and fine fabrics, crystal and silver, the calm and focused lights of closed rooms; yes, among the hands and slowly opening gazes of women to whom the old cress-colored dahlia on the slopes of the Chimborazo (*Dahlia variabilis*), the old "Chou-san daisy," the lost silk-red sweet William of Persia's cliffs would be as distant as the plankton of Lake Thun. The human demi-god who to the left of a beechwood hedge erects the new English garden—the world's new garden—and then to its right steps into a laboratory for the clear and simple purpose, like a farmer who harvests ears of maize and slashes back the canes, of driving one of nature's creatures to produce these short-lived prizes, as personal creative caprice, is engaging both the poles of his only half-mortal mind. He atones for extreme dominion by way of extreme devotion; here he imperiously expresses himself, in order there to efface himself; he alienates himself, to the point of apathy, from the same nature which new capacities for empathy enable him to restore; he flees it, and pursues it; he's there the practitioner of an elegance which rapidly disappoints, and which therefore grows both tiring and once again maladroit—an elegance without composure, and which only the vase can recompose; here he's the soul of a longing in sight of its goal. We are two voices; the truth does not lie midway between them. The middle, said Goethe, holds not the truth, but the problem. Here it was a problem of style, of irreconcilability. The human garden was once again split down the middle, just as in ancient China and Persia. The patient artist whose art is the making of flowers which never existed before stands once again at the gates and every morning passes bouquets of cut flowers through the lattice of this heavy-hearted paradise.

We are two voices—truly and certainly only two? A great deal seethes and works and grows within us but will never find release without having searched for new forms of expression.

We have turned into beggars. We can only count on ourselves. Our fathers had gardeners and helpers, one purchased what one wanted, what one couldn't find in commerce was shipped in from afar, the reins of the world were curtly handled. Even poorer people traveled, since the rich had others travel for them; the poorer too received rewards; there were princes who emulated emperors, and from below one copied the upper classes that strove to behave like princes. This beautiful pyramid has collapsed; on every side we find our tortured way through its rubble. There is nothing more to scale that's worth the climb. But still we can count on the "dual meanings of the elementary words," where "depth" means much the same as "height." Plumbing our depths is now the only thinkable form of self-elevation. If we are a mirror, the stars lie within us, even without any need to turn interrogative eyes toward the pitiless heavens.

The new garden, a poor man's garden, grows from seed. As with Clusius and his peers, the plants which don't germinate easily, and which give a first flower after years, are likewise grown from seed. The same holds true for the cliff-dwelling plants and bushes of which the seeds don't sprout from the ground for as much as twenty months, or even two years. Sophisticated plants that propagate only from cuttings remain desires—like overly costly books—until life celebrates a feast and makes a gift of them. And trades are made, as in the time of the Baroque garden. The gardener—the gardener in the service of the garden's master—surely here and there continues to exist, like the duckbill platypus, but otherwise, universally, the garden's master is his own gardener, with as much occasional outside help as he can afford. He himself has organized, created, lived through everything. He himself has dreamed it all up, pulled it together, split it into parts, laid it out and planted it. The excavations, which, like the construction of his house, would have lain beyond his powers, were events he planned and directed, for spaces of his design. The results of his work for years weren't seen in flowers, or nearly so, and amounted only to soils, and meanwhile he had had to remain content with light summer flora. That's nothing special. Pope wasn't rich, and Addison not until late in life and only briefly; and Pückler, who was, was both bankrupted and made world-famous by Muskau. Very little can be done with nothing but money; not much more than with nothing but imagination. The garden's hope for a new Eden lies in the return of the spade and the seed bag into Adam's hand. The fact that the power of the new flowers, in and of themselves, was of such a nature, while effecting their conquest of the European garden, as to force a return to the seed box attests to one of the period's most defining laws. But only the world's increasing poverty had transformed this law into a freedom, thus humanizing the process and making it aware of itself. Activity alone is a sorry thing. Only what is done with a thousand joys unearths the treasure and wins the ring.

But the depth of exploration that can discover the world within the flower is also a new freedom. It too descended upon us as a law of hard times. The cultivation, contemplation, penetration and comprehension of exotic flowers became one of the very few forms in which traveling through distant lands and attempting to understand them is still allowed to us. These flowers, for us, are the fragments of a lost book; and from out of these fragments we're to reconstruct it. The Romneya—the Matilija poppy—must conjure up the Matilija's waters in our dreams; the Hunnemannia, the Santa Barbara poppy, must show us Santa Barbara; the Dimorphotheca, the salmon-colored Namaqua Daisy, must take us to southwest Africa; *Hesperis nivea*, the snow violet, must show us the Parnassus on which we will never stand. The faces of flowers, their bearing, their movements, their coloration, have taken on passionate meanings for us, and the pain in this passion grows quiet only through its transformation into a higher level of insight. We create nothing dry and impossible; and we know it would be pedantic to want to create a scene here exclusively of the flowering expanses of California, there of the flora of China. But, just as at the time of the Baroque garden, we have invited "the great wide world" to take a seat at our soul's table; and we want to know, and knowing then to feel, and feeling to the full to imagine, that here at the midpoint of the world's flora, into which we have made our hectare of European alluvial soil, two different regions of the globe, as seen in the physiognomies their plants assume, look each other in the eye: regions of the globe—unlike Surrey and Egypt—between which no swallow flies. Here in this flower we want to discover a closed, Peruvian, Indian face, to have plucked that face from within it, and grasped it with our senses; in this other flower we hope to find the Persian who while riding through fields of iris and crown imperial sings the verses of Omar Khayyam. This tulip must be made to disclose a scene we'll never see: things on which we hope to open a dreamer's gaze with the aid of the disk of a small brown seed, by covering it lightly with earth, keeping it moist for a year, caring for the sprout for a good five years until it blooms. From out of this deep, inward longing—an insatiable longing which nonetheless finds consolation—from out of this nostalgia, its reflections and anticipations, this garden too achieves the power to become an order, even while appearing to suspend all order and revert to simple wilderness. As a secretly metaphorical garden, it stands still closer to those of eastern Asia than the English park already had managed to come. It is, and it signifies. It points to what's denied to us. As a European garden, it's the creature of active rather than contemplative men, and a symbol charged with passion, an attempt to grasp the impossible, an act of magic that arises from the depths of mankind's sense of "in spite of everything." This garden—itself disinherited—fulfills the dreams of two great centuries on the ruins of a third, as a legacy for a fourth, which is still unborn.

CHAPTER VII

Sowing, Planting, Spading, Nourishing

THE garden's transformation into a landscape of flowers from throughout the world—a landscape that finds its hidden order in balancing the demands of irrupting flora against human needs and contingencies, while also beneath the sway of human imagination and its dream of an intangible whole—confronts the gardener with practical tasks that have to be performed conscientiously, and with a fine and discriminating hand. It places all necessary tools beneath the gardener's own authority, forces him to kneel to the ground so as knowingly to penetrate beneath its surface into places where plants will unknowingly grow, and gives him sensibilities for sky, sun, wind and rain, for season and time of day, which first of all are new, and which nearly must turn into instincts if they are not to demand from nature what she cannot or will not do, or what if forced would perish in the bud.

Gardens don't begin with flowers. Before flowers can be made to grow, one must first make earth, in quite the most literal sense. Because, again in the most literal sense, it is nowhere to be found. Europe's soils, everywhere and without exception, are more or less heavy, more or less clayey, more or less sandy deposits of products of mineral erosion, created by flooding or weathering, compacted by precipitation, baked by drought. The spade breaks open the compact mass, turns it and breaks it apart, reaches down into the subsoil and aerates it as deeply as it can, allowing atmosphere to penetrate into places where it wasn't before. Loamy and clayey soils are broken down by additions of chalk, which also releases potassium, an indispensable nutrient for all plant life. Vegetable compost provides for phosphates; animal manure for nitrogen, which for animals is death, for plants life. This basic combination, constantly turned, mixed and composted, as well as exposed to water, which further frees its nutrients and distributes them uniformly, is the raw beginning of all intentional settlements of plants on soils which never would have known their kinds without the aid of human beings, and could never have supported them. Peas and leafy cabbage can be grown in it, as well as all sorts of undemanding flowers. It permits itself to be transformed into a tolerably bright and pleasant colony of natural forms for as long as additional nitrates know no end, the sprinkler takes no holiday, and the hoe continues to aerate and again to aerate.

But plants whose natural occurrence would never take place on similar mixtures of soil, plants desiring neither constant food nor constant drink in order to develop their colors and forms, are by far the majority of those that bloom most beautifully. Such plants want to stand in healthy locales, without moisture lying about them which they cannot absorb. They want to grow slowly and not to be driven through their stages of development by a nitrate whip. They ask for certain foods, not for just anything at all. And not too much at any one time. Their diet, as well, should be none too sour in its trimmings, and therefore free of the insufferably spicy humus acids which are always, repeatedly formed by soils that are kept too rich. They want to live in a medium that's constant, modest, and self-sufficient, and not all of them want the same medium, since not all of them are themselves the same. More than anything else, they want no theory, and garden soil is pure theory. They want the exception: their own exception. It's not, of course, that the human being can think the thought that every demand must be welcomed to a table not only specially laid for it, but also provisioned with precisely this and not with that, as though from a hospital kitchen; yet something at least of what the plant might call its natural right, since it's there where it naturally grows, must also be contained in the soil which human beings prepare for it. Where roses bloom, there has to be clay in the soil; and chalk if they're to bloom even close to decently. Rhododendrons want soil that's free from chalk, and decidedly acidic. Where snapdragons aren't too quickly to wilt, the deeper layers of the subsoil must hold sufficient sand and chalk to drain away undue moisture. Leafy plants can be expected to thrive—lettuce or *Perilla nankinensis*—only where the soil is rich with humus, the more the better. Where one wants to see heather, one has to have heath soil; where one wants strawflowers to grow, one has to have sand; but planting beans in sand, or providing lupines with liquid manure—lupines make their own nitrogen—will bring no harvest.

So the greater the number and variety of the plants it hopes to hold, the more different soils the garden has to provide. Its soils divide it into provinces; and not only its soils. Where trees stand, it offers shade, which many of its loveliest flowers search out. Where sun-drunk flowers desire to stand, trees must be banished. Shady, sandy areas are a theoretical possibility, but in practice would be eccentricities, and flowerless. Theoretically, too, trees could be planted in the garden's most torrid spots, and something would grow in their hot, half shadow. But it wouldn't be much. Shadow, humus and moisture form a primordial unit. Sun, aridity and permeable stony sand, or deeply deposited sandy loam of only apparent hardness, are another. As many beautiful flowers grow in dry as in moist places. They have their own reserves and systems for protecting themselves from drought, and these systems shape their whole construction; so they wilt and perish from forced administrations of unnatural quantities of water no less surely than from frost or poison. Flowers are much more modest and selective in their choices of nourishment than their coarse human providers assume them to be. All of their upper organs take nourishment from the atmosphere. One must not make the mistake of thinking that the roots beneath their upper structures have to be furnished with everything they need, and surely not of forcing it on them all at once. And here, precisely, we find the reason why they ought to be brought from the very start into a world that resembles a buffet rather than a banquet table. They should take what they want when they want it. They are not to be served or coerced. Yes, surely there are gluttons and gourmands, crude gobblers and famine victims who have been so thoroughly starved that they won't come back to themselves until having spent years at the human table. But the noble flower at this table is generally an aristocratic guest: "Feed the grape and bean / To the vintner and monger: / I will lie down lean / With my thirst and my hunger."

The host must know his provisions and judge them quite precisely, then lend attention to their preparation and put them away safely and healthfully. He begins with the lightest and most ethereal food, which is plant earth: the natural decay of vegetable life into humus. Next come those in which vegetable decay and mineral erosion—weathered, powdered, turned into mud and washed along by storms—have bonded into a new unit, and one which at first is not unproblematic, since partly it matured under water, and partly under stagnant water, and therefore in anaerobic conditions which turn it sour. Then come the sorts of mineral soil in which living plants have already been at work, riddling it with roots and then decomposing in it. Then comes normal earth, the *alpha* and *omega* of all hardy and tendentially woody vegetation that must nourish great superstructures, and which has to have a medium that doesn't dry out too easily: the loams, whether light or heavy, and the sandy clays that crown them, the soils of gentle flood plains. Their considerable density tends, however, to leave them starved for air and sluggish, and insufficient drainage promotes the production of humus acids. So chalks must loosen their texture and liberate the potassium trapped inside it; sand too must be added, to form an amalgam which its properties as a filtering material will open to the entrance of the atmosphere.

Sand alone, moreover, with slight additions of vegetable decay and animal droppings is quite enough for the nourishment of a number of species of plants that depend primarily on silicates, chalks, atmospheric moisture and the quantities of nitrogen which rain absorbs from the air. And finally there is stone: loose naked stone debris that's highly porous to air, and which again through disintegration becomes a source of nourishment.

So there are heath soils, leaf soils, alluvial soils and earth that comes from moors, earth from grasses and clays, sandy clay and sand, chalk and stone. These are the kinds of terrain offered by nature herself. The human being creates two others. He heaps together his kitchen waste, mixing it well and then piling it up again in layers, douses it with fluids that augment decomposition, then forks it over again and again to aerate even its deepest levels, and finally compresses it all into a mound, which in two years time is a rich, crumbly, darkly colored mass, riddled through and through by earthworms that repeatedly ingest and expel it, enriched with the calcium of their own metabolism: this is compost soil, pure humus, rich in phosphoric acids. Or, again, he heaps up all the dung of his household animals, the more the better: the tough, resinous, slowly decomposing waste of cattle; the steamy, fermenting, quickly active manure of horses and donkeys; the watery excrement of swine and ducks; the hot, corrosive droppings of sheep and rabbits; the seethingly caustic waste of the hen house; the concentrated droppings—the larder of everything most essential—of the dove cote. Collected, mixed and brewed in its own interior heat, covered for protection from dilution by rain, all this too shrinks into a dark, dry, odorless, finely kerneled earth. This is dung-heap earth—when it comes from old manure piles—an earthy horse manure. These are the gardener's stocks of earth, and for the best fulfillment of his tasks, none of it is dispensable.

Heath earth derives from expanses of heather and consists of the fine detritus of its decomposed flowers and leaves. Thick deposits lie on moors, in strata, shot through with the roots of other plants. It has a fresh, brown color and is best removed in large hunks, which maintain their moisture for a longer time. They can remain uncovered, closely packed in the open air, at most beneath the eaves of a shed. They shouldn't be broken apart until use, and in any case not too finely. The coarser the better; and larger clumps, buried deeper in the ground, are natural water absorbers, for draining upper levels of topsoil. The fine, dry texture of this light, lean earth allows the root systems of delicate plants to spread and to subdivide into the subtlest of capillary fibers. With additions of sand, root fibers find an even better hold, and its silicates offer a supplement of slight but effective nutrients. More substantial nourishment must be added separately—compost, manure, dung water—and with that enough will have been done for noble plants. Somewhat coarser plants will need supplementary minerals, and we'll soon see which.

Leaf soil, for the gardener, comes only from the tender, soft-skinned leaves of the green deciduous trees. All remains from conifers, which make for resinous, acid soils, as well as oak leaves, which are saturated with tannin, and poplar and plane-tree leaves, which at least hold traces of tannin, and those of all evergreen trees, inclusive of the alder, are excluded; horse chestnut leaves are again unsuitable. (Earth produced from acacia leaves is relatively close to heath earth). Fallen leaves from lindens, beeches, hornbeans, maples, elms and woodland bushes are gathered into heaps in the fall, beaten together, and covered. Depressions should be made in their surface, for the reception of liquid manure, which promotes more rapid decomposition. Every two months, the pile is pitchforked and overturned and then beaten together again. When half rotted, it is divided in two. One half will be subject to complete decomposition, to the point of turning into earth. The other will find its use in midsummer, when it's thickly spread as a moisture reserve on the ground around the garden's flowering plants, which one has to be sufficiently experienced to water none too frequently, but then all the more thoroughly. For seed beds and nurseries, leaf soil must always be fully decomposed. Otherwise, it continues to rot around the germinating seeds, decay becomes contagious, illnesses arise, money is wasted, hopes destroyed. As well, leaf soil for seed beds must never be too finely sifted. Somewhat coarser, it is looser and healthier. It is essentially richer in nutrients than heath earth, and is capable on its own, with nothing added to it, of allowing magnificent plants to develop magnificent blossoms; and all woodland flowers thrive on it, with a slight admixture of clay. Surely it's acidic, and if used improperly, will sour even more, to the point of becoming poisonous. Small additions of chalk make it healthier (more alkaline), but greater quantities would be harmful, since they would atomize this earth to dust.

Yet acidic terrains are anything but flowerless. Peat bogs and moors all throughout the world show incomparable wonders of form and color, and supplemental acids are greedily absorbed by the roots of countless numbers of the most beautiful breeds. The soils of moors and peat bogs consist of sedimentary layers of fragments of vegetable materials which in standing waters fed by underground springs have been half preserved and half rotted in the absence of air and under pressure, with additions of acidified silicate earths. In the raw, they are deadly poisons, and must first be exposed at length to the air, dried out, broken up, crumbled apart. Where there are sumps and collectors for the run-off from manure piles, one does well for some of the garden's goals—but not for all—to sink large blocks of peat into them: there it becomes healthy and usable, though once fished out must be left exposed to the air, and allowed to fall apart into a dark black, fibrous, crumbly medium of the highest utility. Moor earth is excavated in flat layers, is frequently turned, and ready for use after two years. Both these kinds of earth, as additives to loam, thoroughly mixed together with it, are indispensable for numerous varieties of plants to which one doesn't attribute this inclination, not having seen them blossom in their natural habitats. Sandy moors in foreign lands hold broad, bright, jewel-like expanses of vegetation. Sandy peat soils bloom, amid blackish pools, in all tones of red and cobalt.

Slime deposits, the third of the acidic soils, are the most precious amalgam which nature itself has created of vegetable and mineral earth. Its perfection lacks nothing but alkalization: because this is a soil—one wants, most of all, to take advantage of its clay content—in which acidity must not remain predominant. It is retrieved from drained pools, stored flat and exposed to the air in shady places, and in strata on the order of a foot thick it's given intermediate layers of unslaked lime; it's then again turned over flat some two to three times a year. Already in the second year it's a crumbling heap of broken rubble, in which the layers of the old deposit remain still visible, and as a nutritive medium for plants it's of the very highest worth. Where clay components need to be mixed into heath earth, in order to enrich it, the choice best falls to this earth produced from slime, united with sand, as the lightest clay of all. And rather than sifted it should be broken into crumbs, thoroughly shaken with the sand, and then mixed into the heath or peat earth. For the towering irises of southern Africa, this mixture is the proven source of pure and mighty blossoms.

On the scale of lighter soils, the earth of slime deposits is followed by meadow soil, the daily bread of all artificial cultivations of precious plants. Flat sods are cut from a not too shady meadow of medium vigor, down to the virgin earth below, as seen by the difference in color, and then carried away and piled into squared-off heaps in a shady place exposed to the rain, with the grassy side down, and the whole not more than a meter tall. If the meadow lies on particularly compact subsoil, unslaked lime will be scattered between every two to three layers. Here too, in this solid construction, depressions will be made for dung water, placed at regular intervals. During the first year, liquid manure will be poured into these holes from time to time; in the second year, one can begin with turning over the clods; in the third year, every part of their vegetation, inclusive of roots, will have decomposed, and the whole pile has now become a fresh, healthy, breathing mass of earth, with a strong smell and a pleasant feel as one passes it through one's hands. This soil too must never be passed through a sieve, but only coarsely broken apart and crumbled, since precisely its porosity is its highest virtue, and sifting it would destroy it. And since if shoveled into the ground unmixed, just as it is, pressure and abundant watering would quickly reduce its volume, one is careful from the very start to combine this meadow earth with considerable quantities of sand and pure leaf soil before filling deeper beds with it: the result is an ideal soil for robust plants—rich, soft and spongy—and many more delicate species are also quick to take root in it. What it most resembles is the old, normal humus of the forests of more temperate zones. And if meadow earth has been crumbled up by being passed through a large-mesh sieve—set up on a slant—it goes without saying that the material which didn't pass through it isn't to be thrown away, but instead should be used as the coarsest drainage layer—it nearly always holds anorganic debris, stones, gravel, the toughest roots, pottery shards—at the undermost level of the area that's being prepared for planting.

The sedimentary loam of alluvial lands—the deeper and sandier the natural deposit, the better—will be left where it is, and is only to be broken up, down to quite some depth. That takes place by digging up furrows, the most basic of all the gardener's work: without it, even the best of raw terrain can never turn into land for cultivation, and at most delivers meager harvests. The width of the area to be worked on is divided into tracks, each the width of the spade and marked off by string; the surface soil of the first of these tracks is then broken up to the depth of the spade, removed, and piled into a barrow that runs just beyond and parallel to the last of the outlined corridors. A second spade's depth of the earth in the first of the corridors is then removed and handled again in the very same way: so the far side of the planting area comes now to be flanked by two mounds of earth, one beside the other. The bottom of the trench which has thus been made is next to be thoroughly aerated; its earth is turned over to considerable depth, breaking it apart, and spreading it coarsely but evenly with the point and the edge of the spade blade. It's then to be covered with stable manure, well decomposed, with an addition of sand if the subsoil is particularly compact, or of peat in the case of the most obstinate clay, and the whole is then vigorously worked and spaded. The gardener then turns attention to the second trench, removing its first spade's depth of earth and throwing it into the trench beside it, where it's thoroughly worked as before. It contains that level of topsoil which aeration and decomposition have made most rich in humus and bacteria, is never entirely lacking in nutrients, and is only to be mixed with sand, or at most, in the case of leaner soils, with a small amount of lime—larger amounts of lime would diminish the action of the stable manure beneath it—and the second spade's depth of earth from the second trench is thrown again on top of it. This second level of topsoil is of rawer and lower quality, and stable manure is once again mixed into it, but without being broken apart. It remains in clods, where winter will freeze it and the atmospheric alternation of frost and thaw will crumble it into earth. There is also an alternate system in which the upper spade's depth of soil, as the best of the layers of topsoil, is simply turned over, and only the second spade's depth passes from ditch to ditch. But the suggestion, as here advanced, to relinquish the naturally present advantages of the layer of soil that lies in the light of day has been shown by experience to be finally the more advantageous. Under attentive cultivation, the second, underlying layer of soil will shortly again have reached the quality of the first—especially where the spreading, as counseled below, of half-rotted leaves in midsummer has increased the soil's friability—and that best but now lower strata of earth will provide the deeper roots of the plants with the substance on which to feed an upwards-rising structure and flowering summit. One creates a bed of nutrients which down to a meter is almost uniformly rich, and where the underground stems, for example, of the giant nightshade, the Tithonia, or the arboreal mallows, but also of the flowering trees, can easily extend, without coming up short against hard and impenetrable subsoil, and therefore sending out predatory lateral roots all throughout the plot, just barely out of the light of day, to rob their neighbors of nourishment. It is only in such terrain that giant larkspur and lupine bushes achieve their maximum development. It also drains itself: precipitation sinks deep into the ground—to regions below that sensitive collar where roots and stem conjoin—and waits to be gradually absorbed. The effects of such a thorough spading last for a good six years, but then it must be repeated, if woody perennials have not meanwhile made the plot their own forever.

The natural soils are joined by the two man-made soils, both very rich. Pit compost is prepared in ditches, best if lined with stone and with raised edges—for which rough, singly laid stones suffice. Every sort of kitchen garbage and household waste—rags and feathers (no paper), mown grass and garden weeds—is massed together, covered with boards, doused on occasion with liquid dung, pitchforked at regular internals, divided into separate piles of fresh and rotted material, repeatedly turned, and then finally set to use. The older it is—this stout, oily, now almost coal-black mass—the greater its worth. If poultry manure is available, one mixes it with water, allows it to complete its fermentation, and then uses this scorching fluid, which no vegetable life can withstand, to destroy all still living seeds within it, which might sprout weeds. This soil, once sifted, is soft, black velvet. It's a concentrated food, and readily absorbed; and as an additive to poorer soils, it completes their preparation for gardening. Mixed with ash, it's a nutrient charged with phosphorus and potassium. All stumps and prunings of trees, shrubs cut back in fall, straw, paper, the woody parts of plants and tough roots that don't easily rot, are burned in the open air before winter begins, and the ashes, before being leached by rain, are layered into the compost pit, and then vigorously worked together with it. Whatever the garden throws off must return to the garden as earth; nothing is to be given to the wind, or abandoned to the wilderness.

Stable manure is prepared in the way which was briefly

described above, and treated as farmers treat it: covered for protection from rain, and with reliable drainage to a seepage pit for the collection of dung water. But unlike its use in agriculture—which employs it as fertilizer, to be mixed into the topsoil of the fields—it's transformed into a mass of earth, since the liquid run-off is constantly poured back over it, and the pile is covered with wooden planks, firmly stamped together, and turned with a pitchfork at regular intervals. Before being used for the finer cultivation of plants, it must turn into a delicate earth, light and perfectly uniform, odorless and dry to the touch. Half rotted stable manure, on the other hand, is of value as a top dressing, and as ground protection, but its use must be guided by a cautious hand. Large and immoderate doses of nitrogen are the ruin of flowering plants, no less than they are essential for the production of fodder for animals. Over-nourished plants with a corpulent, thickened habitus, bloated dark green foliage, excessively abundant leaves, and sickly, meager, sometimes degenerate flowers, with signs of malformations on their stems and corollas, are a desolate and dreadful sight. Those who while traveling in southern Europe have seen all its beds of summer flowers protected from evaporation by thick ground coverings of stable manure will remember the lifeless, spoiled, ill-colored and overblown blossoms which are there the pride of naïve custodians. The quantity of nitrogen which the normal run of noble plants require in order to develop their highest level of form, sheen, abundance of flower and intensity of color is minimal. Cultivated varieties which have ever more widely surpassed their natural form in size, abundance, and duration of blossoming will of course make higher and more constant demands; and great devourers of nitrogen, which are also found among exquisitely flowering plants—most of the Solanaceas, for example, and many Composites—as well, of course, as among those plants which are prized for their leaves, are in a nutritional class of their own. Those giant varieties of dahlias, asters, and Chinese asters which have come to us from America at first show peak performance and giant corollas but then fall ever more back into normal blossoms if not supplied with additional nitrogen. The mammoth classes of zinnias and those with dahlia-like blossoms present their show-class blooms for only a month or so, since the tortured plant that wants to mature and die then breaks away from human will—which demands that it outstrip nature, like the sick and fattened goose with a liver that becomes pâté—and produces a sequel of branches with ever smaller blossoms, so as to end up within them as ripe seed and not as a strutting peacock flower. Only rigorous bud removal, the cutting of shoots, continued applications of liquid manure, or of half-rotted top dressing can maintain for a while the production level of the bloom machine, and then the strength of the short-lived plant is exhausted, its structure collapses, buds cease to form, and enclosed in a cloak of leaves the dying creature withers on the cold rainy nights when storm has taken control and October finally triumphs.

The spade works these various earths so as to turn the world of the garden into an image of the earths of the world at large. All soils are both figuratively and literally scattered among each other within it, and mirrored within it. Within this corner of creativity they are to pace out the world which is closed to it, or what Goethe calls "the whole circle of creation." But they're also worked upon—from behind his boxes, pots and shaded trays, from within his little glasshouse, and while bending over his glass-topped growing beds—by the wielder of this spade: the new gardener who has been transformed entirely into a seedsman. The new garden springs from his seeds, and not from his purse; from his attentive, sensitive, nurturing love and lively scruple; everything that is to wave above his head or to break out in colors around his feet must first be created from seed.

Seed is a dormant life form, while looking like a death. An Adam arouses the process of life; an organism sets itself in motion, thanks to his giving it a start, and must thank him again for the progress and further advance of its course: such a mysterious event. Those whom its yearly repetition may blunt to the awesome tenderness of this mute perception, well let them buy their cut flowers in shops, or have a handyman plant some proper-looking something on their properties. Here you'll find the earth and the furrow or the bed; over there the paper envelope with its kernels, or coarse powder, or ethereal dust; there's water here, in the vaporizer, in the finely showering sprinkling can. Seed-bed earth is suckling's food. What the seed at first needs in order to be able to germinate, it brings along with itself, like the child, from its mother's womb. Its only further needs are moisture, warmth, and protection from light, some seeds to one extent, others to another. And for these first purposes, sawdust or sand would be as good as any soil: porosity and a certain constant level of humidity, that's all that's truly demanded of seed-bed soil. The kernel germinates; and only after its exhaustion of the stocks it brings along from what perhaps is the long dead womb of the mother plant, when the capillaries of the first of its underground shoots begin to branch and to search out nourishment, only then does the difference between some one and another seeding soil begin for the seedling to take on meaning. So, the experienced gardener plants as many breeds as possible in the earth that's finest and of greatest assistance to the seedling, since it never hardens, which is heath earth, even while having already decided to transplant them as soon as they have successfully germinated, lifting them as now living creatures from incubation soil and placing them instead in a medium that assures their nourishment. In itself, this is not necessary. In itself, the fine humus of sandy heath or leaf soil is the healthiest nursery food, and sufficient for nearly all newborn plants. But transplantation, this first intervention into the plant's biological processes, also serves to stimulate it. The life process, surprised, stands still for a moment or so, and then redoubles its speed as it leaps beyond the hindrance. The more potent earth in which it's placed makes this effort possible. The digestive faculties of the root fibers that cling to tiny clumps of clay are already capable of absorbing minuscule quantities of nutrients from them. The tiny stem which had remained so pliable in heath earth grows more robust; the upper structure of its leaves develops from the cotyledons; a life reaches out around itself in the light and air, feeling sure of itself and at home.

On the nursery trays, right up close to the glass, we even out the surface of the sandy heath earth with a smooth piece of wood, divide it into sections with narrow wooden slats, placed lengthwise and crosswise along it and pressed down into the soil, and then proceed to plant it, drawing narrow rows into which we deposit the seeds, and then again closing them once they are occupied. We thus accommodate countless varieties one next to another, in little space. Every division receives its name card, the finest drizzle descends on the seeds from the sprinkling can. Seeds, however, which are particularly fine aren't to be covered by soil, and instead will be protected by panes of glass, and then by large sheets of dark paper that cover the entirety of the tray. Pots, both larger and smaller—scrubbed with a brush in boiling, soapy water before being put to use, in order to destroy all possible traces of mold—will be somewhat more than half filled with pottery shards and then topped off with enough seed earth as leaves a rim of a centimeter and a half. The earth is then smoothed flat, seed is placed on it or in it, all the pots are placed in rows in the dark beneath the trays, and covered with dark paper. Cases made from old wooden crates and no more than ten centimeters deep, in order to keep the earth from souring, with rows of holes in their bottoms, cut out with a hammer and a sharp chisel, and filled to a generous third of their depth with gravel, then receive an underlayer of coarsely broken peat or heath earth, and then the finer earth especially prepared for the seeds. These boxes too are divided into sections with slats, and species with roughly similar germinating times will inhabit the same house. Those requiring particular warmth will be artificially heated, and always covered until germination; others will be put in cold or half-warm boxes. These last are warmed by a lower layer of a mixture of autumn leaves and horse manure; the mixture must be well compacted and must also have steamed itself off beneath the closing of a sheet of glass and cooled to a moderate temperature; it must warm, not heat, and stay within the range of moderate room temperature. Once that warmth has been reached, or about five degrees centigrade more, which will quickly dissipate, the box is filled to its upper edge with coarse sawdust, and as soon as the sawdust has warmed, the pots and cases or seed trays are imbedded in it nearly down to their rims. This sawdust will be kept moist with water poured directly from the spout of the sprinkling can. Up until sprouting has occurred, the clay pots and the seeds they hold are never themselves to be watered, or at most no more than very lightly sprinkled; and with the wooden cases even this will be quite seldom. Budding seed needs moisture rather than wetness, and budded seed more healthy moist air than wet ground. The prescription so often found in handbooks, that the seed should be covered to a depth of thrice its greatest thickness, is senseless. Its consequence for zinnias, dahlias, Arctotis and Cosmeas would be to smother beneath too thick a sheet of earth. Aside from a few exceptions indicated in the catalogue, no seed of any plant wants more earth on top of it than serves to bar light from the secret of its birth. Almost all seeds germinate in darkness and humid warmth, uncovered on the naked ground. So, the heavier the seeding earth—and sandy loam is best for the Compositae mentioned above and others—the more thinly it should cover the seed. And the earth that covers the seed must never be pressed. It is the seed that has to be pressed into the earth, and quite energetically with all bulbed plants (onions, for example, are pressed into the ground with a stick). And then, once the bulbs have been thoroughly watered, they are covered with earth which in turn remains untouched and never watered, or only very seldom in the case of plants that germinate slowly. Ground moisture should rise by capillary action from below. The watering from above of seed containers is to offer harmful help. One sprinkles seed before covering it with earth; and excessively dry pots in which germination should long since have taken place should be dipped in water until the upper surface of the soil begins to show signs of moisture—but no longer; never to the point that water rises through its surface. That would amount, in nearly all cases, to the drowning of the unborn plants.

For open-air seeding in shady garden spaces, boards around the chosen areas are set into the ground on their edges and secured on both their sides with pegs rammed into the earth, thus holding them in place as frames, or as sunken, floorless boxes, and these boxes are then liberally filled with loose earth of whatever kind desired. Just as in the instance of glass cases, pots are sunk into it, and only this earth is watered, with the spout of the sprinkling can, whereas the pots themselves are left untouched. Straw mats cover the whole installation until the seeds have sprouted, and these mats are later used as protection from storms or heavy rain. Drizzle, however, is favorable for germination. With this procedure, all the seed of even the most stubborn varieties opens healthily and uniformly, whereas with the usual method of watering the pots only a selection of the strongest escape demise. Here, as in general, the case will be freed of its covering as soon as germination occurs. But it's kept under glass, well exposed to light, until the first transplantation, and if possible, weather conditions permitting, to a bit of open air. Otherwise the seedlings will strain themselves to death in their search for light and air; and once stunted by their lack they collapse and are useless for further cultivation. It's only natural, however, for initial sprouts of more subtropical plants to feel quite comfortable without fresh air, so long as they have adequate light. Those of cooler latitudes are hungry for air from the very start, and want to have access to fresher temperatures; so, weather at all permitting, the cases in which they germinate should have an open ventilation slit beneath the edge of the window that covers them. That won't cause the bed to cool excessively. And even if it did, it would have to be risked, and counterbalanced through the measures described in every technical manual of hot bed cultivation, which here cannot be singly discussed.

All transplantation depends on scruple and a delicate hand. It must always be prepared for by thoroughly dampening the soil, in order that as much earth as possible remain attached to the seedling's tiny root fibers. The finest atomizers handle the job for minute sprouts; hardier sprouts can be sprinkled. Finer seedlings are lifted from the soil on the point of a needle, and the seedling is carried to a hole already prepared for it in the container where the peak of the tiny green dot is again to drop into the soil, and where a fingertip holds it in place to keep it from again being lifted out as the point of the needle is removed. The transplanted seedling is lightly sprayed with the atomizer, is placed in the dark and once again covered with paper until further growth has been ascertained, and then is brought into the light. More robust seedlings will be somewhat more abundantly sprinkled, but not so abundantly as to cause the plant, which has been disturbed and cannot yet resume an intake of water, to begin to rot in the excess. Such stronger seedlings and the earth that clings to their roots are retrieved from the seeding tray with a small transplanting fork, improvised with a v-shaped slit cut into a slat of hard wood, or in metal; holes again have already been made in the earth that's now to receive them; and the tiny fork drops its catch down into them, down to the plant's cotyledons, since here in its new terrain the seedling can be set a bit more deeply than in the soil in which it germinated. To the right and left and around the hole that receives the plant, a flat stick is inserted on a slant into the ground and tilted back up to a vertical position above the seedling's summit, thus pulling earth toward the hole from all sides; mild pressure on the soil around the seedling gives it a better hold; a light sprinkling, and then it's set aside. As the plants develop further, loosening the earth by passing a stick through the soil along the length of the rows is a life necessity: the plants are trapped, crowded into seeding containers, and growth is hesitant. With the vigorously developing seedlings of bushy plants, such as larkspur or Pentstemon, a highly thinned mixture of liquid manure can be poured into the loose earth between the rows every fourteen days. Before further transplantation of the seedlings onto open land, crates and pots must be thoroughly watered, then allowed to drain, and left to stand for a while where they are. Then a knife is passed through the soil in the crates, lengthwise and crosswise between the rows, until every seedling has its separate cube of earth, and these, each with its plant inside it, are then transplanted. The balls of earth in the pots must be delicately split apart. Seedlings which cling together are transplanted together without being separated, and one proceeds in the following days to eliminate all but the strongest. Weeds too which have grown with the plants are never to be removed beforehand from the pots' clumps of earth, since to do so would diminish their consistency; they too are transplanted along with the seedlings and are only later to be plucked out, while two of the fingers of the left hand gently hold the plant itself to the ground. Individual seedlings and their clumps of earth should be relieved of the so-called "felt" which may have formed on the walls of their pot, but not of the drainage material their roots may have embraced. Such material should accompany the young plant, and is a help to it.

No freshly transplanted plant which has been properly sprinkled, as is only natural, after transplantation has taken place, requires more water until such time as it stands up tall in its new position. If the plant looks lusterless, that is surely nothing strange. It's not thirsty; it's just that life is not easy for it, and nothing can be of help to it. But that will pass, and tomorrow or the next day it will lift its head. To give it what it isn't yet able again to drink would be to drown it. The cut or broken root fibers in its cube of earth must stretch new capillaries out into the surrounding soil; the plant must restore itself, adapt to new conditions, and while doing so must only be protected from sun and wind. An upside-down flower pot is all it needs. And no one should imagine to have to feed it for as long as digestion is something it just can't manage. Only vigorously developing plants can be treated with liquid manure, thinned to the point that it barely tints the water, and never allowed directly to touch the plant itself. Three or four holes will be made in the surrounding earth, not too far from its stem, and then poured full, and its roots will know how to find what lies in their vicinity. Spigots on which to screw watering hoses must or should be distributed all throughout the garden. If that's not possible, one will have to provide for a wheeled barrel, to be filled at the tap, and water will be dipped from of it with sprinkling cans.

In the lack of a system of drainage pipes, other schemes must be turned to. An underlying sheet of gravel, a handspan lower than the level to which roots descend, and itself a handspan thick throughout the whole of the planted area, must be covered with a thick layer of leaves, to prevent the soil above it from sifting into the gravel and destroying its porosity. For long, narrow beds, bundles of hard twigs, laid out flat, sunk deep in the soil and covered with a layer of gravel, give excellent service for three or four years. But loose soil, well spaded and worked to sufficient depth, in fact requires minimal drainage, and if sited on a slope, none at all. The more irregular the garden's terrain, the greater its natural drainage. The more sand its soil contains, the better it filters; the more broken stone it holds, the more it stays dry and airy.

But the season of hefty evaporation demands special measures of its own. During periods of heat and extreme drought, thorough daily watering sows senseless ruin among all more noble plants. Plants don't want to deal with dry air, strong sunlight, constant evaporation and cold wet soil all at the same time. It can't be repeated too often: no nobly constructed, harmoniously developed, beautifully flowering plant wants to find the soil around its roots full of water every day. A far cry from the wishes of horses for an always overflowing drinking trough. Its capillary roots mustn't daily be clogged by accumulating waters which by far it isn't yet ready again to absorb. The plant is an active creature, like the hunting animal, and, in order harmoniously to achieve its style and characteristic structure, it wants to secure its nourishment and the refreshing moisture of the soil by way of its creeping subterranean (and not only subterranean) organs, and through the burgeoning of this desire for growth and movement to flourish. Ground moisture should not be daily increased by the double of the quantity that evaporates, but instead should be protected, for as long as in any way possible, from excessive evaporation, and from time to time gently reintegrated. This is the purpose of what the English call "mulching." A handspan depth of half-rotted vegetation—leaves raked together in the fall—is spread on the whole of the freshly watered garden grounds, and then once or at most two times a week thoroughly drenched. On evenings after very hot days, the plants themselves will be lightly sprinkled. The moisture in the well-watered mulch seeps slowly and gently into breathing, friable soil, in which the result of protection and sunshine is a cool damp temperature. Decomposing fragments of leaves sink deeper and deeper into the topsoil, and their substance is absorbed and transported by the organs of the plant. Protected, yet wisely left to its own life processes, the creature thankfully develops toward its predetermined form; a natural condition has been recreated, a superior humus of the wild, rich land, in which the foot of the beautiful creature rests and breathes, undefiled. In a very few days, the color of the covering of leaves adapts to its surroundings and is no longer seen as different and artificial. And soon it's entirely hidden by luxuriant, ever more natural vegetation.

What mulching is for the vegetation of deep, loose, and naturally moist soils can't be the same for their opposites: for naturally dry, deep sandy soils, or the arid stony soils of chalky or clayey declivities. But the new garden holds primacy over all former gardens for having included precisely these terrains in its paradise, striking brightly colored sparks from the desert and the wasteland. It can make no pedantic copy of the desert, since desert flora is a briefly explosive, rapidly subsiding burst of magic: a fleeting, flowered rainbow. The garden likewise can only pursue a vision, never a reproduction, of the vegetation of the wasteland, which after a quickly finished display of amiability, turns everything to straw, economizes, tortures itself into ghostly distortions of its life forms. Garden sand is rich, shot through with humus and heath soil, with layers of earth bearing nitrogen and phosphoric acids; they hold for a while the moisture of evening waterings before the sand absorbs it; so the desert children of California and southern Africa, while never losing their characteristic form, are able, quite to the contrary, to bring it to a higher level, since they nourish themselves on food of which the endurance in ensured. In this case, the layer of mulch is shifted to below the ground, for a lower strata of moisture-retaining subsoil. The situation, moreover, is natural, since desert vegetation, for example in Australia, lives on water reserves which are far beneath the sand, but which the hollow, tubular roots of acacias know how to reach. Flowering wastelands, on the other hand—which again would be poorly served by excessive watering—discover the hoe to provide those benefits which mulching elsewhere supplies. Evening work with the hoe, loosening the soil, must never rest around Eremostachys and mullein, poppy shrubs and the pea tree. In well-aired soil, capillary action causes subsurface water to rise, while air and atmospheric moisture descend from above, and the solitary plant knows an unaccustomed comfort that ameliorates its life. Here, finally, manuring is in place. Water here, when given, should also offer nourishment, since in the form of liquid dung it is charged with gummy substances that bond moisture for a longer time with the topsoil. The human being stands here at his limits. This is the moment at which he cannot grasp nature without enhancing it. Just as at other moments his every attempt to grasp it fills with longing admiration for its sacred, prior knowledge of miracle. His garden stands between these two extremes, and is in this sense a symmetrical place, conceptually, like Eden, with its center in the inexhaustible, insatiable, indomitable human heart.

Postscript

THE reader with whom the author of this book has still the luck, after so many pages, to converse—like the host who, when other guests have gradually departed, remains among only his few most intimate friends—this most understanding of readers has of course been aware for quite some time of spending his hours with no gardener's garden book, and indeed with no botanist's book, nor even, finally—no matter how strong these pages' defense of the stature of such a figure—with the book of a simple *amateur.* He has been in the company of a humanist. And if now he has the impression that the garden can be seen, or must be seen—like everything truly important for the human being—as a voice of the human spirit's oneness and indivisibility—since this alone is the whole of *humanitas*—then the effort of this book has not been wasted. It will have been seen that here again All is in Everything, that history and the natural sciences, that politics and poetry, that the laws of society and of individual life, indeed that philosophy and the intimation of immortality all come once again together in this point of the orb which is ourselves, in order to make it a reflection of a beam of eternal light. It will have been seen that the routes from the highest and proudest castles which men have the privilege to inhabit, from every science and every art, from every assumption no matter how bitter or sublime of responsibility for the life of humankind, lead as lightly and freely to the garden as to Shakespeare or Plato, as to Alexander or St. John's Gospel, as to Beethoven or Kepler or any other of the wondrous doors into the labyrinth of the understanding of life as tragedy. The garden—like the stage and the museum, like the library and the star watcher's dome, like the orchestra, the temple and the throne room—is a sacred circle that describes our highest worth, and communicates with all of them, just as all of them communicate each with all the others.

So even if its author can see this book—as some of its readers will know—as a deviation from the purposes pursued by his life's activities, that's not to say that it comes into existence as a codicil, since in fact there are no such things. It has been written with the firm intention of discerning a connection, heretofore not established, between the human garden and the human spirit: a connection quite different from the one foreseen in most of the literary propaganda in favor of gardens and flowers, or so-called "garden literature." There seems to be a general tendency to want to make gardens and flowers "accessible." And there is surely no need to elucidate the large and conspicuous merits of all efforts to extend the practice of gardening more and still again more. Extending, however, is one thing, and flattening, clearly, is something else. If broadening gardening's base means finally, as well, to dismantle unremarked the summit of a grandiose pyramid, a process of leveling has begun, which always, as we know, starts out with the look of good business, but always ends up as bad. This tendency to make gardening "accessible," and to present it as cheaply affordable, has led, as is generally recognized, to quite the opposite result: to the ever broader feeling and more widely heard complaint that "gardening is costly." And from there to even more mistaken attempts, guided by even more erroneous calculations, to make it still again "less costly." Which again is still further to flatten and cheapen it. The error in the calculation doesn't lie in the estimation of gardening's various costs—rent for terrain, the price of labor, expenditures for gardening equipment, and for plants acquired as merchandise. It lies in false assessments of the nature of the human being: in a false relationship to *humanitas.*

Such erroneous practice and faulty theory presumes to find its client and customer—and in its literary guise, its reader—in a type of individual which it must first of all construct, so as then to be able to convince the general public, to whom it proposes to sell its wares, that he represents the normal run of those who ought to have a garden; which is also to convince this general public to plant what this practice has in stock, and what this theory recommends. This person can be described as follows: his home is always and only in the least hospitable territory his country has to offer, with the most unfavorable soil and severest climate, pure clay, stony ground, pure sand. The world's flora divides in two before him: a smaller part made up of plants which survive in such conditions, and endure such winters; and the endless profusion of everything else, scornfully declared unsuited to such soils and latitudes. Plants that "don't survive our winters" are summarily condemned and set outside the door. Because our curious type of individual, this Eskimo in a territory which convention alone calls temperate, has so little interest in his plants, and is so indifferent to them, as to see no gradations; and he would rather die than take the slightest precaution for the winter survival of a beautiful plant. If this barbarian breed of garden owners had ever been the rule, no stock or rosemary bush, no peach or myrtle tree, no tea rose would ever have crossed the Alps, and the relations which gardens articulate between peoples, times and latitudes, as created by the great historical notion of acclimatization, would never have been shaped. Our gardens still today would live on acorns. There's also more: in addition to being so impassive to the life and death of his plants, this type of individual is also so lazy and loveless as never to allow us to imagine him involved in even the least of those activities that make up the life and essence of gardening: husbandry, stewardship, careful attention, thoroughness, diligence and constancy. The slightest hint of such requests is already cause for consternation. His garden can expect no more from him than what the jailer must to throw to his prisoner, for pure and simple survival. Any demand the plant might make beyond that barest condition of being allowed to live already bans it from this man's garden. His garden has the duties of a paradise, but barely the rights of a brick wall. Once the bills have been paid—from the garden architect and the shrub nursery—the planted grounds can themselves be viewed as a living corpse. Their proprietor is a cold-minded egoist who at best paces back and forth across them, shows them to his friends, cuts bouquets from the midst of them. Woe on this garden if it ever complains; if it ever offers resistance; and woe above all if one of its tall slender joys, exhausted by the weight of its flowering beauty, should want some slight support, some modest prop: out with it! And in its place some nursery creature that stands up straight as a pole and asks for nothing. Ask, and you make yourself bothersome. Because this gardener has no time. No time at all? Not so much as a minute? Not that regular minute which even the poorest manage to find, the owner of the Schreber garden, the proprietor of the allotment, that minute in the evening after work, that minute of love and passion? No, no, no! He does not have it, or to tell the truth—we'll keep it among ourselves—he *must* not have it: he is complimented for not having it, encouraged not to have it by his best well-wishers, one pats him on the shoulder, this busy man, and waves him on to his car. He also lacks imagination, has no drive to experimentation, no flexibility. He thinks up nothing of his own; he looks for no expedient that could help him attain what at first appears impossible; he is a stick; he is a stone; he is passive. He accepts the suggestion that professional life is so impelling as to allow him the possession of no other garden than this one: the cheapest; which as well, at the very same time, is the most expensive. Since surely it must be the most expensive in light of the measureless effort required to set up a perfectly fool-proof installation which nonetheless, from a certain distance, resembles what people call a garden. One can only conclude that this type of individual would never have been so painstakingly constructed, so loquaciously promoted as the present-day replacement for the old, true, authentic forms of humanity, were it not for his being so desirable a client: the most solvent and least demanding, surrounded and served by salesmen as though he were a prince, but dealt with as a mass, like proletarians, for the purposes of balance sheets.

The tendency to cheapen gardening has nothing to do with making it inexpensive for the poor—for the pauper in pursuit of a dream nothing can be sufficiently costly and rare—but for those among the rich who would cheapen the world, and pay only a pittance for it. In short for Dives. This isn't intended in social terms, in terms of the enjoyment of luxuries and millions. The tendency is all too well aware that true wealth nourishes dreams which are nearly as fabulous as those of true poverty, and which pay no attention to other people's rhetoric. It coins itself for the Dives who lives in all of us—just as other unbeautiful qualities live in all of us—for the Dives of the Gospel who excuses himself from the summons by saying "and *therefore* I cannot come," and surely he was no great nabob but only a little philistine from the ranks of the "up-scale professionals," or a little snob of this "breathtaking age." Yet, in any case, this tendency to make the garden amenable to philistines, in order to be able to acquire and guide such clients, is only a part of that larger tendency, throughout the world, to render things more saleable by declaring them to be much easier that they're generally held to be. It's the sister of the literature that bears such titles as *Greek without Tears*, or *Philosophy Made Easy*, or *Around the World in Thirty Days.* Now, we know there's no such thing as an art for making things easier than in fact they are. But there's an art for making human beings more foolish and insipid than they are: one convinces a man he can buy things cheap and then boast of how valuable they are. Such an art quite surely exists, and it brings in all the greater profit since everyone finally is poorer for it, other than the salesman. The human garden is a vast democracy; and it needs no one to make it more popular than in fact it already is. It is not the only democracy that clumsy advocates can drag into the danger of finding itself dehumanized. And democracy without humanity is plebeian with the very first of its steps, and vulgar already with the second.

This book, therefore, could never have aimed to present the human being only and fundamentally in the form of the worst developed print from a plate which itself is good, thinking later to restore its lights with much retouching and at great expense. It sets itself the opposite task of presenting the human being at the highest possible stage of development. Pale copies of the original are things that life will supply on its own. Rather than find its point of departure in the poorest possibilities, this book sets out quite purposely from the highest. It candidly invites the reader and the gardener to more than they can deliver, since it knows that nothing more advances the human being—and therefore, with time, is of greater practicality—than precisely such an invitation. One springs as high as one possibly can only when aiming a little bit higher than the mark one sees as one's true capability. The leader who wants to know what his men are truly worth has only to throw the flag among the enemy. Those who today in gardening matters promote the flattest, simplest level of things—and who thus indulge in the snobbish abuse of seeing every reader and every gardener as nothing but an object for "clear and informative tips, one hundred percent reliable," and for all the accompanying dozens of expensive bushes, mass-produced by the shrub dealers—have no idea of truly human endeavor, or of its wealth of historical experience. The grape was planted in England and in central Germany by Roman legionaries and by monasteries, pressed and made into wine, to be cellared and even drunk. The insolence of demanding that acclimatization perform an impossible feat required whole centuries to push back the limits of its cultivation, mile after mile, to the point where they stand today. Up until the end of the last century, before inexpensive ocean steamers made it unprofitable, Europe's large-scale production of pineapples found its center, believe it or not, in Silesia. Stock is surely not "winterproof," and European wallflower at least has no such reputation, but

Scotch varieties of stock, along with Dresden and Königsberg wallflower, have proudly maintained world fame until today. Window glass has been once and for all invented, and can be broken, but no longer dispensed with. There are doubtless such things as flower pots, and their existence too won't be reversed. There are even such things as stalls and stables, and the farming communities of Tyrol and Bavaria—whose begonias, carnations and fuchsias attract the understandably envious eye of sophisticated travelers—have known how to put them to excellent use, for protecting their much loved blossoms from bitter winters. Love is far more telling as a criterion of suitability than any question of being "winterproof." The man who loves something is an adventurer and a stubborn suitor, inventor and wooer. The man who himself desires to create and bring forth something that will truly give him pleasure prefers to listen to every fable and to every curious scrap of news than to all the "one hundred percent reliable" information of the rascals who take him for dumb. — The author, a number of years ago, when the daily press had printed one of his notes on real and unreal plants, received letters from perfect strangers who proved to him that the mystic, flower-raising weavers of the seventeenth-century Midlands continue to live unchanged into the twentieth. The people who wrote them were village school masters, rural storekeepers, country postmen, and they burned with the desire to cultivate only the plants which were most exotic, and which never had been seen before. They wrote about the contraptions they had improvised for themselves, in order to be able to match the performance of greenhouses and prize-winning installations. They were poor, hardworking people. And apparently blessed with time. They saved what they needed to create their pleasures, and didn't complain, as the rich will do, about "the great expense of gardening." It would have been small and shabby to reprove them for mainly longing for things which partly perhaps they failed to understand. That, after all, is why children are always such a wonderful audience. That, after all, for a good three quarters, is the secret of the power of poetry. "Clarity," "information" and "guidelines" have their place, a place where they belong, in a purely mechanical and practical order of things. But the delights of the human heart connect with things which are neither entirely clear nor wholly reasonable. Otherwise, cobblers and smiths would never have become such potent mystics as Bunyan and Böhme, and the Bible's darkest books would not have remained throughout the centuries the common people's favorites. This book would hope to be equally accessible to the uneducated and the highly educated; and its greatest pride would lie in being seen by the half-educated as a book with seven seals, and finally—which amounts to the same—as scandalous.

So, this book proposes a radical reversal of that general fashion of the times which seeks the guidelines for a country's gardens and cultivated plants at the lowest level of its possibilities: in precisely those regions where its soils and climate are most extreme and inauspicious. The continent's gardens should find their orientation in its wine-growing regions and areas of abundant summer rain; the English garden in the island's south and southwest corners; and so on for every country. Neither reasonability nor profitability would allow lean cows to prescribe the fare for fat ones, and to force them to share their own modest diet. In political life, both in Europe and elsewhere, the nineteenth century witnessed a victory of the north over the south, but its aftermath is still regarded with enthusiasm by an always smaller minority. The tyranny of the northern over the southern garden—in breeding trends no less than in terms of propaganda—is a further reflection of this shift in political realities. We are told, for example, that bushes and roses bred in Holland fail in the dry, continental climates of central Europe; or that plants raised or bred in England won't adapt to the prevailing weather of other countries. Breeders in the center of the continent boast of only selling varieties with proven survival capacities under the most unfavorable soil and atmospheric conditions, and in circumstances of almost total neglect. What makes these postures so damaging and senseless isn't however to be found in the simple raising of iron-sturdy plants, which indeed is a merit: it's a merit that even such problematic lands—such as certain parts of northern central Europe—and even the most neglectful of the garden owners among their populations, should be provided with a last-ditch guard of varieties of plants that can promise to withstand all possible forms of adversity, inclusive of those produced by human beings. The damage does not lie in growing such things, but in demanding that nothing else be grown; and in pretending to set up laws that also hold for landscapes which don't have the character of steppes. The senselessness lies in undermining the gardener's art, and discouraging the spirit of experiment. The author has had the experience of planting in happier latitudes plants which had been bred in those beds of pain of the far north, with the result that in the second year their growth was rampant and ceased to obey any form; in the third year, malformations appeared; and finally they had to be eliminated. But when planting shrubs from moist climates and mild soils in dry climates with poor earth, he lost only those plants that remained without the benefit of the especially protected site and more attentive care which they of course required. The demonstrable nonsense that the Maréchal Niel and La France roses "tend to die out" likewise finds its only encouragement in a lack of attention to the needs of noble but more delicate forms. Finally, there is something degrading in always, repeatedly hearing the praises sung of the types of plants which have been bred to such degrees of indestructibility that the dimwit's check will also buy the assurance that the more they're mistreated the better they bloom. A garden that does not owe at least half of its creatures' strength and vigor to the gardener's constant love and attention, a garden which instead is so "ready made" that love and hate can make no difference to it, is simply a whitewashed grave. The acclimatization of plants brought in from somewhere else, and even if from only a couple of hundred miles away, can never be dispensed with for noble subjects, and never takes place on its own; and acclimatization is more than half of all the work of making a garden. There is no acclimatization except through seed, and since climate and soil conditions vary from one locale to the next, from one elevation to the next, there can be no narrowly standard type of seed with guaranteed acclimatizability for all climatic variations in any given zone. Vegetable gardening knows quite well, and grain production from a long way back, that there is no one wheat, no one beet, no one potato for everywhere. That's why highly selected Scottish potatoes have become the rule for England, because the goal is a harvest of tubers, and not bouquets of roses: because the South American habitats of wild *Solanum tuberosum* go from very wet to almost boggy, and experience has taught that high quality seed-potatoes are more impossibly won from soils with too little rain, even if in the south, than from others which are relatively too far north, but wet. Analogous laws are no less clear for flowers. The chance to adapt a wonderful wild or cultivated plant to the situation of one's own garden—through observation, care and repeated seeding—should be taken away from no one.

The author must go even further, and must quarrel a bit, for a change, with a few of his friends not only with whom he enjoys a common ground, but whom, precisely, he himself was the first to note for their distinction in the independent adaptation of the wisdom of foreign traditions of gardening to local conditions. Among the tendencies from which he wants to stand apart there is also one which, even though not in intention, is effectively nationalistic. It strikes him as utterly perilous for certain local possibilities—for example, "the German garden"—to place the plants they cultivate, and their literary propaganda, too exclusively beneath the sway of the notion of creating a compendium of "what's truly at home in our climate," and all too dogmatically to exclude from this fiction whatever apparently confuses it. This book has been written with a view to affirming, by way of historical exposition, that none of the premises set forth in this theory hold up to scrutiny or accord with fact. The only German garden which history knows as an original creation on the part of this one of the great gardening peoples—the German Baroque garden—developed along a semicircle, open above, that arched quite logically from Vienna through Silesia and into southern Germany, and then further up the basins of the Main and the Rhine, and into Holland; and from there it was able effortlessly to press its conquest forward into central and northern Germany since the people of those regions—at least the equals of southern Germans in passion, imagination, the spirit of adventure, and inventiveness—were entirely up to the task of forcing foreign flora to accept their straitened climates. The northern German was no fatalist, and no determinist. He wasn't "the product of his environment." He was no nationalist, and no rationalist. The oriental hyacinth, which he imported from Haarlem, was by no means "winterproof" in the regions where he lived. Yet still he had the finest beds of hyacinths. How did he manage? That was his business. No freezing, rotting, or degeneration of his prize possessions was finally able to prevent him from having what he wanted, and with no restrictions as to "what's truly at home in his climate." Man was the master and measure of things. He protected, covered, wintered, terraced, tirelessly seeded again and again, made heavy soils light, and light soils heavy until finally he saw and was able to pluck what first had hovered in his imagination. When settled by large-hearted peoples, the poor, raw lands which human beings have come to inhabit are in everything poor and raw except in the kind of man they breed. His passion grows in inverse proportion to his failures. The apple, the grape and Hellenism take on their most authentic flavor at the outermost edges of their range. This isn't where they find their origins. And what, here, might on its own have found its origins? Surely not the human beings, since the human beings were driven there, have migrated and immigrated. And surely no floral cover worth speaking of: the flowers which after the ice age came to join the few remaining residues of arctic flora were brought along in the Holocene by the rivers that flowed from the Pontic steppes. Human and plant migrations came together there, and wherever the human being appears, unadulterated nature halts; and wherever he stamps his foot, history subdues it entirely. So, what one calls the "German" landscape, just as for what one calls the "English" landscape, is an historical landscape, regardless of the absence of any ruined castle or any stump of a tower, since the will of something immortal has shaped it. And it's only in a spirit of play that the will of this something immortal will ever again submit to the once broken yoke of climate and terrain. Where for mile after mile there are summer crops of Mesopotamian wheat, Uruguayan potatoes, Mediterranean beets and South American beans as the defining characteristics of fields where wheat, for example, would freeze and die in the winter—where the fruit trees lining the streets are from Asia Minor, where in peasant gardens India's *Rosa sinensis* sleeps out the winter in a mantle of straw, and well-protected Chilean strawberries have no fear of it—the notion of "winterproof" vegetation, which agriculture has long since left behind and eliminated, must first be artificially reintroduced. The notion of nature on which it's based has nothing, in fact, to do with the reality of rural life and cannot deny its origins in the romanticism of the city dweller. In Schiller's terms, it is not naïve but sentimental to countermand the path of southern plants which migrate north and there sink their roots, and to declare that the landscape of "nordic" plants must return to the north and recognize itself "for what it is." This "nordic" landscape is either a violent or a nearsighted fiction. Already wherever an acacia stands, with the dull blue-green of foliage which for Europe is impossible; wherever horse chestnuts flower, with great pyramidal blossoms perched on wooden limbs, again displaying a habitus which Europe couldn't have produced; wherever the cherry tree is wrapped in pinkish foam and stands over fields that rape paints yellow in all directions (masses of colors and form which would here be inconceivable, if not thanks to imported plants)—compendiums like those which are mentioned above may on their own be interesting experiments, but as dogma become ridiculous. Things must keep on going as they have gone till now. Immigrations must continue, just as before. Further acclimatizations have to be attempted and accomplished, more and more. Wealth must dispense and distribute itself, since only wealth can do so. Poverty must consent to be colonized, and humanized, as it learns from its place in history; and then, with experience, to reshape, transform, transmute, broaden and refine itself, as is its mission. But the point at which the notion of the "only semi-frostproof," or not truly winterproof, becomes unavoidable and has to be discussed is not the point where the problem comes to an end: it's the point where it truly begins. One learned to cut fine cucumbers, and later melons, in open fields of the north from vines that formerly yielded only squash. Whoever feels a shiver on hearing himself encouraged to raise a few of the flowers discussed in this book must only dare so passionately to desire to see these flowers as the gourmet desires to taste and grow those melons. He must dare first of all to risk failure: his failures won't be limited to flowers from Chile and California. He will have to struggle just as hard and just as long around the cultivation of any number of thoroughly northern gentians that germinate quite readily from seed. Even on the shores of Lake Constance, it will cost a great deal of work, the most demanding and the most rewarding, to raise the Romneya or the new varieties of Nierembergia to perfect and enduring forms. But even in the luckier exposures of temperate lands, which are here quite consciously proposed as thresholds which selected plants can first be asked to cross, the threshold is no easy one: it's an upwards step that demands an exercise of will.

But these places also count as thresholds for other and deeper reasons. The history of the human garden has made it a place of gods that bind peoples together: the garden is their sanctuary. The garden is a oneness, and the selfsame oneness in all zones and latitudes, a symbol of the oneness of the human spirit. The fact that as such it finds itself between subtropical extremes on the one hand and subarctic on the other—that nothing which reasonably resembled it could be kept alive in Norway or in Mexico—serves only better to define this concept, not to invalidate it. The limits at which the garden shrinks to a few species of plants contrast with its high and maximum levels where nearly none are excluded: the great reservoirs, rich with experience, of the history of acclimatization: California, Crimea, the French Riviera, the Lake of Geneva, Florida, Italy. Along the descent from these higher levels to those which are greatly restricted, capacities of reception and diffusion by no means diminish schematically. Hills, mountains, oceanic influences, warm currents greatly vary them. Every warm and temperate region that also holds high mountains has a little arctic of its own within them. Hot countries, but with continental climates, will also have cold zones. Cooler countries where sheltered hollows and valleys have formed between mountains with a southern exposure and abundant precipitation have warm and sometimes very warm zones. The scholastic classification of climate zones—the tropics, then banana, orange, olive, grape, and apple-tree zones—offer no more than a highly schematic overview. Olives stop at the Apennines, but only to reappear beyond the continental climate of Lombardy in a paradisiacal landscape of subtropical flora at the edge of the southern side of the Alps. The orange dies out in Calabria, but in Ventimiglia once again stands heavy with fruit in free and open orchards. North and south alone mean nothing at all: the decisive characteristics are found in the lay of the land, the proximity of seas, amounts of precipitation, the sizes and courses of streams and rivers. "Climate" alone means nothing at all, since the human being is decisive. Italy at the time of the Scipios had a characteristically northern landscape. Forests of beech, as now in Rügen, rolled down to the Ligurian coasts. The colossal, century-long process of cultivation and importation which was to turn the peninsula into the center of acclimatization for the cultivated flora of the whole of the Mediterranean changed the climate, and made the country in part subtropical. So, the scholastic classifications, mentioned above, of zones of vegetation bear the names of cultivated plants which were constantly on the move as the limits of their areas of cultivation pressed always forward, and they never corresponded to rigidly definable latitudes. They represent mobile limits, of which the placement and overlapping at any given time have always depended entirely on the human hand.

It follows, therefore, that nearly all the great historical peoples of Europe and North America have been so distributed throughout their spaces as at least to graze the southerly and northerly extremes of subtropical and subarctic possibilities. The historical migrations of cultivated plants were to exploit this extraordinary situation—which hinges in Europe on the continent's incomparably subtle articulation—in the most remarkable ways. Limits as defined by various zones of cultivation are also superimposed—in ways that differ from country to country—on a second group of limits, as defined by the areas that mark transitions from one country's plants to its neighbor's. Such areas of transition stand all around Italy—the great historical center of Europe's achievements in acclimatization—like so many bridgeheads of the forward advance of flora from throughout the world: age-old portals of adaptation for invasions of plants from south to north. Provence is such an area for France; western Switzerland and the Canton of Vaud for Helvetia; for Germany the provinces of the old Roman Germania. Political and botanic frontiers are much the same: the place where the pulse of advance beats strongest, of the battle for the further penetration of cultivated plants into soils which, again and again, are wild and new. No matter the country, these zones of transition speak the accents of a culture of colonization and concentrate it, naturally enough, in their areas of greatest climatic vigor, as centers from which to develop and expand. These are the sites of the first embattled nurseries, and where the first adversities are overcome. It's from here that expansion toward new adversities continues tenaciously forward, in order finally to break and tame them once again. Every country, in the course of time, thus creates its own new center of adaptation as the basis of its own maximum performance; and it is on terms of this once-established maximum that it defines its character as a new homeland of cultivated vegetation, and as a unified floral landscape. An ideal asserts itself, and infuses the whole of national feeling into the country's mildest skies and the nobility of the soils beneath them, their abundance and inexhaustible variety, their cultural antiquity, their link with the Floras and Pomonas of the world. Italy calls itself "the land where lemons bloom," on the basis of those very few areas of enormous vigor where in fact they do; France sees itself as *douce France*, in the light of its gentlest expanses; and Germany, at least in its poetry, through the widely opened eyes of Hölderlin, dares to see Lombardy and Swabia as sisters. Such sisterhoods are the hinges of the oneness of the human garden. Provence and Savoy, Lombardy and Alemannia, Flanders and southern England are age-old welding points of a great chain: places where the historical process of adaptation derided all limits and boundaries, which human expansions leapt across by way of legs and feet, expanding plants by way of their seed. In names like *choux de Savoie*, or *Wirsingskohl*, or "walnut" (the Welsh nut), the meanders of the process have recorded themselves in language. It is a great and amazing process—and amazing not only for its unforeseeable consequences—since the primacy of man over nature, as expressed through laws of climate and terrain, lies at the very basis of the oneness for which it aims: of the oneness of which the vehicle is the further primacy of the rich landscape over those which remain still poor and wild; and of which the goal is the inter-relatedness of the best of the areas of cultivation of all the countries of the world. It is also amazing in its unabashed audacity.

The human being has reached and grasped superlative possibilities, thanks only to having desired and attempted to do what can't be done, and to having attacked the wilderness all at once along all fronts. He has managed, as said above, not only to plant the grape in regions well beyond anything thinkable, but as well has drained swamps, cut back woods, cleared rocks from soil, and created stone-walled terraces that turn the face of the land directly toward the sun; he has refined damp, stifling, unhealthy summer sultriness into dry mid-summer heat; he has cleansed the air over stormy, flooded plains and readied it for seedlings. This wisdom too was nothing the north invented out of necessity; it migrated from the south, as already traditional knowledge. Protection was one of its indispensable elements: the unconditional, impelling, self-certain will not to allow this plant—precisely this one, and precisely that one—to be lost for any sort of reasons of climate, saw no validity in frost limits, either for the plant or the human being. Plants were pushed daringly forward, into the open air, so far as in any way possible, under roofings, on ample sites before walls with southern exposures, or espaliered, or covered with leaves when pitiless lows in temperatures approached, or provided with the housings in dung which Germany's ancient monks had invented as winter quarters for women and children. Protection isn't limited to the north, nor is it only in the north that southern plants receive it; the protection of plants didn't first begin, as foolishly misconceived, as any unwilling northern invention. Wherever gardens stand, whether near Naples or Quedlinburg, they always stretch beyond their apparent climatic limits. In Palermo, bananas and tropical leafy plants are sheltered by walls and roofings; in Pisa the orange is espaliered and shielded by mats, like the peach in Quedlinburg; in Milanese gardens, the passion flower is swathed for winter, as grape vines are treated in Erfurt; in Tuscany, fuchsias are transplanted in springtime from vases out into the open land, as in Scotland is done with stock. If Holstein and East Friesland can be too proud to enrich their gardens' humble souls with will-o'-the-wisps that ask for care, defense and winter protection, bountiful Italy, where everything comes from, has never felt that way, and for exactly that reason became the mother country of European acclimatization. The smallest and least pretentious of Italy's gardens, the most rustic and rule-of-thumb, have always had, and continue to have, their unassuming measures, a shed or cabin, for the frost-free wintering of the plants one loves: something built, maintained and patched for a pittance, by no means very beautiful, but there, and suited to the nature of the property. If these primitive, timeless expedients hadn't likewise traveled northwards, the great semi-northern transition zones would never have turned into new homelands for further regions of garden flora and fruit, and the chain that links all peoples would never have been forged.

There's a tendency now to slight these zones of transition, the historical links of the chain, and suddenly to strike them out of it, seeing a country's most elastic terrains, and thereby the natural home of its cultivated flora, as at best its least significant appendage, in no way useful as a guide; they're seen as an exception to the one true rule, and are bracketed between parentheses, and the rule itself—the body of laws that govern the country's gardens and flowers—will be coined henceforth only and on principle in bronze, or on the basis of the minimum rather than maximum possibilities which the country's climate offers. We know that as a praxis this tendency stems, as all will find it easy to see, from commercial speculation and its tactics for the increase of profit; and justifications for such a praxis are something that businessmen can be left to discuss. But when it makes its appearance as dogma, and promotes itself as propaganda, yoking human beings to the inflexible givens of a country's harshest climate and most joyless soil, it amounts to crude naturalism, wrecks the whole of the garden's and the flower's humanism, runs counter to history, and mutilates itself: "the little fox that lost its tail would happily take a knife to all of us." In the Heidelberg countryside, ripe fruit falls in groves of fine chestnut trees just as in the province of Lucca; in sheltered areas, figs ripen nearly without a shed roof, and in others need no enclosures: they have immigrated here just like the chiselwork and pilasters, the balconies and palace windows of the ruined princely castle that commands a view of a transformed historical landscape. Must one always and only eat and drink in order to be aware of what such skies and soils have been taught to do? Or must one give up the shade and sight of these plants simply because they probably wouldn't survive in Uckermark?

Years ago on an empty, nearly boggy stretch of the shores of

Lake Constance, the author saw a field of tomatoes which a man of imagination—no gardener—grew as a wilderness, without poles or bindings or pruning, allowing the plants to riot uniformly on a half hectare of warm, active soil, almost completely covering it with color and fruit. Where such a thing is possible, must one give up collecting experiences which will surely result in acclimatized precocious tomatoes which then can move further northwards and be acclimatized again? Must one truly prefer, as fashion demands, to compliment a northern poverty on its virile barrenness, its rattling tenacity, its heroic recalcitrance. The author finds it high time, now that the poorest landscapes have been sufficiently praised, for the rich landscapes, neglected and relegated to corners, to be allowed once again an awareness of their unconditional primacy; it's time for the old landscape of cultivated plants on the southern side of the Alps to be restored to its role in the final, maximum expression of the human garden, as presented in this book; these rather than those should be seen as its basis and canon. The result would be for this form of garden to propagate northwards on its own account, just as in the sixteenth and seventeenth centuries, thanks to its simple magnificence, if trade and commerce can be hindered from falsifying judgment. Indigent regions must experiment as they best see fit; and the work and concentration with which they attempt to summon for themselves a satisfying selection of flora from the gardens of the world must never be denied the attention and admiration which so stubborn an ambition on the part of able workers deserves, even when it goes astray.

But the gardens in which Germany can lift itself through patient work to the level which the gardens of our century have achieved, and thus establish equality with the other nations—the gardens where the *amateur* can work with new flora from all across the globe, and where society can peruse and review the results—these gardens belong in much the same place where Max Leichtlin's world-renowned garden once stood in Baden-Baden: that garden to which the English unjealously owe so much. They belong on the shores of Lake Constance, on the banks of the Main and the Rhine and the Mosel and the Neckar, on the southern slopes of the Black Forest, in the Markgrafschaft, on the Danube, along the old Bacchic roads in the tracks of the god who made his way northward in a chariot drawn by panthers. What was right for wine was also allowed to fruit, greens, and subtropical vegetables; and what was allowed to these must also, finally, be allowed to the flower. In the middle of the lake, as a residue of the botanical conquests of the nineteenth century, stands the princely creation of the Zähringers: that always green, always flowering subtropical wonder-garden in the open air of the island of Mainau, both memento and monument. As memorial it reminds us that the era of collections of overseas oddities, all of them planted together, the era of Chatsworth and Woburn, has reached its historical conclusion; the flower has grown beyond them and has taken possession of the new garden, dashing the horizontality of the old, and growing upwards and downwards across it in all directions. As memento, it tells us that the future too will discover, just as here, that possibility is born from enthusiasm, and that nature even at its most luxuriant, blessed like the islands in the Gulf Stream, must strive to go beyond itself: that the garden is no instrument of pleasure, but of magical evocation, and that the daemonic drive to which this book is dedicated, the human need for the garden and the flower, rises out of the irrational so as then to pass through reason to a higher level of irrationality. That, conversely, it is absurd to want to sober this drive toward the reappropriation of lost paradises—this drive which itself is no less absurd, but wonderfully absurd, and therefore moving and creative in its unredeemability—and to force it to live a monogamic relationship with so sour a bride as "the climate." If such a suitor buckles to a thing like that, he is lost; and the climate too gains nothing; in the long run, she profits a great deal more from him if he flees, and on coming back brings the great wide world into the cold house.

And here the author adds a final ballot against tendencies and fashions of the times. This book has no illustrations. It is a text to be read, not a picture book to be leafed through. This is only very slightly, if at all, a willful asceticism that he forces on himself and his readers; in greater measure, it certifies the poverty of the times. The large majority of the plants this book discusses have never been drawn, and in order to find a draughtsman whose pencil might have flanked the pen, as in the splendid flower books of the sixteenth through the early nineteenth centuries, it would have been indispensable to create a link between the best of gardens and the finest of talents. It is a childish mistake to imagine that photography—a mechanical process for fixing reflections passed through lenses and reduced to the crudest patterns of shadow and light—might be capable of representing so complex a creature as the flower: complex in and of itself, and also in terms of the sensibilities of the various different human eyes that take it in. The lens—dumb, stiff and non-human, like storm and lightning—can never create an image which the human being has not first arranged and predisposed: it perceives no being, experiences no living impression. It preserves, like a footprint in wet sand, no more than the crudest impression of a material pressure to which it was materially exposed and subjected; and in preserving that impression must exaggerate its crudest details, while scumbling its median features and finally ignoring its finer and finest subtleties, which are physiognomically determining. A flower is more than simply its blossom. Its carriage, the angle at which it branches while growing upward, the way that angle plays against weights, the texture and tonality of the flower's tissues, its attitude, as expressed by the flower's will to attract or to hide, by purity of line or sensual presence: all of this contributes to its habitus, though by no means completely defines it. And what's to be said of the blossom itself?! It doesn't, like a human face, have a front and a sidewise view, a face and a profile; it has neither a smile nor magical eyes. Yet, how many arts must the photographer deploy when simply addressing the young Phyllis or the earnest Timon—with what variety of screens, veils, supports, lamps from above and below, and full and partial scrims will he not attempt to dematerialize and spiritualize the raw light that falls so stupidly onto the scene; through how many nuances will he have to adjust the turning and lowering of the head before obtaining the shots of which perhaps no more than one will strike him as worthy of serving as the basis for the true and proper work of humanization through further arts, and then retouching, and the choice of the grain and tone of printing papers? And only this work will be able to imbue the mechanical process with something of what he wants to reproduce not simply because it is "there," but because he loves it. Only the eye which has peered in this very same way into the visage of the flower will be able to convince the lens to follow it. Those who are acquainted with the flower painters of seventeenth-century Holland and their followers throughout the rest of Europe will know that they stripped the parrot tulip, the buttercup and the fire lily of everything non-essential with the same grandiose gaze of the spirit through which van Dyck and Goya consigned their human subjects to immortality: the painted flower gives undying life to impressions which the real one made on the enraptured eye for perhaps no more than a second; so, rather than provide an already extant external reality with a further external expression, it bathes something passing in the light of immortal delight. Such a training of the eye for the flower will have to proceed for still some decades before it will have taught the lens even to want "to see" what the eye sees. There's a barbarism in filling up books on gardening with page after page of phototype paper—made of calcinated wood pulp and already repulsive to touch—on which crude prints from mediocre plates present some something in expressionless black and white of which only the caption has anything to do with a flower, all of them alike, and always misrepresented. Schematic reproductions were usual up until the turn of the century, with modest sketches of the approximate botanical image of the overall view of the flowering plant, at times assisted by accompanying sketches of details—a method initially developed in France for the simple preliminary registration of new arrivals (then further developed in our own country, exemplarily, by Haage's and Schmidt's portrayals of newly imported flowers)—and these small-scale wood-cuts, discrete and unpretentious, were all that the gardener and the *amateur* needed as a point of reference. Today, it would be fundamentally more important to revive the drawing and painting of flowers—in constant decline since the middle of the last century, and then finally annihilated by Impressionism—than to develop and refine the photography of flowers. Color photography too, for the latter possibility, has only further coarsened an already coarse procedure. Its scale of available colors far from matches the flower's. The flower does not always and unchangingly have the look of bathing in a Bengal sunset. Stiff, severed stalks with bright lacquered corollas, all set against a black background, don't amount to flowers. A spray of scattered flowers on an old Meissen cup, no matter how perfunctory the craftsman's painting, has more to do with what Flora shakes from her apron onto the edge of the path than these brazen, empty fictions of total resemblance. It just won't work without the human being, since things in general don't work without modesty, no less than without love. Wisdom stands between them, and has aspects of aesthetics and morals as well as of knowledge. All three are contained in the words of the old Greek prophet: "A fool has never suspected how much more the half is than the whole." The "whole," whether as nature or the human spirit, is a riddle, irresolvable, indivisible, and has no "halves" at all. Love, too, even when its efforts are most extreme, is never more than half victorious. Yet, where it realizes and is content with this, there's a higher sense in which it possesses the whole, since this feeling contains at least the intuition of what remains to be achieved.

A Catalogue of New, Lost, Rare, Misunderstood & Singular Plants

THE following compendium results from many years of practical experience on the part of an amateur, who hopes in turn to be of practical service to other amateurs. It draws attention to a number of plants which today, to the best of the author's knowledge, have disappeared from commerce, the conditions of which, along with their causes and possible ways in which they might be remedied, are elsewhere discussed in this book. To whatever extent these notes are desirable, they appeal first of all to the expert, specialized levels of the seed trade, which despite being overly burdened by responsibilities of every kind—and regardless of its public's meager appreciation of its spirit of service and self-sacrifice—has never grown thoroughly heedless of these sorts of indications.

The fortunes of Germany's greatest establishment for the importation of seed, Haage and Schmidt in Erfurt, have fluctuated greatly in the period since the war, and one doesn't know if the company today is a memory or a hope. One hopes, however, to see it remain the latter, and once again become the pride of German tradition. Erfurt's world-famous Benary company, which administers a prudently restricted assortment with the greatest conscientiousness, and which even in leaner years never frugally bolted its doors against the new, has a fully proven right to the gardener's trust, but can address no more, naturally enough, than a portion of the present-day garden's needs. England's classic firm is Thompson & Morgan, in Ipswich, with today some five thousand species and varieties that with negligible exceptions can all be entrusted, or at least be lent, to spaces in the open air. Elliott's Sevenhills Nursery, in Stevenage, Hertfordshire, deals in South American specialties; Blackmore and Landgon, Bath's famous specialists in delphiniums and begonias, also has a great reputation for hardy lupines; Rivoire et Fils, in Lyon, has till now preserved a number of species, including the *Leptosyne arborea* and the true "Japanese mountain chrysanthemum," from being totally forgotten. Sutton and Company, in Reading, the enormous establishment that caters to England's luxury gardening trade, has a circumscribed stock of mostly well known and primarily florist breeds, of excellent quality at exclusive prices, but nonetheless offers a number of specialties. These remarks are made exclusively in the interest of purchasers, are based on experience, and dealers can disregard them only to their own disadvantage. Enormous institutions that import and distribute seed from all around the world merit a gardener's thanks, and thanks can be given even by those who once among a hundred orders may have suffered a true disappointment. Those who for a pittance offer the garden what elsewhere cannot be found at all must also be allowed to continue to market the wares they'd surely have abandoned if the effort of supplying thousands of different sorts of things left them time to test every packet before its release. One does best to hold a generous attitude, and always to think of the bigger picture.

The signs employed below have the following meanings:

A	annual
B	biennial
P	perennial
PA	perennial that blooms in its first year
AP	perennial which in Europe is mainly annual
Ph	woody perennial
bu	bulb

tu	tuber
co	corm
	climber
	creeper
︿	winter protection
⌂	elevated winter protection
⊓	temperate winter housing
T	cover in winter with a sheet of glass

Soil specifications: lower case letters for seeding earth, capital letters for general soil requirements.

H	heath soil
HT	peaty heath soil
L	leaf mold
S	slime deposit soil
D	pit compost
R	meadow soil
M	manure soil
C	normal compost
Y	general garden soil
Z	poor soil
S	sand
LE	loam
Gr	stone rubble
K	chalky soil
OK	chalk-free soil
tr	dry
f	moist
w	very moist
○	full sun
◐	half shade
●	shade

Numbers, in this order: height (in cm), month of flowering, spread (in cm square). All figures approximate, variable according to location.

Only the fewest of the plants below have names. The Latin designations with which they are presented are not "names," but conventional terms into which they have to be ordered for clear international recognition and exact differentiation.[†]

Attempts to replace such official terms of classification and recognition with imaginative names in each of the various languages would not only betray the striving for a clear overview of the world of plants, but would also run counter to the nature of language.

Names aren't given arbitrarily. They either derive from familiarity, which grows only slowly, or result from an instantaneous reaction on the part of the organ of linguistic creativity to compelling sense experience. Names are also given by jokes and games.

Greek and Latin designations for plants cannot be translated into other languages, if not at the expense of grotesque malformations, since they themselves are mechanical composites of unrelated pieces of words from those languages, and in this sense barbaric. *Anoiganthus* makes no sense in Greek, *Salpiglossis* is the roughest of approximations, *Verbena* means "soft stick."

Latin names for plants must be accepted much as we accept such words as meter, kilo, volt, gram, or decagram. We today make use of dahlia, zinnia, fuchsia, begonia and heliotrope no less lightly than we talk of roses or lilies or the gillyflower, since the images of the blossoms belong by now to everyday life, and these conventional designations immediately call them up. So they have turned into "names," without any need that anyone invent or tinker with them.

The common people, who are the most authentic of all name givers, naively make do on their own. Begonias in Tyrol are known as *Fettenstock*, or fat stock; Matthiola is *Veigelnstock*, or violet stock; *Funkia liliiflora* is known on Lake Constance as *Plattenstock*, or flat stock. South Africa's English population refers to the local flowers it has come to love as the "Natal

[†]In any given article of the Catalogue, Latin nomenclature appears in italics for the species or varieties of plants to which the article is dedicated.—H.M.

daisy," the "Namaqua daisy," the "Transvaal daisy," or the "black-eyed Susan." Americans refer to their native bushes not with botanical terms, but with names like "woolly blue curls," or the "snowdrop tree," or the "dogwood." Such names are local and would resist introduction even more strongly than conventional labels in Greek, since no mental image supports them. "Coral drops" says no more than *Bessera elegans*, if we are not familiar with the flower.

We give names to what we love, and to what we hate. We can give no names to things we have hardly yet begun to know. After fifty years of revolution, the new European garden can be spiritually and sensually repossessed only at the cost of a measure of sacrifice, and the effort must be freely made. As we grow more friendly with it, names, perhaps, may come on their own, if we are lively enough to throw them off spontaneously. The Baroque garden, in happier and simpler times, knew how to solve the problem by organically setting up links with things it already knew. "Indian cloves" (Tagetes), "Chinese carnations" (*Dianthus sinensis*), "Turk's cap" or *Türkenbund*, the "Pentecost rose" (the peony), "Easter bells" (*Anemone pratensis*) and the "Turkish lilac" all showed the way. Why shouldn't the *Loasa* one day take the name of "Mexican nettle"? Or *Arctotis grandis* be known as the "moonshine aster"? But "stoneweed" is a useless substitution for *Alyssum*, *Duftwicke* ("odorous vetch") for *Lathyrus odoratus* a sheer linguistic horror, and whoever might dare to say, "My bouquet still needs some three or four 'pretty faces,' 'trumpet tongues,' 'sunlight wings' and 'bee's companions' (*Calliopsis, Salpiglossis, Helipterum, Phacelia*) would be talking like the pedant in a farce, a comical figure. Those who think themselves important might first inquire as to what they see as so important about themselves: their energy, or their indolence.

Abronia umbellata AP, difficult to keep throughout the winter, W→S ○ 25 V 40. Nyctaginaceae, native to the California deserts. Gray-green, thinly growing creeper; flesh-pink, verbena-like flower clusters, with light aroma; very pretty;

flaccid stems. — Leguminous seeds which germinate slowly and easily rot, in pure s, transplant to S, cease to water as soon as leaf buds appear, later attend to cautiously. Desert gardens. The *grandiflora* somewhat better.

Adenophora potanini P rich LR, ◐ 40–50 V 20. Campanulacea of southern Siberia, in thin deciduous forests. Lovely pseudo-bellflower, with broad, open, sky-blue bells that hang to one side from gracious stems; fresh foliage. — Seed sparsely in lrs, thin immediately, keep in half shadow, transplant early to garden site, in dense groups, blooms the second year, roots attract mice. Do not remove the leaves that fall in winter.

Adlumia cirrhosa P CK ○ and ◐ ≷ 200. North American Fumariacea, the Alleghany vine, where it grows in thickets. Extremely dainty climber with split, fine to fern-like foliage, a fresh pale green, climbs on spiraling stems, with hanging blossoms, pale pink to scarlet red, shaped like the *Dielytra* (bleeding heart), a tiny jewel. — August in sl, seeds often do not germinate until the following spring, thin early, flowers the second year, protect somewhat from winter drought.

Agapanthus umbellatus var. pendulus ⊓ P MCL ○ 50 VII 50. North African Liliacea, in damp, compact soil. The *pendulus* variety, or Lily of the Nile, is far more beautiful than the commonly-known Agapanthus, showing a noble stalk with long, narrow, fine blue hanging bells among Kniphofias and Galtonias at the edges of iris-bearing plains. Seed in sh, keep warm, very slightly cover, keep in shade, with seeding tray bottoms in water, never sprinkle, otherwise seed will rot, sprouts should first be thinned into pots when cotyledons fall, continued ⊓ until root stock is pencil thick, then divide and transplant yearly, fertilize with liquid manure. Flowers after four to five years in the open.

Ageratum conspicuum AP ⌒ C ○ 50 V 30–40, later up to 60. Mexican Composita, common in middle elevations. A pure white variety, by now rare, with a dense growth of woody stems; dark, serrated, nettle-like foliage and abundant, umbrella-shaped inflorescences like those of the Eupatorium, and quite vivacious thanks to the single, roundish blossoms that spring out from them. — Seed sparsely in warm cs, thin promptly, transplant early to garden site, nourish well; can flank Alonsoa and Angelonia, Cuphea miniata and selaginoides, also on stony, sunny slopes. Precisely the same for *mexicanum*, larger and known as "géants Russes," up to 90 cm tall, with enormous, more abundant inflorescences, as well as requiring more terrain, liquid manure. *Lasseauxii*, dusky, pinkish mauve, loose, thinly blossoming panicles, fond of F with supplements of HT, will tolerate ◐, in sunken gardens. All *Agerata* ⊓ for winter survival, indispensable for *mexicanum*, placed with roots in a ball of earth in well-drained pots of not too large a size, kept fairly warm, somewhat pruned, prudently watered only as necessary.

Alonsoa warscewiczii AP ⊓ SC ○ 90 VI 40. Low Peruvian shrub on rocky heights and in stony soils, Scrophularina, with a typically South American grimace. A thick, pale green, broom-like bush, with pendulous, grape-like blossoms, scarlet to tomato red, among slender foliage; *acutifolia*, from Central America, with notched, myrtle-like leaves, vigorous in growth, with less abundant flowers, flowers larger, intense cinnabar, pendulous visages, late VI flowering season. — Warm, in sl, sparsely sown, promptly thinned, transplant to garden site in good, not too heavy C; in front of rockeries, good between stone outcrops; an always tousled and disheveled appearance, which one mustn't attempt to "fix." Occasional nourishment with liquid dung assures luxuriant grown: ⊓ for winter survival, prune, keep warm but not too moist, in medium-size pots, otherwise divide.

Alyssum idaeum P w→ KLGrY ○ IV 40. Cliff plant native to Crete, demanding tr conditions, Crucifera. A dwarf, creeping, gray-green carpet with abundant, lively, yellow blossoms, striking, compact, and sweet smelling, nobler than *saxatile.* In well-drained sly, with additions of old plaster rubble. Four leaves must appear before thinning, increase chalk dosage as soon as new rosettes begin to bud; at garden sites, inclusive of dry stone walls, keep at a distance from drainage courses, since it otherwise rots in summer rains. Old sheep dung and pigeon droppings, thoroughly matured into earth, can be carefully dosed at planting site. *A. spinosum var. roseum*, from various shores of the Mediterranean, with thick, thorny, single rosettes, late VI, enchanting somewhat dusky pinkish flowers, in cracks and clefts, in tiers each above the other.

Alstroemeria aurantiaca P tu L HT MYS in equal parts, ○ 40–50 VII extremely rank. Splendid Amaryllidea, from Mexico southwards, a mountain plant of middle elevations in rich, humus-laden soil. Clear green, sheath-like leaves emit naked shafts with tiers of steeply standing blossoms, split lengthwise, the roof petal thrown to the rear, rust orange, speckled or striped in red; *pelegrina*, Peru, the "Inca Lily," *psittacina*, Mexico, as above, scarlet red with grass green, the latter speckled as well, up to 60 cm. — The medium-sized, spherical seeds in sh, in holes 3–4 cm deep, warm; sprouting irregular, often after 1–2 months, often one or two years; seedlings immediately into small pots, for further nursing, then slightly larger pots when the soil is riddled with roots, transplant to garden site with the whole clump of earth; the bulbs grow rank, and hate disturbance; when division is required, dust damaged bulbs with abundant charcoal powder. Rich root bed, as above, thorough drainage, minimal quantities of thin liquid manure, no sprinkling. Individual plants in three years time multiply to an area of a square meter, choking all neighbors. Stems keep in water for two weeks, if cleanly cut at the base, but will dry if broken off, owing to the fleshy, non-porous foot by which they're attached to their bulbs. Hardy in warmer exposures without ⌒, otherwise provide with an overturned basket, covered with straw. Half-sunny clearings, boggy, but drained.

Althaea ficifolia P YK ○ 180–200 VII–VIII 70. Solitary plant of the Tartar steppes, to as far as Siberia, in tall prairie grass. An imposing mallow with large fig-leaf foliage directly attached to the stem, and large, simple, deep yellow blossoms, far superior to the garden mallow as a proud, elegant form. — Seed in zs, relatively thickly covered, protect from mice, which dig them up, continue cultivation without interruption in order in September to plant magnificent growths at garden site. Deeply worked terrain, with only earthy, fully matured manure. Fresh manure encourages mallow rust, whereas additions of chalk will hinder or reduce it. — In grassy expanses, as well as steep, bare slopes, along with sage bushes.

Amarantus salicifolius A YS in equal parts, O 60–70 summer 50. Amarantacea of tropical Asia, leafy plant without flowers, and hidden sexes. The loveliest of all the Amarantus, with fine, flat, twisting leaves, spiraling out in all directions, a copper green that blends toward crimson, yellow, scarlet, white; the twisting and curling of the plant contribute to its fairytale quality. — Quite warm in sh, to trays with additions of Y after seedlings develop their first four leaves, then when half a palm tall into earth that's not too rich, where they preen and take on their colors. Never in the company of Celosias: Coleus thyrsoides and rehnaltianus, Torenias, Roscoeas, Commelinas. Warm, dry slopes. — Seeds a matter of trust, not everywhere authentic.

Amaryllis (Hippeastrum) hybr. These magnificent amaryllis cultivars, crosses of a number of wild South American varieties, blossom twenty-one months after seeding, reliable sources resulting in perfect flowers. — Seeds in warm sh, barely covered, kept in shade, watered from a saucer below, the surface of the soil must never be wet, immediately thin in the seeding pot, leave undisturbed until cotyledons fall, transplant to sheltered bed when the plant has developed two tongue-shaped leaves; dig up in fall, allow to dry, winter frost free in the dark beneath heaps of dry earth or ash, plant in the open in CM after last spring frost, simply placing the bulbs on the ground, lightly pressing them in to a third; weekly feedings of thin dung water, in fall as above, will bloom this year or the next.

Angelonia (grandiflora hort.) salicariaefolia AP (⊓) CSM ○ 70 VIII 40. Scrophulariacea of the higher elevations of Ecuador. Fresh green leaves, toothed and lancet-shaped, powerfully growing stems, violet, impish faces, thrust forward like those of the grassy Cupheas, a faint, slightly acrid odor. — In sl, sparsely, thin promptly, will strengthen at garden site. With plentiful nourishment, tolerates slight shade. A plant with character, can stand among highly different plants, whether tall or short. — The white variety is a dirty white.

Anoda lavateroides A Y ○ 100 V, topples over, at intervals of 30 cm. Mexican Malvacea, a badlands weed. A tall, compact bush, covered with pretty mauve-pink flowers. Undemanding cultivation, also at garden site; fills empty, sunny spaces with masses of flowers, makes do anywhere.

Anomatheca (Lapeyrousia) cruenta P bu A CK ○ 15 VII in colonies. A small bulb, Iridacea, from the Cape of Good Hope. From out of narrow, grass-like sleeves of foliage, the thinnest, stiffest stem bears an outwards-jutting panicle with up to ten steep, hand-shaped blossoms, of a bright, shimmering, brick-red pink, speckled at the bottom with blood red. In appearance, fresh and extremely gracious. — The spherical seeds go into a pot with three quarters pebbles, one quarter sc, are lightly pressed down, scantily covered, and always watered from a saucer below; seed germinates quickly; do not disturb until the pot is full of densely growing tufts of grass; then empty it, turning it upside down, and transplant the seedlings, careful not to damage their roots, as follows: half insert a trowel into previously prepared earth and tilt it back and forth to open a slit; place the seedling within the slit, with the bulb a finger's breadth beneath the surface of the soil; close the slit by inserting the trowel at either side of its outer edges, press lightly, sprinkle. If planted in a hole, the seedling's roots will wither for the current year. Cared for as here described, seedlings bloom two months later; in winter ⌂. Exemplary bulb for rockeries, passes up through carpeting creepers, will also bloom in half-sandy terrain.

Aquilegia P LRSK ◐. The new species *akitensis* (Japan, blue, low), *buergeriana* (Japan, yellowish brownish white, low), *fragrans* (white or pale red, sweet-smelling, California), *pubescens* (cream colored, velvety, California) are still under observation. The lovely *A. clemataquila*, a large, simple, deep plum-purple, Clematis-like star on a sturdy columbine structure, has again disappeared from commerce; its native habitat remains unknown. The remaining newer sorts are: *viridiflora* 60 late VII 35, a transparent creature as though of blown glass, or cricket's wings with gold and bluish reflections, one of the greatest wonders among the new importations, delicate in growth, native to California; *longissima*, North America, 100 VII 40, a giant-spurred derivation from *chrysantha*, with less abundant blossoms, more spidery in habit and structure, paler yellow blooms, a highly delicate wildflower; *ecalcarata* 40 VI 20–30, a brownish-reddish Japanese dwarf without spurs, and an odd, impish form; *hybr. Mrs. Nicholls*, the blue giant columbine, the maximum further development of the North American *coerulea*, 90 V 40, perfect flowers, flexible bearing. The older sorts include: *Helenae hybr.*, with a narcissus-like trumpet form, broadly spread, deep blue petals, snow white spurs, 40 V 20, skittish, plant very dry; *glandulosa* (true seed a matter of trust), in dark silky blue and molten enamel white, exquisite tissue, the Altai region, 100 V 45; *skinneri*, 100 late VI 40, Guatemala, scarlet with green tips, spurs primrose-yellow, tense vibrant structure, loves ○, the family's highest, most sumptuous form. Seed often mixed with poor reddish-yellow species such as *arctica* and *canadensis*, very hard to come by fully pure, and should indeed today be freshly imported. — Sow in sl with additions of fragments of charcoal, a month will pass before germination, thin at the appearance of two true leaves into trays kept in half shadow, never allowing the soil to sour. Transplant in fall to garden site LRS, drainage, slopes, dry exposures. Very fleshy roots susceptible to rot; keep mice away. When flowering loses vigor, remove the plants and reset the young ones. In sour earth, fungal blights appear, wreaking havoc on the plant's entire above-ground structure.

Arctotis grandis AP ⌒ LESK ○ 90 VII 40. South African Composita, of dry locales. Pliant, silver-gray construction with slightly downy, round-lobed leaves rising from half rosettes on bobbing, limber, gray stems with large, silver-bluish white flowers, petal underside in violet blue, corolla bluish violet, the whole growth as though bathed in milk and moonlight. Grows woody in suitable exposures. One can attempt, after cutting the plant, to cover it with rounded mounds of dead ash. — Seed germination after 3–4 weeks in ys, very small seedlings to be left undisturbed until the growth of four leaves, development then quite rapid. Stone and rock as setting and background indispensable. *Scapigera (hybr.?)* P ⌒ 40 VIII 30, thick, crinkly, fleshy leaf rosettes, robust woody stems with bronze-colored star-shaped flowers, black-blue corolla, a dusky magnificence, highly sensitive to moisture. — In 50% s, seeds quite lightly covered, thin promptly, seedlings tolerate at first more moisture, transplant with six to seven leaves, to above-mentioned soil mixed with Gr. Pot before winter, keep cool in ⊓, never water if not in emergency before the return of vegetation. Same cultivation for *speciosa*, taller growing, deep bronze orange; *breviscapa* A ○ 25 VI, creeps, a lovely, ochre to cream-colored summer Composita of southern Africa with dark corolla, fleshy leaves, plant tr, water only exceptionally.

Aristea capitata P bu ⌒ HTRLE ○ 150 IX 40. South African Iridea on ancient swamplands. Tall reeds with panicles of bright blue gullets, of enormous splendor. — The large seeds are deeply pressed into sh and lightly covered, then kept warm, preferably in trays in a tepid greenhouse, otherwise in pots in hotbeds; germination in 3–4 weeks; the newborn plants immediately thinned, transplanted a finger tall to garden position, bulbs dug up in late fall, wintered dry and frost free, replant in spring after final frosts; in the second year, when the plants have grown strong, and after their foliage has withered, cover with piles of palm fiber, held in place with brushwood; the plants first blossom after growing into stouter bushes. Together with large Crocosmias, or with Dieramas among Tritonias.

Arnebia echioides P KGrRS tr ○ 30 VII 30. Boraginea of Asia Minor, in chalky, thoroughly-drained terrains. Gray, raw-leafed half-rosettes, rough, downy, bristly flower stems, inflorescences of round, primrose-yellow blossoms with deep violet spots that pale as blooming flowers ripen, then reappearing on new buds; the Prophet flower of Arab legend. — In 50% s with k, the rest r; use shelled seed only, often lies dormant at length, seedlings to remain undisturbed, only thinned, set at garden site in fall. In wet winters, cover with an overturned flower pot. Will rot unless soil is perfectly drained. Never water, except when threatened by drought. *Cornuta*, the A variety of the same plant, very similar, black spots, looser bearing, more voluminous, coarser. A splendid one-year plant for stone rubble, among Myosotis rupestris and welwitschii, Omphalodes, Moltkia petraea; for rock slides and step gravel slopes.

Asphodelus liburnicus P ⌒ RZ tr ○ 90 VI 60–70. Liliacea of the shores of the Mediterranean, on poor, stony, wasteland soil. Rosettes like bubbling springs of gray-green swine cress leaves, with runners in all directions carrying new rosettes, central stem with a golden yellow, thyrsus-like inflorescence, from which tightly packed buds emit single blossoms with yawning faces and extended, tongue-like pistils; a severe and noble form. The *luteus*, similar, without runners, more robust. — The large seeds are pressed in deeply, slightly covered, kept uniformly damp, not wet, in darkness; germination can occur after very few days, *never keep warm*; thin when seedlings have three or four yellow root shoots; when pencil-thick at base, plant in a spade-made cleft. Stony slopes, near single boulders, with Eremostachys and the final irises.

Aster californicus (tenellus hortorum) A SHT ○ 50 VIII 30. Moist, shimmering, fibrous foliage, toothed and grayish green, on a rich, well-balanced, well-tiered structure with a loose pyramidal inflorescence of perfect flowers, orchid-lilac-colored petals, a corolla the yellow of the Maréchal-Niel, exquisitely pure and fresh; among the finest, but also lightest, most delicate summer flowers, nowhere found in cultivation. — In bowls with s earth, thin, transplant to dry shelves in the rock garden, tends to topple over, should be supported with stones. No other aster should be planted nearby, would look coarse. Bushes of Ismelia broussonetifolia behind it, flanked in rocky cracks by Platystemon poppies and Hunnemania. The *capensis (Felicia amelloides, Agathea caelestis)* variety, Ph YK ○ 80 VII, 80 and more with older plants. Bushy Compositae of the Cape of Good Hope, on cliffs and dry stone walls. Gnarled, bristly, half-spherical mounds of hard, leathery, dusky foliage, an erect stem surmounted by copious blossoms with pure blue petals, often crinkly, surrounding a yellow corolla. Grateful for additions of H, occasional liquid manure increases blossoming. ⌒; in raw exposures remove to ⊓. — Seed in sandy normal earth, thin in the pot, transplant after seedling roots have formed a clump of earth, onto embankments, dry stone walls, always higher up. Taller plants, Digitalis canariensis, Delphinium sulphureum, in the near vicinity.

Babiana tubiflora, ringens, among others, P bu ⌒ ○ 30–50 VI in colonies. Bulb from the Cape of Good Hope, in all colors, with panicles like those of the Ixia, more delicate; a decorative wonder of colors, in paler tones. — Press seed into hs, cover sparsely, medium warmth, in darkness, seeding soil kept moist, remove from soil in the fall, small tubers to be stored frost free and dry, to garden site after last spring frosts, blooms two months later. Sandy terrain, somewhat enriched, Nemesias fairly close by.

Baeria gracilis A YSK ○ 10 V 30. Dwarf California Composita, common on uncultivated land. Delicate, matte-green foliage, small golden crown with a wheel of truncated petals, uncommonly abundant flowering, heap on heap, completely fills up borders, always and only in large-sized colonies. — In fall at garden site, seedlings thinned; in colder exposures, plant in March.

Belamcanda sinensis (Pardanthus sin.) P R with a measure of SMK, not too light, ○ 80 VII 40. Magnificent Chinese Iridea, often with a penchant for cultivated terrains, appears along the courses of rivers. Its rhizome lies half above ground, strong canes, leafed stems, widely angled ramifications of conspicuous yellow iris blossoms with red spots, truly a showpiece, vigorously bushy from the ground up. — The large seeds slightly covered with sandy earth, sprouts after 5–6 weeks, remarkably fast development, transplant soon to garden site, reaches 30 cm height the first year, blooms the second year. In exposed positions ⌒. Powerful groups develop in the course of the years. Nothing too colorful nearby. Warm hollows, Echium aculeatum.

Bletia hyacinthina P DLES with T, ○ 40 V 30, later twice as broad. Chinese terrestrial orchid, the loveliest field-growing orchid of temperate climes. Stands of crinkled foliage, partly sterile when growing from fibrous roots without tu, fertile plants sending up the hardest, thinnest flowering stems, large pale-violet blossoms with dark velvet-violet trumpets, crenate and speckled. Flowers keep for days in water. In raw exposures ⌒. Easily subject to black aphids, immediately to be fought; seed untried, and likely to thrive only in the plant's own soil; divide the plants in spring, they quickly grown strong again.

Browallia elata A CS ○ 100 VII 50. Mexican Solanacea, of a genus extending to northwest South America. A brittle, woody bush bedecked with small, dull-violet, mask-like visages (like those of the Achimenes) that stand out beautifully from lustrous, deep green foliage. Additional calcium somewhat reduces fragility. *Viscosa* P (sow only the variety *compacta sapphire*) a smaller (15 VII 20) more robust bush with lapis-blue flowers, whitish at the center, standing singly. *Roezlii* of a looser build, only 40 cm tall, satisfying only in soil with additions of M. *Speciosa*, poorly constructed, inclined to topple over, with coarse foliage, dull-violet oversized flowers in purely gullet (petunia) form; overflowing with blossoms in CMS. — All Browallias warm in hs, gently press the fine seed, sprinkle lightly, slightly cover with a sifter, keep in shade, transplant with two or three true leaves into stronger earth in trays, strengthened with soil from the garden site; *viscosa* ⌂; *elata* self-propagates in warmer exposures to the point of becoming a nuisance. With Alonsoas. At the bottom of large rock gardens. In deeply deposited soil *Browallia elata* and *roezlii* become stupendous.

Bulbinella semibarbata P bu DS ○ 30 VCII 20. Liliacea presumably from North America, precise original habitat unknown. Stands alone, rapid growth in very few months from seed to robust bulb, abundant foliage and tireless flowering. Bright green crown of moist, vigorous, lymphatic, leek-like leaves, the inflorescence a sideways standing thyrsus heavily laden with small golden-yellow star-shaped flowers, habit of Gageas and Ornithogalums; unsightly when it withers, though constantly producing new inflorescences. — Seed in hs, rapid germination, development visible, do not thin, stronger plants to rich soil where they bloom quite soon. Invaluable for quick, luxuriant effects, the thick, lucent, deep green foliage is already sufficient reward.

Calandrinia umbellata P ⌒ SDK ○ 8 VIII 30. Portulacacea,

Chile; thick, ruffled phyllodes, succulent, woody stem, the whole plant a dwarf bush, large, glowing, violet-purple chalices, one of the noblest plants for rock garden slopes with southern exposures. Hardy with careful protection (T, straw covering against frost), otherwise ⊓, in warmer climates limitless self-propagation in cracks and fissures.

Calceolaria chelidonoides, mexicana, scabiosaefolia A and all quite similar to one another, vigorous herbs with fresh green foliage, Y ○ 40–80 VII, 40 and more, with highly abundant primrose-yellow, pouch-shaped flowers. The P *crenatiflora, tenella* and *biflora* need HSML with slight additional R, love ◐ or northern exposures, and easily suffer from moisture. The *polyschiza* P 5 VII 10 needs S supplements, and ◐. All, without exception, extremely gracious and delicate, exquisite creatures in search of shelter, in winter T, and thoroughly well-drained soil. — In bowls with pure h, half warm, seeds simply strewn on lightly sprinkled seeding soil, cover with a sheet of glass, keep in shade, keep cool after germination, thin with the point of a needle, in small pots until fully robust, then plant with their clump of rooting earth at garden site.

Callirrhoe involucrata PA Y ○ 10 VI W→ up to 100. Creeping Malvacea native to Texas. Builds carpets of abundant silky reddish-violet blossoms, handsome and mallow-like; colors very fresh and precious, flower tissues strong and noble. — In ys like all mallows, not too damp, seed takes some time before sprouting. Droops wonderfully down when planted on terraces or retaining walls. The *pedata* A, redder flowers, creeps less, taller stems, generally coarser, same treatment. Lovely plants which first found use in landscape gardens.

Callistephus sinensis, the China or "summer" aster, A LEF, deeply worked, supplements of K; humus acids promote diseases. — In ys, sparsely seeded, tr, thin promptly. The seed of these highly-bred plants is up to 25% sterile, germination at times no more than 50%. Garden position to be changed each year, otherwise total failure. Fully developed blossoms only with careful cultivation, rich nourishment. — Old varieties on the scale of blue-red-white and 90% of experimental forms have all died out in the course of development. Tones of blackish blue, golden yellow, pale blood red, glowing crimson, thistle pink (heather), and all shades of salmon have been achieved. Purification of lilac tones remains to be accomplished. Pure peony and petalled thistle forms predominate. Abundance of blossoms remains limited. The enormous American breeders concentrate on washed out colors of colossal cut flowers in chrysanthemum forms, not suited for the garden. Garden varieties include the *Hercules* 40 robust, perfect form, pure colors, *Victoria*, exquisite, along with *Micaéla, Deutscher Prinz, Miss Roosevelt, Jungfräulein, Leuchtfeuer, peony (Grabelotte), surprise, terracotta, color queen, cactus, King of Spain, ruby, aurora, red and white giants, youth, deep blue-red, record*. The *sunshine class* with a butter-yellow center, an intermediate circle of white and brightly colored petals, has the look of a Phyllocactus. The yellow (pure yellow) *Dr. Dürr* and *sunlight* are sheer perfection. All from Benary. Normal spacing for classes, expanded spacing for varieties.

Calochortus, the "Mormon tulip," or Mariposa lily, P bu, deep SMY ○. A California tuber (Liliacea), tall (40) *venustes, splendens, clavatus*, as well as shorter (20) *flavus*; solitary desert bulbs, all fond of sand, three petals, floppy, heavily speckled, hairy interior, blooms that bob and beckon on thin, pliant stems. *Kennedyi* short (15) and resembling a poppy, scarlet flecked with black; *plummerae* tall (50) deep lilac with yellow hairs, astounding; *vesta* (40) with the look of a Godetia, whitish-lilac flecked with red. Magnificent English hybrids among all the species. — In 30% h, 60% coarse sand, firmly pressing down on the platelets, lightly sprinkle, cover with a sifting of fine sand, keep in shade, half warm; germination mostly not till after several months, grass-like seedlings, allow them to wither in winter, do not disturb, winter the tiny bulbs frost free under sawdust, planting them after the last spring frost, cover in winter in rougher climes with palm fiber and straw, smaller plants flower in the third year, larger in the fourth.

Camassia leichtlinii, the white Quamash, P bu YML ○ 90 VI 50. Liliacea of western North America, precise original habitat unknown, with wonderful lily-like shafts and large, hanging, Scilla-like, bell-shaped chalices, myriad stems, moist gray-green foliage. — Seed only slightly covered, sy, seedlings promptly thinned, into stronger soil for rapid development, blossoms in the third or fourth year, sometimes sooner. The bulbs attract mice. In clusters at the edges of clearings along with large *Campanula lactiflora*.

Campanula (annual) *macrostyla* A Y 100 V 30 Greece and the Orient, with stiff hair and voluminous build, fragile stems, abundant ramifications, widely gaping, middle-violet chalice, with dark violet veins, bristly, angular, gawky, conspicuous. The *mirabilis* P Y tr 100 VI 50, native to the Caucasus, a compact bush with pale blue bells, sheer perfection; the *vidalii* Ph YKM tr, a woody shrub-like form from Madeira, with wonderful cream-white flowers, sweet smelling, a paragon, ⌂ in colder exposures, to be planted in corners in the rock garden in ways that allow the creation of ⊓ with sheets of glass. — All *Campanulas* in sr, the fine seeds as thinly scattered as possible, do not disturb, but scatter widely, thin, to garden site in fall, all love tr, solid soil. Mice attack their roots. — All on arid slopes, as well as dry stone walls and faces of rock; *Campanula medium* grows wild in Italy as a decoration of country walls, but is beautiful only there.

Canarina Campanula P tu ⇞ CK ○, up to 200, V, needs 40 cm on all sides, perennial only in sheltered positions in warmer climates, the Channel Islands, Lake Constance, the valley of the Rhine. A climbing Campanulacea, native to the Canary Islands. A sharply rising spike from thick, fleshy bulbs, notched, pale-green foliage, pendulous primrose-yellow bellflowers with blood-red veins and a faint odor; vigorous climber by way of peduncles on leaf stems. — The seeds, barely distinguishable from those of the radish, warm in hs, shortly followed by germination, seedlings transplanted into pots, blooms the second year after planting.

Cardiospermum halicacabum AP ↟ YK ○. South African Sapindacea. A luxuriant climbing plant with beautiful, feather-shaped, fresh green foliage on hairy, reddish stems, leaves divided and alternate; VIII and later; delicate bunches of silky whitish blossoms with a golden yellow interior, and puffed seedpods which in fall are papery balloons. — The pea-like seeds in ys in furrows, transplant immediately after germination. Reaches full beauty only after several years. Tolerates ◐, flourishes into thickets, covers, fills, drapes over everything.

Castilleja. Of all the many delightful species of the Indian paint brush, *Castilleja indivisa* is nearly the only one to be currently available in commerce, since it's seen as the "easiest." Marshland Scrophulariacea of Mexico and southern North America with mainly red bracts that beckon from a distance, and somewhat less attractive flowers. P HTRSM ◐ to ●: sow in pure h, keep moist. The *affinis linariaefolia,* like the former 40–50 VII 40, with pinkish-reddish bracts and tongue-shaped foliage, more dainty. Both love marshy but porous terrain, half-lit exposures. Ignoring these conditions results in failure; plants that cannot be cultivated in ordinary gardens.

Cathcartia villosa B HTS ○ 60 VI 40. Heathland Papaveracea, native to California. The whole plant covered with down, like the Meconopsis, attractive yellow poppy flowers. — In hs, seeds lie dormant at length, germinates with difficulty, and unpredictably, thin cautiously, careful not to harm or knick the tap-root, plant in fall in a spade cleft, flowers and dies the following year. With Anemone hupehensis, japonica, a wasteland flower.

Celosia spicata A SY ○ 50 VII 30. Amarantacea of eastern India, very much different from the vulgar cockscomb (*cristata*) species with coarse tissues and impure colors; a delicate pant with small leaves and slender habit, silvery, bobbing panicles with a flush of pink, at times pure pink with a shimmer of silver, in form like the Statice suworowii. — Smooth round seeds quite warm in sz, germinates slowly, at start to be treated with great care, transplant soon into small pots to be inserted into earth under ⊓, water only the surrounding terrain. In the warmest position possible, at the edges of desert gardens, with additions of Y.

Centaurea americana A YSM ○ 130 VII 50. North American Composita, a sturdy, heather-violet fleur-de-lys on a thick, coarse shaft, abundant foliage, rustic flowers with considerable character, develops broad with powerful perimetric flowers. — Can be sown directly at garden site, otherwise normal seeding. Prairie flower. The white form impure. Subject to damage from beetles, whose larvae destroy its receptacles; blow pepper into the flowers.

Cephalaria tatarica P Y ○ 250 VII 80. Giant Composita, native to central Asia's flowering steppes, with beautiful, notched foliage, tall, leafy, richly ramified stems and large, pale-yellow, Scabiosa-like flowers on long, thin stems, a faint smell of honey. — The Scabiosa-like seeds in dry c, rapid germination, normal further handling, the plant flowers in the third year, and as years go by grows imposing. Of great effect as solitaries in flowering steppe-like tracts, grows poorly in barren spaces, flourishes in the corners of rock gardens.

Ceratotheca triloba AB CMST ○ 90–100 VII 50. South African Pedaliacea, a biennial that often blooms and dies in the first year; covered entirely with soft, downy hair; richly developed foliage rising up to inflorescences of large, hanging, dark pink blossoms, like those of Digitalis or Martynia, exceptionally beautiful — Hammer-shaped seeds kept warm in ys, promptly thin for forced, precocious blooming, warm exposure, abundantly watered at times of great heat, otherwise never, but weekly applications of liquid manure. Weak and inclined to droop, should be staked.

Cheiranthus linifolius Ph KYS ○ 30 VII 20. Crucifera of the coasts of the Mediterranean, always on rocky terrain, forms dwarf trees with broad, thick crowns and sweet-smelling, pale-lilac flowers, as though stuck into them. The driest sand, the most porous terrain. — In kys, treated like all the gillyflowers, do not transplant until strong, younger plants extremely humidity-sensitive, older plants more hardy. With Linaria ericoides, Myosotis traversii, Arnebia, which require the same soil and treatment. The *kewensis* species, presumably a cultivated hybrid, is a prettier, somewhat more delicate gillyflower in three colors, cream yellow at first, then tending to ochre and violet, all on same plant; resembles lantana, is sweet in smell, declines in bearing from the third year on if not in particularly chalk-rich soil. An exceptionally beautiful plant for very hot rock gardens. — Seeded like all the gillyflowers, quite dry and healthy, allow it to thirst.

Chrysanthemum japonicum, a mountain plant, known to the French as "chryanthèmes de la montagne." The nomenclature is dubious and perhaps misleading. The commercial varieties are highly blended, transformed by a history of cultivation. PhA YMSL, improved by additions of leaf mold, ○ 130 IX and later, 90, hefty bushes with small leaves, and strong odor, summits covered with clusters of small, bright, star-shaped flowers in unbelievable quantity, in all colors except blue. Special varieties with larger blossoms, crinkly petals, spoon-like shapes. Numerous commercial names. All from Rivoire, in Lyon. — Seeding in early spring gives first year blossoms only if the young plants are forced through repeated transplanting. Normal seeding procedures, in rich dry seedbed soil, highly porous. *Mawii* PA YSKM ○ 20 VII 30, Composita from California rock slides, delicate, silvery, feather-like foliage, compact bushes, myriad, eloquent, pinkish, star-shaped blossoms.

Early seeding in ys, promptly thinned, transplanted early. Sensitive to winter moisture. ⊤ advisable. Treatment with nutrients enables it also to live in sand.

Clitoria ternatea PA ⥉ CMLS ○ very warm 300 VII. Leguminosa Papilionacea of the American tropics. Typical habit and foliage of beans, velvet green, extremely vigorous with adequate heat and nourishment, large, glowing, pale blue blossoms with strange white niches at their centers; showy and beautiful for warm moist terrains, well-watered and rich with humus. — Bean germination is quick and easy, transplant to bowls when the first feathery leaves appear, to garden site not before summer. Will not survive the winter. Poorly tolerant of fall transplanting back into pots.

Codonopsis clematidea P half ⇝ HSR tr 15 VIII 30. The Himalayas, Campanulacea, in recesses and on terraces. Lax bearing, with evil-smelling, gray-green tendrils covered with downy leaves, and ending with anemic inflorescences, weakly built and porcelain blue, of bell-shaped flowers bent and slightly flared below with stripes of black around a yellow center, pendulous. — Sow like the Campanulas, do not transplant until the fleshy roots are half as thick as a pencil, very porous terrain, without it the plant will immediately die. The *ovata* shows bells with livelier colors and no interior markings on even limper shoots.

Coleus The garden forms that derive from constant crossings of the colorful Southeast Asian Plectranthaceae are too well known to need comment. *Coleus thyrsoides* Ph ⊓ CMHD ◐ 50 VIII 30, Labiata from tropical Africa with mottled leaves, abundant, pale-violet inflorescences, stays low, loves half shade and moisture, and the richest humus. *Coleus rehneltianus*, from Java, a rank, tropical, carpet-building plant with tightly intertwining and self-enveloping ground shoots, thick with small, crimson-purple leaves edged in green and yellow, sprawls mat-like across the ground in warm, moist locales, enlivened by small, pale violet inflorescences. — Both warm in sh, lightly covered, long dormancy, then immediately tough and resilient, highly rapid development, transplant late. *Coleus rehneltianus* also in O.

Commelina PA tu, in every sort of soil, rampant in richer soils, O 60 VII uncontained. South America Comelinacea. The *coelestis* a pale blue beauty; *sellovina* more of a climber, deep cobalt, from Uruguay, an aggressive, strangling plant with primal, typically American energy and lax shoots that root on touching the ground and send out subterranean stolons, deeply and quickly established, winters without protection in mild exposures. — In sh, rapid germination, transplanted seedlings bloom after 3–4 months. Indispensable for quick improvisations. Overwhelmingly abundant blossoming of only three-petaled corollas, both species the purest blue. Volume as great as half or three-quarters of a cubic meter is not at all seldom. Where troublesome, remove after frost.

Cosmidium burridgeanum A Y O 50 VII 30. Composita of the flowering Texas prairies. Resembles the Calliopsis, but is clearly superior, with purer colors, finer tissues; golden yellow with lively brownish-scarlet stripes. — Normal seeding, normal attentions for large summer flowers.

Cosmos dahlioides P tu RSM O 50 VII 30. A tuberous Mexican Composita with the habit of the Bidens and the dahlia's basic structure, a borderline form. A pretty dwarf shrub with profuse, highly dentellated leaves and long, thin stems carrying single, pink Cosmos flowers with fine, solid tissues. An interplay of whites and scarlets. Bulbs not tightly packed. *C. diversifolius atrosanguineus*, the "black dahlia," much as above, with darker, more luxuriant foliage, a heavier bearing, and vigorously rising flowers almost velvet black. — Seed in good ys, thin with two leaves, transplant promptly into meticulously prepared soil, gives satisfaction only with abundant fertilization. *C. aurantiacus* A (?) woody 300 late X (?) 100; even in the warmest exposures it often blooms until frost sets in; exquisite, deeply notched, dark green foliage; thick and bushy; moist, glowing, orange blossoms with a light as strong as the orange Trollius; now often supplanted by the dwarf form *Orange Flare*, which after 3–4 months gives a great abundance of splendid blooms. Among steppe flowers half its height. Seeding as above, seeds only lightly covered, otherwise it immediately dies.

Cotula barbata A YSK ○ 30 VI 20. A new Composita from southern Africa. A small bush with golden yellow spherical buttons, blossoms abundantly. In all soil. For improvisations in new rock gardens, next to Viola gracilis and Felicias.

Cuphea. A beautifully blooming Lythracea in herb, bush or shrub form, from Mexico to Peru. The tallest and most beautiful, like the *C. roezlii*, have again disappeared from our gardens. *C. miniata* A Y ○ 70 VII 80, a Mexican herb, fresh green, slightly rough, vigorous, bedecked with small, bright, capricious faces of vermilion to brick-pink blossoms with lively gullets with accents of whitish violet. The *silenoides*, similar, with flowers of a fluffier pale lilac (fading toward white, toward pink). Both are invaluable, undemanding, gap-filling mounds of color that will grow in any corner, the colors of the *miniata* enchanting for their freshness (Haage and Schmidt). *Zimapani* with more tubular flowers, of a dark, velvet plum color, the whole plant sticky, with a stiff, meager bearing, always branching at the same angle, characteristically American. Ph *platycentra,* known as "dropped matches" on account of its helter-skelter criss-cross of little red stick-like flowers with whitish, blackish rims, a shrub with fresh green foliage, generally known as a hedge plant. — In good ys, the latter species requiring more assiduous care, the former in warmer exposures going endlessly to seed spontaneously.

Cyclamen ibericum P tu LDMK, ◐ but also ○, 10, X and III, migrates. A Caucasus mountain violet. Beautifully marbled leaves, relatively large flowers, very luminous crimson with purple reflections, through and through the early springtime blossom. — The spherical seeds into flat depressions of the best ls, germination after 4–5 weeks, transplant tiny tubers with about four leaves into pots, keep in half shadow with further cultivation until withering, the bulbs must not be completely covered, IX to garden position, supplements of L and K, in sheltered exposures.

Cynoglossum nervosum PA RS tr O 40 VII, a bush with a width of 40 cm and prone to topple over. A newly imported Boraginea, origin unknown, rough, thick, grayish green, vigorous growth, lax shoots, apparently inclined to be pendulous, bunches of blossoms at branch ends in splendid bright dark satiny blue, regrows after cutting, securely and toughly anchored. — In tr rs, don't pamper, thinning not necessary, early to garden site, at the tops of embankments.

Cypella herberti P tu YDS O 70 VII 40. Iridea from Rio de La Plata, closely related to the Tigridias, flowers among grasses. Broad, somewhat crispy sheath-like leaves, from between them a succession of short-lived flowers, each with three petals, around a bowl-shaped throat, crumpled and twisting and golden yellow with dark brown spots. *C. plumbea*, Argentina or Brazil, similar, leaves more creased, dull blue-gray with leather brown, very showy. — In sl slightly covered, fresh seeds germinate immediately, thin in trays, leave them in place until withering, they often bloom in as early as the following year.

Dahlia maxonii P tu LEMD, spaded before planting, O, 500 and more, X and later, 200. An arboreal dahlia of imposing size from Guatemala, its tuber a giant star-shaped bulb, its trunk as thick as a fist and with knots that send out meter-long branches of foliage resembling elderberry leaves; inflorescences stand at the summit and are over a meter tall, with tier after tier and sub-tier of Cattleya-colored cups. Planting in pots anticipates normal November flowering by about three weeks, the pots buried in the ground. The lovelier *D. imperialis*, slightly smaller in all proportions and daintier, bears inflorescences with pendant, reflex, lily-like flowers of the pink-to-white magnolia scale with a crimson, golden gullet, one of creation's greatest wonders: blooms in Europe at the end of November. — Normal seeding, March, keep warm, in rich sandy earth, every seed sure to germinate, quickly continue cultivation, transplant to the open when pencil thick, with a hefty subsoil layer of stall manure and leaf mold, water abundantly, and weekly treatments of liquid dung, will blossom a meter tall in the very first year if provided with a warm, sunny southern exposure, protected from northern and easterly winds. The *merckii*, a dwarf dahlia, 70 VII 30, Mexico, pretty foliage, small cups in tender resplendent lilac, an exotic "meadow flower." — Store all bulbs frost free beneath heaps of ashes.

Delphinium The new California species *linariaefolium*, *trolliifolium*, *tricorne*, *luposum* still untested, under observation. Bulb-building P tu LRKS, ○ to ◐ (with caution). *D. sulphureum* from Abyssinia, 100 VII 40, a splendid, noble, golden staff, notched and highly fibrous leaves; the variety from Kenya much the same, dark blue, with pale crowfoot foliage, medium size; *cardinale* as above, a broader bearing, dusky coppery flame red; *nudicaule*, a hood-shaped form, dull brick red, only 50 cm tall, both Californian. — Seeded in ys, sprouts after 23–25 days, instantly thin in pot, to garden site with their clumps of root-filled earth. The clods of earth must not fall off, disturbance leads to wilting, most often to withering of the tiny tuber; in the first year only attend to carefully, never disturb, if foliage in any case withers, mark the spot. California varieties do well in rock gardens, on terraces, or at their edges. — *D. cashmirianum* with a generous addition of leaf mold, only 60, VII, slightly villous, large more fluted flowers, from a distance seems like a Campanula; *brunonianum*, western China, much the same, dusky blue, sweet smelling, unsightly bearing. From China: *bicolor*, powerful blue with brown scar, voluminous, highly moisture sensitive, drain its site with stone gravel; *grandiflorum*, with wonderful cultivars (Blue Butterfly, Blue Gem), glowing gentian blue and white, low, with myriad thin, stiff branches, demands much humus;

additional D. The commercial forms *barlowii, formosum, bellamosum* (*belladonna* crossed with *formosum*), *speciosum,* all presumably of hybrid origin, with more or less largish blossoms in exquisite deep marine blue, 120/60. *Duhmbergii* and *pylzowii,* Siberian, naked voluminous branches with impure flowers, but which visibly improve under cultivation; *vestitum* a splendid Himalayan species, the whole plant woolly, deep violet flowers in tall inflorescences, up to 200, older plants spectacular. The *cheilanthum,* Portugal, north Africa, atypical, with a loose, gray, sub-tomentose build, ash lilac blossoms, 100 VII; *welbyi,* related, smaller, grayish blue. Present-day stocks give the garden's every corner its own breed of delphiniums. — All seeded essentially as above, with immediate thinning nearly all bloom the first year. Commercially offered true-to-type seeds of white *Delphinium hybridum* with generally impure colors, little vigor, meager flowering; the most satisfying true-to-type hybrid seeds, the mauve-colored (*Wrexby, Samson*) sorts with enormous inflorescences of mainly thickly-filled, carnation-like blossoms, up to 300, as well as races produced by Blackmore & Langdon, and Thomson & Morgan's first class mixture (*Superb*), a fifth of which are continuations of the most exquisite brand-name sorts, and the best of which, in a few years time, can be multiplied tenfold. All delphiniums are lusty gourmandizers, demanding constant additional nourishment, even in the deeply aired and humus-rich soil that has to be prepared for them. They hate greedy neighbors. The hybrids regress after 4–5 years and must be newly transplanted; they otherwise revert to species norm.

Dendromecon rigidum Ph bushy YS O, taller than a full-grown man, VIII 150, a splendid arboreal poppy, California, with gray-green foliage, golden yellow, reflex, cup-shaped blossoms (cyclamen form). — In y with 1/3 s, a little plaster rubble, seeds seldom fresh and often lie dormant for as much as a year, in pots until growth is sure, transplant to garden only when strong, and to sunny, sheltered well-drained sites. Related to China's *Eomecon sinense*, with white flowers and sadly no longer found in commerce, a plant of great nobility.

Dianthus winteri Of unknown origin, most likely *hybridus hortensis*, recently introduced, a feathery, pulvinate carnation that develops in its very first year into richly blooming cushions of simple to half-filled flowers of every possible color, in various zones, with a sweet and powerful odor; a healthy and vigorous plant throughout, and with older plants in astounding masses on dry stone walls. — In pure sand, press but do not cover, keep in shade, carefully sprinkle with fine sand once germination begins, carefully water from below when cotyledons start to form, thin with two small sticks into ys, transplant again, as little bushes, to garden site. P YS with good R and K, thorough drainage, O, protect when winters are wet.

Diascia barberae AP SYK with additions of H, O 50 VII up to 50. South African Scrophulariacea, with snapdragon needs and habitats. Delicately built, stemmed flower, gracious foliage, an unusual, reclining habit and a great abundance of small, double-spurred blooms in salmon pink, with curious, capricious faces, survives at length in warm, dry terrain, among the very best of cliff-side plants. — Seed like the snapdragon, thinning not necessary, promptly transplant to garden site, for dry stone walls.

Dicranostigma franchetianum AB deep YSR tr, O, up to 200 VI 40. A new Papaveracea from western China with beautifully undulated gray-green sheaths of typically Meconopsis foliage at the base of tall, richly branching, frosty-bluish shafts, buds a frosty violet, and abundant, glowing, buttercup-yellow blossoms, voluminous bearing, in overall effect like the horned poppies. Shorter and with smaller flowers in the case of first year blooming. — in ys, seeding bowls to be kept in shade in the open air, sprouts after 3–4 weeks, leave unthinned until at least five leaves appear, transplant to garden site when already strong; despises moisture, therefore slopes and declivities, in the neighborhood of Michauxia, Campanula peregrina, Campanula phyctidocalix.

Dierama pulcherrima P tu SHTR ○ and ◐, up to 100 and more, VIII 40. A tall South African Iridea, the narrowest, toughest, ribbon-shaped leaves with stemmed, upshooting panicles that slowly release, like quaking grass, a growth of buds on hair-thin threads which turn into pendulous sky blue bells; sheer enchantment; forms in pink and white have also been developed. Setting and cultivation like *Dierama* [...]. Blooms at the earliest after three years, fertile blades don't grow until after clumps have formed. Cover in winter with leaves, as a precaution.

Digitalis canariensis P YK ○ 90 VIII 50. A Canary Islands foxglove, with a stiff, leathery, ground-hugging rosette and a stem that's charged with angular, bronze-colored bell-shaped flowers; stiff, hard, magnificent carriage. — Seed very sparsely in 1/3 c, 1/3 s, 1/3 y, thin, transplant the most developed, plant when strong at garden site. In larger groups, only in characteristic surroundings; for rock gardens, in fissures near Felicia bergeriana.

Dimorphotheca ecklonis PhA YKS ○ 60 and more, VII 50. A suffrutescent Composita from the Cape of Good Hope, with abundant leaves on strong, fresh green shoots that turn woody close to the ground, creating thick, knotty bush; at the ends of the powerful stems, large, solitary, bluish-whitish star-shaped flowers with rounded petals, a bluish underside, and a small blue central eye. — Seed in sy, slow development, thin out the stronger, transplant seedlings to garden site as soon as they grow robust; they only grow tall in the first year and do not bloom, maturity in 2–3 years. A lovely form, plant close to Aster capensis, Pyrethrum partheniifolium in large rock gardens, in protected exposures, is damaged by harsh winds.

Downingia elegans pulchella A SH over a deep bed of gravel, ◐ 15 VII 10. Mexican Lobeliacea, from stony, jungle terrain.

An extremely graceful herb with marbled pixie faces in gentian blue, white and yellow, superabundant blossoms, extremely shy of moisture. — In pure h, uncovered, shaded, germinated seeds give a fine grass, do not thin, instead transplant whole tufts into sh; leave only one plant standing, disturb no further till strong, transplant into fissures in piles of stones which have been filled with SH and protected from heavy rains by overhanging rock. The charm of the plants is sufficient reward for all such efforts in cultivation, with normal planting they immediately die.

Echium. The species of "The Islands of the Blessed" are easily raised from seed and after transplanting grow quite impressive in the same year as sown, but do not survive the winter except in special exposures in England and on the shores of Lake Constance. They need rich, porous soil. Instructions on pot cultivation are not necessary here. *E. creticum,* a worthless weed. *E. plantagineum,* even in its improved commercial forms, can very much be done without. Walls with southern exposures and glass protection in winter should lead to favorable results, but no personal experience can here be offered.

Erodium pelargoniflorum P SLY ○ 30 IV–V 40. South African Geraniacea, rocky terrain. Tall, woolly, bushy, robust plant with luxuriant foliage around countless central flower stalks with a profusion of whitish-pinkish blossoms showing lively striations like those of the Pelargonium, highly eloquent. — In y with 50% s, thin when the plants have two leaves, promptly to garden site where it often flowers the first year, and later grows ever more beautiful. Thorough drainage. Same blossoming period as the primrose, blossoms long-lasting.

Eryngium pandanifolium P ZY ○ 400 VII 200. Giant thistle from the Andes, similar to the agave. Stiff, gigantic, leathery rosettes, protected by thorns like those of the agave, give rise in spring to tree-tall flower-bearing shafts, highly branched, with small, crude, spherical button flowers, of no account. — Seeded in sy, normally thinned plants grow rapidly; tolerates transplanting even at an early age, indestructible. Preferably the poorest earth, given measureless development in richer soils, or the latter only in situations of total isolation. A powerful, defining feature of its landscape. *E. bromeliaefolium,* somewhat smaller, same procedures.

Erysimum pulchellum, pumilum, purpureum P KYGr ○ 15 IV, V 10. Cliffside Cruciferae of Mediterranean coasts and higher mountain elevations. Small, flat rosettes and short-stemmed flowers with thick umbrellas of blossoms on the yellow-orange-violet scale of fresh springtime colors. — In ysk, then thin, then redistribute with several leaves, transplant before September to garden site, into wide cliff fissures; in year one the plants must firmly root in order to be able to survive the winter. Rock garden pearls, seen far too seldom; remain demure, whereas other *Erysimums* grow immediately tall, then gaunt and ugly.

Erythrina bidwillii P-bush ⌒, in raw exposures ⊓, LEMD ○ 100 VII 100. Arboreal Leguminosa from eastern India. The most beautiful of the tropics' cockscomb and bean trees, with bunches of protruding, dangling, drooping rods among bright, green leaves, then turning into panicles of enormous, deep crimson blossoms. Perfect flowers, free from the hard red tones of the other *Erythrinas,* in a deep, glowing, silkily enameled color. — The beans, warm, in sd, at best in trays in the hothouse, very moderately damp, and no less so after thinning first to smaller and then into larger pots, to garden site only when tubers are solid and robust. Drapes wonderfully from the edges of terraces. A heap of ash for winter protection, or ⊓, but in that case keep totally dry.

Eschscholtzia caespitosa A S or SYK ○ 8-10 IV–V 10. California Papaveracea. "Eschscholtzia grass." Forms delicate, balanced, miniature gray-green bushes in which primrose-yellow poppy flowers stand up straight and tall. — Can be sown anywhere in the rock garden, or on open terrain, also in fall. Desert gardens, dry stone walls. The other *Eschscholtzias* PAh, true shrubs, turn woody in dry, warm exposures and yearly grow more beautiful, with ever larger blossoms, only then becoming truly themselves.

Eucharidium breweri A YR ○ 60 V 40. California Onogracea. A very pretty plant related to the Clarkias; gray-green lance-shaped leaves like those of the willow-herb; when sown in place in fall on soil that's not too light, it develops great heaps of flower-studded vegetation, in mounds across the ground; properly nourished, the tattered, foamy, lilac-colored blossoms develop a glowing silky tone. A space-filling plant in broad, flowered tracts, like Cupheas; goes to seed, spontaneous propagation.

Eucomis P tu DRLM ○ ◐ 60 VIII 40. South African Liliacea, on rich moist soils. These fairy-tale plants that resemble Bromelias have large bulbs that develop great palmettes of richly undulated, deep green leaves, mainly with conspicuous crimson-blackish dots; from the center of the leaves a powerful shaft, its whole length covered, like the pineapple plant, with small, stemless, scale-like, star-shaped flowers, greenish-white, often with dots, and at its summit a great tufted pineapple flower. — In sd in rows, lightly cover, press well, provide with shade, keep warm, do not disturb, sprouts in four weeks. Dig out the tubers when they reach the size of a pea, continue cultivation in trays with dsm, bulbs when the size of a hazelnut to sheltered garden position. Blooms in 4–5 years. Heaps of ash as ⌒: No strong colors nearby, white Crinum, Zephyranthes candida, Hymenocallis, Aquilegia viridiflora, Thalictrum dipterocarpum var. alba, Benninghausenia, Eupatorium ageratoides, Alstroemeria psittacina viridis.

Euphorbia heterophylla APh DRS ◐ 90 (with thorough-going cultivation) VII 40. The Mexican wolfsmilk bush, woody. This lovely plant—also known as the Mexican fire plant, and the poor man's Poinsettia—presents naked shafts with bunches of deep dark green, round-edged wolfsmilk leaves that rise into bright-red to rose-pink bracts with tiny, nearly invisible flowers. — The spherical seeds half warm in pots, cover relatively heavily, with sl, they quickly sprout, thin into rows in trays, still subsequent thinning results in stronger plants. The same demands as Poinsettia for richness of soil, moisture and exposure; belongs in half-shaded, nicely moist terrain, where it reaches full development. *E. marginata* with foliage mottled white, white bracts, known as "snow on the mountains," has a stiffer carriage and needs full sun, but is also grateful for additional humus; A ○ 100 VII 40. *E. heterophylla* should be potted before winter, radically pruned, kept dry. Its classification as annual, an old wives' tale.

Exacum affine A ⊓ TMS in open summer fields ◐ to ● 20 VII 20. Gentianacea of tropical America, in the humus of the Brazilian rain forest. The small plant quickly takes the form of a miniature tree with thick, regularly branching, pale-green foliage studded with small, round, orchid-lilac-colored flowers with a sweet, slightly bitter smell. — In hothouse trays in hs, only press the seeds, spray lightly with a vaporizer, cover with glass and dark paper, air briefly every day, keep glass dry, sprouts after 20 days, thin, do not disturb, remove the more developed plants to trays with old h and sifted peat, somewhat sandy; rapid development, keep shaded and in open air during summer heat; to garden site in the above-described mixture of soils at midsummer, warm, shaded, moist terrain. Lives in the same conditions as Impatiens holstii sultani, long since cultivated in open fields. Delightful in abundant quantities.

Felicia Annuals: *bergeriana* A (?) SLH ○ 5 VI and VII up to 30. South African Composita, precise place of origin unknown. This magnificent dwarf, one of recent years' most lovely new importations, forms small, ground-hugging mats with creeping, dark-green tendrils and tongue-shaped leaves, and, rising above them, small, star-shaped, daisy-size flowers with petals of a fisher martin or hummingbird blue, a color never found in nature in any other flower, and a mild yellow central disk. The rolled-up petals stretch fully out only in sunlight. — In sy in rows, repeatedly thin so as to strengthen the plants before transplanting to garden site. The plant is difficult to keep alive under normal garden conditions, where its root collar usually grows diseased during blooming, but it likewise fails on shelves of rock and develops well only in dry but rich terrain. It survives on slopes in light, porous soil, but remains unimpressive. When planted, however, between loose stones in the rock garden in the mixture described above, with the further addition of a measure of light, sifted loam, it blooms in abundance and runs its course. A luxury undeserved by all who aren't disposed to offer it every extra attention. *F. tenella*, the same as above, tiny nests with small, blue, dainty daisy flowers, less delicate, the blue of the petals pure, petals somewhat longer, porous terrain. *F. rotundifolia* P LKSH 10 VII 30, small South African perennials, for the terraces of ordinary rock gardens, large flowers, pure blue petals, a transitional form toward Aster capensis.

Fuchsia Ph-shrub *fulgens* P tu LHDRS ◐ 100 VIII, IX 50. Peruvian Onogracea. Bulb-building plants with soft, pendulous shoots; long, flesh-colored, cylindrical corollas from short violet crowns. — In moist sh with absolute shade, warm, germination unpredictable, tiny, bright green seedlings immediately thinned with the point of a pin into th, keep strictly in shade, warm, not hot, spray lightly, do not drown, raise in pots in shady places in the mixture as above, blooms first year. The *var. President Goselli* more colorful. The Columbian *corymbiflora*, an arboreal fuchsia, up to 300 VIII 100, in the mixture above, same seeding procedure, a slim tree with large, pointedly elliptical leaves, dull mat green with red veins, the ends of its branches with pendulous bunches of long, cylindrical, crimson reddish flowers from short crowns of a lighter red. Blooms the second year. Prune radically before repotting, eliminating weaker shoots. A handsome and easily cultivated plant, effective in landscape gardens only when the impression of natural vegetation is preserved, so never in isolation.

Funkia liliiflora. Seeds of the only *Funkia* truly worth cultivation, in the highest sense, are commercially unavailable.

Gaillardia picta AP YS ○ 80 VII 45. Composita of the flowering grasslands of Texas and northern Mexico. This sparsely leafed and voluminous plant with a typical steppe habit has thin, hard branches, somewhat rough and often twisted, and covered with handsome, wine-red pistils with notched rims and yellow-tipped petals; a somber form, severe and with character. A more beautiful species than the full, played-out *lorenziana.* In arid soils a true bush, every year richer and with flowers of ever more perfect form; with appropriate care, the growths take on more branches, stems are shorter and stronger, yet the plant tends still to grow full. — In ys, no further cultivation. Seedlings set out in fall give more abundant blossoms.

Galtonia candicans P bu RDS 100 VII 40. South African Liliacea. From a limp rosette of fresh green, fluted leaves, a powerful round shaft up to a meter tall with a pyramid of large, short-stemmed, stiffly pendulous "snowbell" (Levcojum) blossoms, pure white. — Sown as normal for bulbed plants, undemanding seedlings develop quickly, often blooming in the first year, surely in the second. Full beauty only when the bulbs reach maximum size, with bellflowers more than a meter tall rising in expanses of Iridaceae over gladiolas and Montbretias, at the side of the tallest Kniphofias.

Gaura lindheimeri AP Y ○ 150 VII 50. Onogracea of Texas and northern Mexico. Habit of the willow-herb with slender, pendulous, woody stems and spotted, tongue-shaped, closely adhering leaves, white terminal inflorescences that blend to pink as the flower fades, and with crimson stamens; the overall effect of the blossoming branch of a fruit tree, tender and graceful. Blooms in its first year. — The hard seeds in ys, where dormancy persists for weeks, thin promptly for rapid further cultivation, in Y at garden site. Not for flat expanses, to be allowed to dangle over edges. Leave unsheltered in warm soils and exposures, otherwise a heavy covering of leaves. Too beautiful a plant to be allowed every year to freeze.

Gazania AP P South African Compositae, even for the reputedly A. The *longiscapa* DHRS in four equal parts, leaning toward a bit more sand, ○ 30 VIII 40, sprawls along the ground. Dark green, creeping, fluted leaves, silver on their underside, somewhat fleshy, the growing shoots becoming robust stems with flowers a wheel of dark yellow petals, at its middle a black, white-eyed zone designed to frighten and a yellow disk; cultivated forms with enormous flowers, color variations to fire orange, of great magnificence. — The shelled, wrinkly seeds into very sandy y, water with caution, thin into more substantial earth, do not pamper, promptly out into the open air. Hybrid *splendens* and other botanists' varieties with long, creeping shoots require quite sandy soil, but also abundant nourishment; in all colors of fire, copper, rust, with and without central markings. Highly porous soils.

Gerbera jamesonii P very rich DHRSM ○ and ◐ 40 VII 40. Transvaal Composita, known as "the Transvaal Daisy." Markedly undulated sleeves of large, stiff, dark green leaves around a silky stalk surmounted by a great, star-shaped flower from vermilion pink to carnelian orange with long, pointed petals around a small, maize-colored disk with a list toward pink; reflowers again and again. — The needle-thin, blade-like seeds will germinate only if inserted point down into holes, in dry sy, water cautiously even from below, seed will die from excess moisture; do not thin, forcing the plants is useless; when the plants have four or five leaves, remove to deep thinning trays, with an addition of manure soil, then into the open, in a sheltered place.

Gerberas root deeply, and die in rock gardens if their roots encounter underground obstacles. The stiff bearing and pointed petals of the countless brightly-colored hybrids make for a particularly aggressive, mannered, affected habit: fashionable cut flowers, useless for the garden; though the natural species may be bizarre, they remain unrivaled by the hybrids.

Gilia A S with additions of H and R, Polemoniaceae of California and New Mexico, in deserts and flowering prairies. The *abrotanifolia*, *achilleaefolia* and *capitata*, 40–60 V, ca. 30, foliage green to gray green, linty and sometimes fibrous; umbrella-like flower clusters from whitish blue to lilac; the whole very light and delicate in bearing, tissues, transparency of color. The *aggregata* and *coronopifolia* (also known as the Ipomopsis), the former 50, the latter up to 100, B, slender and candle-like with stiff, spreading, needle- and hair-like foliage, from burning scarlet to vermilion red, dotted with long, cylindrical flowers. The dwarf *Gilias* that take the name of *Leptosiphon*, inclusive of *G. dianthoides*, build small thick or rigid cushions of serrated foliage with the daintiest of pink and bluish chalices, these too A. — The A species in the open air, the B species in sh, very thinly seeded, kept very dry, housed in well-drained pots in the open, frost-free in winter in a bright, dry unwarmed greenhouse; avoid all moisture on the leaves, water only from below and only when thoroughly necessary; to garden site in the second year. — Except for the stiff and insignificant *tricolor*, a summer flower for smaller gardens, *Gilias* are unable to hold their own and lose their colors and visibility (are simply overlooked) when planted too close to the flowers of temperate alluvial regions. In strong, healthy sunshine and proximity to the sea, these delicate triumphs of color, from pure light and pure sand, create a world of special forms that define a particular landscape. For sand gardens, among their bulbs and bushes.

Glaucidium palmatum P SLY ◐ 35 VII 30. Papaveracea of the

mountains of Japan, in shadier locales. Gray-green to green-gray foliage, like that of the horned poppies, broad, notched leaves, gray flower stems with pointed buds, and large, very beautiful, pale-lilac flowers with golden pistils. — In syh in small furrows, seeds remain long dormant; thin; do not remove to trays before the growing seeds get in each others' way. Then, as above, into deep-soiled, well drained trays. Transplant to the open in September. Observation remains to be made on how this lovely new plant adapts to garden conditions.

Glaucium anatolyjaënsis AP SY ○ 100 VII 50. Anatolian Papaveracea. Sleeve a dull gray-blue, hard and with crinkly edges, strongly nerved, stands close to its neighbors with the overall effect of a thick, bushy bearing; moderately branching flower stem, large, deep orange to ocher poppy flowers, speckled, in transition to *G. leiocarpum.* Majestic, imposing, unique creature. — Seeding like Glaucidium. — Only recently imported, yet already no longer to be found in commerce.

Godetia hybr. hort. carminea-aurea 40–50 cm, hybrid cultivar of California's *Oenothera amoena,* large deep carmine flowers with broad, lively, yellow rims. An especially beautiful and surprising variety, 30, with small white flowers, on every petal a sharply circumscribed red fleck. The *Mandarin* variety, 40, greenish, yellowish, silky chalices, abundant blossoms. — The one-sided breeding of *Godetias* for use in "colorsheets" has forced these lovely species, a joy of older gardens, out of commerce; they're nowhere any longer to be found, and should all be newly bred from the pink and yellow *Oenotheras* which originally were crossed to obtain them.

Habranthus (Amaryllis) pratensis P bu RDMS ○ 60 VIII 40. Amaryllidea of higher Brazilian elevations, survives in good exposures without ⌒. A smaller version of *Hippeastrum vittatum,* a supremely beautiful scarlet lily; seeded like the Amaryllis; blooms a year and a half after seeding.

Hebenstreitia comosa serratifolia AP KY ○ up to 80 VII 40. North African Resedacea. Thick bunches of tongue-shaped leaves and long, flexible, weakly-constructed stems covered with small, reddish-greenish, mignonette-type flowers with a highly noble fragrance. — Normal seeding, fairly hardy, blossoms the first year. Must be placed where it isn't expected.

Heliophila leptophylla and *linearifolia* A, A SY ○ 30 to 40 VI 20. South African Cruciferae. These lobelia-blue Cruciferae with extremely delicate build and never-tiring blossoming belong to recent years' most beautiful new introductions. — Seed in the open. More robust neighbors heighten their effect; for rock gardens, sand gardens, they flourish exemplarily in humus-rich sandy soils. Among Nemesias, which lack these tones; also with lobelias, such as the tenuior and ramosa, which the *linearifolia* greatly resembles, to the point of being mistaken for it. Near Ursinias.

Hesperis nivea P KSYD ○ 50 VII 40. Crucifera of the higher Greek mountains. From gray-white, tongue-shaped, stock-type leaves that hug the ground, a short, rising shaft thick with snow-white, sweet smelling blossoms, of pure, noble form. — Seed like stock, promptly thin, allow to thirst, the root collar is highly sensitive to moisture; to garden site only when fully formed. Thick subsoil layer of gravel indispensable, the plant in its native habitat grows on stone rubble. *H. tristis*, the old "night violet" with insignificant flowers, same cultivation, but common garden soil, nearly no longer planted, yet its loss would rob the garden of its finest, richest, night and evening perfume.

Hibiscus diversifolius† A LY ○ 50 VI creeps for as much as 120 cm. Malvacea of tropical Africa. Departing from the base of the principal stem, which bears arrow-shaped three-pointed leaves, ground creepers move off in every direction, covering the ground with a thick mat from which new flowers spring; flowers are large, moist and lemon yellow with a crimson gullet and golden pistils protruding from a bright green navel, highly expressive; blossoming ground shoots give the impression of fallen but still living flowers. — Normal seeding, thin promptly, very rapid development. Transplanting however causes a notable suspension in growth, since the plant takes some time to establish its roots. Seeding in the open possible only in warmer areas.

Homeria collina and *var. aurantiaca* P bu SDLR ○ 45 VI 20. Liliacea of the Cape of Good Hope. The telescoped and slightly crinkly canes release a splendid orange to vermilion flower, often with a yellow eye, in form like the Acidanthera flower, colors glowingly pure. — Seeded like Dierama, to garden site in fall, protect in rawer climates, or reserve for sheltered spaces, blooms the second year.

Hunnemannia fumariaefolia AP SKR tr ○ 80 VII 40. California Papaveracea. Moist, shimmering, blue gray greenish leaves, daintily dentellated. Roots thicken out into club shape, the plant would like to be arborescent, the flowers rigid tulip bells on long stems, solid tissues, lemon yellow with a soft, deep quiver. (Keeps for a week in water.) — Seeding: one cuts out squares of grass with a spade, turns them over, and smoothes their earthy side as well as possible, waters them well, leaves them lying for several days, gives them a sprinkling of fine sand, then works it lightly into the soil with a small wooden stick; one sows the relatively large-sized seeds (the size of cabbage seed) by pressing them into the soil, sifts them over with sand, places the clods in empty crates, which then are stored in the shade; shoots appear after twenty days; thin out the plants to 4 cm between them, allow them to grow robust. When the plants show a pair of feather-shaped leaves, use a sharp knife to cut up the clods into as many squares as plants, then place each square

†The plant which appears in botanical literature as *Hibiscus diversifolius* (the swamp Hibiscus) shows little if any resemblance to the one to which Borchardt ascribes this name. The plant to which Borchardt refers remains unclear. The description here is also slighty at variance with the description offered in Chapter IV, p. 86.— H.M.

at its previously well-worked garden site. Following these instructions, along with the use of nourishing, well-drained, chalky earth, assures successful development. T in winter is sufficient to assure their survival.

Iberis linifolia B YSK ○ 45 IX, Z 40. Crucifera from Asia Minor. The rich, pale lilac inflorescences of this lovely autumn-blooming shrub enlivens rock gardens at their moment of greatest emptiness. Its dark green foliage the narrowest tongues, its bearing erect and gracious. — Normal seeding, in fall at garden site, slightly prune the shoots; it blooms at the very same time as Zauschneria, their colors harmonize.

Impatiens olivieri P DMLS ●. Balsaminea of tropical eastern Asia. The palmettes that rise sleeve-like from node to node up turgid, viscous shafts conclude at the summits of a sap green structure in sterile tufts, beneath which hang, on slender threads, the large, spurred, milky lilac mask-shaped flowers so similar to Miltonia orchids as even to be mistaken for them. — In sd, very warm, moist and shady, remove immediately after sprouting to the same soil mixture in small pots, and then with the arrival of certain summer heat transplant with their clods of root-filled earth to shady garden corners with rich, porous humus. In masses, for a powerful effect. Retransplant to pots with the same earth mixture before cold nights return, prune, keep half warm and dry throughout the winter. Every section of the stems, inserted in the hothouse into hs, roots within 14 days.

Incarvillea olgae P YSL ○◐ 90 VII 40. Bignoniacea, from northern China through southern Mongolia to Siberia, a woodland bush of deciduous forests, in form like foxglove, erect, with nicely dentellated foliage, and pendulous, thickly placed, lilac pinkish trumpets, a unique and highly noble form. *I. variabilis* A Ph YS ○ 40 VIII 40, uncertain native habitat, smaller yellowish fading to pinkish, also pinkish to lilac trumpets on wire-thin stems, extremely elegant, still not widely seen, the color scale of the freesias. — Both with large seeds in sl, germination in 3–4 weeks, normal further rearing, the *variabilis* early to garden site, on slopes, which it mounts and beautifully covers, among poppy species, like Papaver atlanticum and californicum.

Ipomoea setosa A ↟ LDRK ◐ also ○ VIII-IX. Convolvulacea of tropical America. Enormous grapevine leaves, stems thickly covered with stiff red hairs, highly rampant, flowers a milky orchid lilac with a crimson gullet, white pistils, faint odor. —Large seed in moist, warm hs, thin into pots, to garden site when nights are no longer cool; flowering must be forced by pruning all new shoots as soon as the plant has reached the height desired; the plant will finally obey and leaf axils send out short, flowering tendrils with numerous buds. — The lovely *saguinea*, with small, luminous, bright red flowers, has now for many years been unavailable in commerce; likewise for the heavily fragrant *umbellata*, in need of greater warmth and with even smaller flowers, white, in bunches, and in form like those of the Mandevillea; and again for the velvet red *scarlatina*, with the fingers of its lovely, deep-cut foliage. The *preacox* variety of the *rubrocoerulea* which today is generally sold shows little vigor and bears few blossoms. The species is preferable to the variety, and can be forced to flower as above; grown over criss-crossed hoops for wonderful sky-blue bowers.

Ismelia coronopifolia Ah (?) YS 100 or more VII 100. A reputedly annual California Composita. The loose, dentellated foliage, reminiscent of swine cress, branches always sideways as it grows, resulting in a tangled, airy, regularly spherical bush, studded with countless simple, white, star-shaped flowers. Since it grows in a single year, the plant is invaluable for the temporary enlivenment of barren spaces, but in any case is charming and good. (Exclusively from Haage & Schmidt).

Isotoma petraea PA LYRS ◐ to ○. Violacea of uncertain origin, a very pretty pseudo-violet, violet in color, with abundant blossoms, creates small clumps between stones, long stems, effective only in groups. — In ys, thin, transplant promptly to garden site, in good exposures needs no ⌒; branches of fir prove sufficient in others.

Ixiolirion tataricum P bu YS ○ 80 VII 40. Amaryllidacea of the near Eastern steppes, also known as "the blue narcissus." Foliage in the form of steppe grass, with loose clumps of violet, dull-blue flowers which from a distance resemble the narcissus, uniquely beautiful. — In ys, slightly covered, half warm, shaded. Germination unpredictable; thin seedlings after they develop some 4–5 stalks of grass; late bloomers, bulbs form very slowly.

Kniphofia P tu DRMS ○. South African Liliaceae, same cultivation for all: *rufa* 90 VI 40, blooms repeatedly, with tall, peaked roofs of copper-red spicules, very beautiful; *tuckii* VI 40, yellow, delicate, ⌒. —Press seeds into drs, cover slightly, provide with shade, every kernel sprouts, with the point of a needle thin out seedlings even with seed still attached. Allow to strengthen, no further disturbance until the base of the seedlings is a pencil thick. Then to garden site. Though constant hybridization has produced show plants, it has also suppressed a number of highly distinctive species and as well had the sad effect of making commercially available seed quite undependable; worst of all, it's nearly impossible now to obtain true seed, as with the *aloides*, of which the commercial seed produces only hybrids: the true plant has a very different appearance.

Lachenalia. These magnificent Liliaceae from the Cape of Good Hope, with hyacinth forms and the most unimaginable combinations of colors, are extremely easy to raise from seed, but do not survive winter frost and in part bloom too precociously. In warmer locales on the Channel Islands, they make themselves thoroughly at home, but must nonetheless be dug up after blossoming, since they have to experience a dry season. Acclimatization would involve no more than the tasks which the Dutch of former eras carried out so beautifully; such work is more important than hybridization.

Lardizabala biternata Ph ≸ LYK ◐ III–IV. Chilean Lardizabalacea. A climbing shrub with abundant foliage of round, slit, lightly frosted, doubly trilobed leaves and sweet-smelling, violet flower clusters; in sheltered exposures needs no ⌒. —Seeds often lie dormant at length, easily rot, very sandy soil, pieces of charcoal in seeding earth, and as well: old, thoroughly seasoned l; thin in its pot. Seed now nowhere stocked, formerly with Haage & Schmidt; much more beautiful and with far more character than the related, everywhere common Japanese Akebia.

Lavatera assurgentiflora P-bush YSL ○ 300 VIII 300. Near Eastern Malvacea with smallish, fresh green leaves and a compact body with numerous stems, quickly reaches the height of a man, then filling out to the sides and below, blooms abundantly with pretty, fresh red, mallow-type blossoms; wants sheltered positions, but not in isolation, will die from broken stems from wind exposure. — Normal seeding in ys in furrows, easily germinates, thin into pots; seedlings very hardy. In flowering meadows, over shorter plants, scattered.

Leonotis leonorus AP-shrub LYSK ○ 200:100, flowering: as annual in July, older plants in late fall; Labiata from California (?), if that's its true native habitat (?) — there are reasons to believe it comes from Africa. A strong, woody shrub with erect branches and a dense foliage of dentellated leaves, the whole plant with a strong aroma of sage, the foliage arranged in whorls; tiers of buds at branch ends appear in October; large, flaming, brick-brown, slightly woolly sage-type blossoms encircle the branches, above one another, in rings, standing out horizontally, gullets downward, like water spigots. — Large seeds in normal ys, thin promptly, transplant promptly to open air where development is uncommonly fast; soft, non-woody shoots give abundant blossoms mainly in July, so training the plant to bush form serves to provide for blossoming branches up until November. Winter in ⊓; after potting prune away all woody stems (if not keeping them for the purpose mentioned above) preserving only the principal trunk. An incomparable sight in full bloom.

Lepachys columnaris (of which *pulcherrima* is only a variety) AP YS O 60 VIII 40. Composita, Texas. This exaggerated Rudbeckia, reducing here to nothing more than a protuberant, conical receptacle and a few vestigial, stunted disk flowers, is given charm and character by the small, reflex ray flowers that support the cone from below like rings of golden foam. Light, loose construction, small, segmented leaves. — In ys, normal seeding, promptly to garden site, which must be open, visible, and isolated; the plant is a specialized concentration of its genus, as developed on mountain terrain; for slopes, along with Stokesia cyanea, propped up with stones.

Leptosyne A (P) light SDRK, O, California Compositae, *arborea (gigantea)* up to 100, arborescent, VI, 50, with a ground level club-shaped thickening, moist, slimy, sap-rich crown of a dark green color, foliage richly fringed, large, undulated star-shaped flowers in soft, luminous, canary yellow; *stillmanni*, rapid blossoming (V) A, 30:30, more frail in all its parts; *maritima* SD, "the beach Coreopsis," with large-sized flowers. — All *L.* in 50% sand, thinned out into stronger soil. They flourish only in the lightest, most porous soils, and otherwise die before fully grown. Semi-succulent constitution rules out sites that are constantly watered.

Leucocoryne ixioides P bu SD O 40 V 20, Chilean Liliacea, specific locale unknown. From thin, fluted leaves, a thin, rigid, wiry stem with pale blue blossoms, whitish at the base, sweet-smelling, very fine and singular. — Cultivation is successful only as follows: seeds in a large pot with sdy, well sifted and mixed and with excellent drainage, seeds slightly pressed into the soil, sprinkle, lightly cover, keep half warm, provide with shade. Germination gives fine, grass-like shoots, do not thin. Water only from below, only when necessary, at most spray lightly at times of great heat; when development is well underway, move gradually, sheltered, into the open air, removing back to ⊓ in case of heavy rains. Allow to wilt in fall, empty the vases, store the small bulbs dry throughout the winter, most will bloom when replanted in spring, the development of bulbs is slow and slight. — If touched or forced in the first year, the seedlings immediately die.

Lilium Obtaining lilies from seed is entirely a question of patience and love. With normal precautions, there are no real difficulties. The seeds, lozenge-shaped platelets folded back over the germ like a doubled wafer, in color from cinnamon brown to reddish-gray, will rot if incorrectly handled. Artificial heating to hasten germination spells their ruin. In the cool house, starting in March, the seeds go into pots with old l and abundant s; the pots are sunk into beds of cold manure, and the material around the pots, but not the pots themselves, is thoroughly drenched. Germination quite regular. Thin when the cotyledons fall from the tips of the seedlings, then leave undisturbed for the first year, allowing the plants to wither; transplant the following spring to the open air. Cultivation requires particular knowledge, to be found in the specialized literature, since root structure is singular, and must be studied; different sites also call for different treatments. Some sixty species are available today as seed, and they can be grown by every gardener who's aware of their demands; in addition, some thirty individual hybrids can be had, as well as ten to twenty in mixed assortments. *Lilium tenuifolium* always flowers, *concolor* usually, *regale* often in the second year after seeding, like any other shrub; lilies raised from seed grow and bloom with exceptional vigor.

Linanthus densiflorus A S with L ○ 30 V 20, California Polemoniacea. This lily-like plant ("California Phlox") of the daintiest, glassiest structure, with fibrous leaves and hoods of lilac pink, yellow-eyed flowers that rise from the joints of branching stems, demands treatment and placement like lilies, and languishes among unsuitable neighbors.

Linaria P and A all more or less in very light SKR, ○. Scrophulariaceae, nearly all from the mountains and coasts of the Mediterranean, inclusive of Spain and North Africa. For the most part no longer cultivated, and yet the daintiest and least demanding tenants of new rock gardens whose perennial flora has just begun to be set. *Hendersoni ericoides* PA 30 VI, with heatherlike foliage, a lovely reddish lilac, highly abundant flowers, grows every year more beautiful; *macroura,* 10 with enormous spurs; *multipunctata,* with uncommonly plentiful blossoms, pale lemon yellow with splattered dots, spontaneously goes to seed into great yellow clumps of itself, blooming in March, in various corners of the rock garden; *triornithophora,* Portugal, AP, pure sand with additions of HT, smooth, blue-gray foliage, large, perfect blossoms, violet and yellow, a flower vase and a bundle of straw are enough in winter to keep this lovely plant alive; *triphylla,* P, similar, only 25, less delicate; *tristis,* very beautiful, pure yellow with a dark gullet; *verticillata,* P, yellow, 20, compact, enchanting. — Sow *triornithophora* in very dry sh, thin, move promptly to the open air; all others at garden site, with pinches of seed in cracks, corners, fissures, hollows.

Lindelofia spectabilis P R with hefty additions of K and L, ○ 60 VII 50. Boraginacea of the Himalayas, rough, dark green foliage, pointed like the leaves of the Cynoglossum, robust stalks with excellent bearing, ending in a cluster of lungwort blossoms, dark sky blue blending up from red, reddish buds and calyx throats enriching the color effect. Excellent in the company of Arnebias, Hesperis tristis, Dracocephalums. — Seed germinates after four weeks, seldom earlier, rots easily, sandy soil, thin out into deep trays. At the forward edge of the rock garden, stony corners.

Lisianthus russelianus Bh ⌒ HTRMS ◐ 50 IX 40, Mexican Gentianacea. A lovely dwarf shrub, presumably perennial in its natural habitat, with grayish leaves, a thick bushy build and large, violet, tubular, gentian-like flowers with a faint perfume. — The plant's cultivation has been turned by professional gardeners into such an occult science as to frighten away all laymen, thus forcing this lovely plant in effect to remain unknown. In the first year, like all subtropical biennials, on the order, for example of the Ipomopsis, it must mainly be kept under glass, for which a hotbed is quite sufficient. — Seed in a mixture of heath soil and old meadow soil with a large admixture of sand, well drained, do not cover the seeds, provide with shade, keep warm; commercial seed is often useless, if seeds don't sprout within eighteen days at 20° C, immediately complain, demanding replacement, this germination time has been tested; when the plants have 4–5 leaves, thin out into moor and heath soil with much sand and a bit of loam, allow them to strengthen in pots, never in the burning sun, moderate moisture; in short, common sense and good measure. In the open air, in shadow, in good weather, winter at medium warmth, in shade. In the second year, the pots will be filled with roots, transplant to larger pots with the addition of old, well-seasoned meadow soil; during midsummer heat keep mostly in a warm, shady place, and then like every other plant out into the open air, where they bloom at length and beautifully.

Lithospermum petraeum (Moltkia) Ph KRS tr ○ 30 VII 30, Boraginacea of the higher Greek mountains. This silver-gray plant with narrow tongue-shaped leaves and deep blue clusters of flowers ornaments Hellenic limestone heights. — Seed in flat, well-drained bowls (drained by pebbles) in a mixture of gravel and r; with 3–4 leaves, thin out into trays of the same mixture, gradually adding y. Must be strong and well-developed before placement out of doors, best kept as a potted plant, finds acclimatization hard. *L. graminifolium* sky blue, smaller in all its parts. *L. breviflorum* and *canescens,* both yellow to orange, up to 50 and 60, of entirely different habit, and of unknown origin, still under observation.

Lobelia P MHT moor SR ◐ and ○, Lobeliaceae of central and southern North America. Only *L. erinus*, here not discussed, a common border lobelia, from southern Africa; *ramosa* reputedly Australian. *L. cardinalis*, the Carolinas, 110 VIII 50, a thick, ground-hugging rosette beneath a strong, leafy, upright shaft with imp-faced flowers, bright scarlet red, made even more alarming by white stamens; red in all parts of the plant; damp, swampy environs, will tolerate ●. *L. fulgens*, Mexico, smaller, flowers a glowing crimson. Hybrids of both up to 150 and 180 with giant, magnificent blossoms. *L. syphilitica*, Mexico, a woodlands plant with thick, abundant, nettle-like foliage, ash-violet flowers in thick cylindrical inflorescences among the stands of leaves, as well as a lovely white variety, and a pink variety that still remains impure. *L. cavanillesii*, a splendid Mexican lobelia, P tu with white, rampant taproots (up to 80–90 VIII 100), lax, pliant, half-winding reddish shoots, green, willow-like leaves, red to rust-red tubular flowers with five yellow tips, dangling down from thin stems, very beautiful. *L. tupa*, bronze-brown imp-faced flowers, 60, moist environs. *L. glandulosa*, low (30 VII 30), solid, dark-blue inflorescences. *L. sessilifolia*, "the moor lobelia," with full-blue flowers. — All seeded the same, half warm in pure h, do not cover, provide with shade, thin directly after sprouting with the point of a needle into the same soil mixture with additional sand, keep shaded and moist; the plants at first make little progress, but then quite rapidly; as soon as they start, as is typical of the species, to "eat down" into the earth, transplant to the open air. *L. syphilitica* also tolerates full sun, the *cavanillesii* demands it, all others prefer ◐.

Lopezia coronata A SYL ○ 50–60 VIII 40, Mexican Onogracea. Nicely built gray-green plant with long shoots and pinkish whitish, crimson-spotted flowers of bizarre form perched among the leaves. — Normal seeding, like zinnias. The seeds of these lovely plants, once eagerly sought for sophisticated gardens, are hard by now to obtain (Haage & Schmidt).

Malva miniata (Malvastrum) APh SRY ○ 80 VIII 40, California Malvacea. Gray-green, heavily downy plant on arid terrain, with small, oak-shaped leaves and a rich profusion of small flowers, terracotta pink, very gracious. — Keep seed dry, water the sy only if truly necessary, in deep, well-drained trays, blooms first year. Arid slopes, the plant tends to fall.

Malvastrum coccineum PA S with additions of HT ○ 40 VIII 30, California Malvacea. The "California desert mallow," shimmering, fluffy gray, low, compact, with brick pink to rust pink blossoms. — In sht, water if needed only from below, allow to thirst, remove to sand boxes with additions of HM, then set in the desert garden along with Salvia carduacea, Gilias, bulbs.

Martynia fragrans A DMLRS ○ up to 100 VII 100, Mexican Pedaliacea. This gray-green plant with widely divaricated branchings, and everywhere bathed with a mucous secretion, presents large, open trumpet flowers, in tones from chamois yellow to chamois pink, their interior flecked with red spots and vivid yellow stripes. In form like gloxinias. — The large seeds into any warm seeding soil, with a first few leaves transplant to the open air, as soon as the season has settled. Fill a deep hole—40–50 centimeters—with the mixture indicated above, stamp firm, cover with good D, set the seedlings, heap up a mound of earth around it, thus leaving the plants in a depression, the edges of which can be watered in midsummer. The vigorously developing plants soon conceal the artificiality of the planting, and their roots, which otherwise would deplete their surroundings of all nourishment, remain deep in the ground.

Maurandia (Lophospermum) scadens, erubescens (? a variety ?) P tu ↟ LKMR ○ 300 VIII–IX, climbing Mexican Scrophulariacea with notched, pointed, slightly woolly, dull green foliage, climbing leaf peduncles, and very large, open, pink, late-blooming bells, like foxglove; *erubescens* a pure, deep, rose red. Bulbs perennial with ⌒, in any case keep frost free. — Moderately warm in sh, do not disturb until the seedlings show three tiers of leaves, then transplant to garden site. If several plants are planted, their dead leaves are highly valuable. Creepers, however, are jealous, solitary lords of their sites, even with the richest nourishment.

Melianthus major P DRLM ○ 100 and more, IV-V, 150, South African Zygophyllacea. The powerful, whitish-grayish-bluish, fan-shaped leaves with sharp tips and abundant undulations of this imposing shrub are crowned in spring by deep reddish, plum-blue panicles of flowers, rigid in shape, and with heavy drops of honey in their throats. — The large seeds willingly and easily germinate in any shady, half-warm soil, seedlings develop quite rapidly, but ought to remain in pots for the first year, then in their second spring to be transplanted out of doors in the rich mixture described above. Heaps of straw for frost protection; but plants that succumb to frost will sprout new shoots. So, protected settings not only serve as shelter from frost, but also provide the closed landscape in which these plants make their best impression: as a solitary it first of all would be overlooked, and only secondarily might suffer from cold.

Mesembrianthemum criniflorum A SZGr ○ 3 VII 40, a Mesembriacea of unknown origin, presumably a hybrid; perhaps from tropical South America. The lovely, new introduction of the most colorful and richly blossoming of all the Mesembrianthemums is of little avail, since, quite to the contrary of its admirers' claims, it simply cannot be grown in normal gardens, where the watering needs of the one are in outright opposition to the other's. Can only be grown in piles of stones, with the poorest of earth in their interstices, or in cracks and fissures in dry stone walls, where water is never sprinkled. Cultivation demands the greatest care and cunning.

Michauxia campanuloides B YSK ○ 180 VII 40, Campanulacea of Persia and Armenia. The first year's highly crinkly, protuberant rosette sends up a single robust stem with few ramifications and skewed, pendulous, whitish-pinkisk lily-like blossoms with bent-back tips and speckled interior. — Sow the fine seeds sparsely in ys, thin, then transplant larger seedlings again into ys, in deep trays, since the fleshy roots grow long; once strong, to garden site, where the basic requirement is thorough drainage; slopes. A fundamental feature of its native habitat; can be used as a fulcrum, constructing whole landscapes around it.

Mimulus AP, seldom A, HTMRS, seldom SHT ◐ to ●, North American Scrophulariaceae to as far south as Mexico. The monkey flowers, nearly all of them rank and carpeting, with pale green, moisture-loving, ground-hugging foliage, surmounted by stalks with tiered verticillate blossoms; ground runners found with even the anomalous *M. cardinalis* (up to 60 VII 40) with large, dark crimson, somewhat flattened flowers, very much demanding of expert cultivation; the monkey flowers live in woodland clearings to the side of streams and brooks: the *ringens* (up to 45 VI) dark violet and very beautiful; the high yellow *implexus*, with dark speckles, like the ground-covering *primuloides* (the former 15, the latter 10); the pink *fremontii* that grows in sandy, moor terrain (additions of SHT), an annual, some 20 cm tall; the *lewisi*, from British Columbia, with panicles of striated rose-red, throat-shaped blossoms, still under observation. — All *M.* in hs, cool and left uncovered, very sparsely seeded, thinned out into the same mixture, transplanted outdoors as soon as they start to "curl." Must always stand in places where they're least expected.

Mirabilis longiflora (violacea) AP tu RD ○◐ 100 VIII 50, a Peruvian Nyctaginacea. An exuberant plant with abundant foliage that rises from node to node, and which stands on a hefty bulb; the shoots come to an end in panicles of large-throated, sweet smelling blossoms with the form of a five-pointed chalice, and which open at night; the pale violet forms are especially beautiful. — The hard, plump seeds, warm in pots with dr, take some time before germination, but then develop quickly, and blossom the first year. Conceal in thickets; the tubers should be placed in rough terrain, and raised like potatoes.

Morina longifolia P, light KSRL on an underlying layer of gravel, ○ 70 VII, VIII 40, Dipsacacea of the limestone mountains of Greece. One of the wonders of Greek alpine flora, not easily domesticated. A thistle-like habit with extensive, well developed, undulated foliage, giving rise to a stem with a verticillate, thistle umbrella surrounded by tubular blossoms in white and scarlet pink; in full bloom, an inflorescence of extraordinary beauty and nobility. — Seeds in lr with sk, and protected from mice, which dig them up whenever possible, rapid germination, thin out into pots or deep trays. At a suitable spot in the rock garden, one then digs out a funnel-shaped hole, 60 cm wide, 70 cm deep, which is then 3/4 filled with limestone gravel and finally topped up to ground level with the mixture described above. Stir the whole with a stick until the empty spaces have filled with earth, then abundantly water, to check on drainage, and then top up again with earth, again to ground level. Dig a hole into its middle with a trowel, plant the seedling, heaping around it the quantity removed of earth and gravel. This treatment has proved to keep the plant in good condition for quite some time.

Myosotidium nobile P RHMD with a measure of S ● 50 VII 40, New Zealand Boraginacea. A stately borage plant with large, dark blue flowers, edged in white, very singular. — The large, black-hulled seeds are known to rot in 90% of all attempts at their cultivation. Placed between moist leaves, layered in sand, and stored in a warm place, they slowly sprout. A fairy-tale plant in need of winter protection.

Myosotis azorica Ph LRSK ◐ 15 VII 20, Boraginacea of the Azores and Canaries, a dwarf suffrutex. The soft, woolly, round-edged umbels develop into small-sized bushes tipped with mounds of smallish flowers in deep, velvet blue or violet; the stem turns woody, and the diminutive flowering tree grows more and more beautiful year by year. — Normal seeding in sl, normal thinning, transplant early to shady garden site, keep under glass for the first winter. The moraine forget-me-nots *welwitschii* and *traversii*, the first a gentian blue, the second a lemon yellow, a dwarf Arnebia, are sown as above, and are both of such great beauty that attempts at cultivation can't be ended even by repeated failure.

Nierembergia hippomanica APh SY ○ 30 in all directions VI 30, a low Solanacea shrub from the mountains of Chile. A small, robust bush with fine, strong branches and delicate leaves, for a very light general impression, and everywhere thickly covered with pale lilac to dark violet, bellflower-similar chalice flowers. Since the plant falls over in all directions, it produces whole mounds of flowers, singularly beautiful. — In hs, slightly covered, allow the grasslike seedlings to grow robust before thinning out into rs, and then transplant with three to four stems to the rock garden. Prune to the ground in fall, once blossoming is over, protect in inclement exposures.

Nolana A YS ○ 15, creeper, VII, 40 and more, south American Nolanaceae. The *atriplicifolia* and *lanceolata,* both blue, resemble bindweed, with abundant flowers sprawling on the ground, strong and pure in color. Sow in the open.

Nomocharis P bu RLS ◐ from 30 to 60 VI 40, Liliacea of western China. The new pseudo-lilies of western China, creatures of half-clear areas of deciduous forest, show broad, lanceolate, semi-verticillate foliage surmounted by fantastically spurred and piebald lilies, open and upward slanting, browns over pinks, carmine over white, chocolate tones over yellows. The *mairei,* 60, silky white with crimson and lilac; *pardanthina,* with flattish flowers, 60; *nana,* 30, pale lilac; *salvensis* 60. — In ls, highly porous, half warm, moderately moist, in darkness; seedlings sprout rapidly; transplant when cotyledons fall to small pots, to be kept in shelter in the open air, transfer as they grow to larger pots; keep under glass for the first two winters, allowing the plants to die, always maintaining moderate moisture; transplant third year to protected woodland sites, where they bloom in the fourth or fifth year.

Odontospermum sericeum Ph ⊓ or ⌂ SHT with a measure of R O 100 and more, VIII 60. Bushy South African Composita, with soft silk-green, slightly notched, unpleasantly odorous leaves, a magnificent silky silver sheen and highly compact carriage, chrome yellow star-shaped flowers as though stuck into a pin cushion; with age the plant develops into an enormous, regular, spherical bush, studded with stars. — In sh, thin out into the mixture above, in small pots, transplant to sandy places with their whole clumps of earth once the seedlings are strong, winter with ⌂.

Papaver A SR c*ommutatum* 60 V 20 explosive red with black spots, quite elegant; *horridum*, a rough, hairy red, from southern Africa; *caucasicum*, 70 red, precocious; all of them new, summer plants that characterize their native landscapes; all to be sown in the open air, at best in fall. The *californicum* P up to 70 V 30, with long twisting stalks, salmon-colored flowers. Of the older poppies, the glowing silky blood red *P. laevigatum*, from Persia; and the tall, lithe *P. glaucum*, with cup-shaped flowers, all too seldom seen; *P. hookeri*, India, the pride of older gardens, full and pink with blue rims, by now no longer found in commercial assortments and cultivations; the *pilosum*, resembling the *californicum*, and the *rupifragum*.

Passiflora gracilis AP ↟ RM stays low VII, a South American Passifloracea. An extremely attractive plant with typical, hand-shaped passion-flower foliage, on a smaller scale; blooms with quantities of smaller, typical, grass-green flowers; climbs even the thinnest trees and bushes. — Plant warm, in ds; soon germinates; thin immediately into small-sized pots, and then promptly to the open air; never at the feet of other plants, maintaining at least a half meter distance. Perennial in warmer exposures.

Pentastemon P sometimes AP, mostly YRMS with supplemental

L, O. Of the many newer species of this characteristic plant from Central and central North America, the *antirrhinoides*, with somewhat gray-greener foliage, and large, narrow, deep-yellow chalice-shaped flowers, up to 90; the *cyananthus brandegei*, a cold, silky, sky-blue reddish color, 45, subfrutescent; *gordoni splendens*, dense panicles, deep violet bluish, 70–80; *speciosus*, nearly pure blue, with long, dense inflorescences, 60; *spectabilis*, likewise bluish violet, 90–100. All others under observation. — The seed in furrows in lrs with m, treat like delphiniums, thinning out stronger seedlings into the same soil mixture. ◐ or O, in front of woody plants and trees.

Perezia multiflora AP S, supplemental D, O 80 VII 50, Canary Island Composita. A stiff, compact shrub with pale blue, star-shaped flowers with notched, pointed petals, drawn together to shape a capitulum. — In any dry soil, the stronger seedlings directly to the open air, extremely shy of moisture, aerate the soil if high in clay.

Portulaca grandiflora parana (hort.?) A SHTR O, creeper, VII, a Brazilian Portulacacea with strong, tightly packed, crest-like phyllodes and densely covered with enormous flowers like those of the Phyllocactus, of a liquid crimson violet. Sow amidst rocks in warmer exposures. Forms superb cascades.

Pyrethrum ptarmicaefolium, a bush, SYK O 200 IX 100, a bushy Composita from the mountains of the Canary islands, with the finest fringe of white-green-silver foliage that rises in clumps and tufts into a feathery, quivering structure; insignificant yellow flowers; numerous older plants on slopes a splendor that compares to nothing else. — In very sandy r, poor germination, very slow development, in the first year barely a handspan tall, 3–4 years for full development.

Ranunculus gramineus PA S with slight additions of RH, O 45 VII 10, Moroccan Ranunculacea. A radial umbel of gray-green leaves with upright central stems bearing flattish cups of earth-yellow buttercup blossoms, very beautiful; *pyrenaeus* similar, smaller, with white blossoms. — Seed remains dormant for quite some time; do not overwater; thin; transplant to highly sandy soil, mixed with gravel; highly moisture sensitive. Avoid bad neighbors.

Rehmannia angulata PA LMRDS ○ 100 VI, very rank and expansive. A Chinese Scrophulariacea, of unknown local origin. A bush with rich, handsome foliage and large, rose-smoke-reddish trumpet flowers with highly spotted yellow gullets, in form like those of the trumpet creeper. For rough terrain, where rhizomes lie dry beneath sand. — Seed in sl; Seedlings fare better with drought than with excess moisture. Let stands grow as large as possible.

Romneya coulteri, trichocalyx, nearly identical in height and cultivation, the second slightly smaller in all its parts, with reflex petals. Bushy P, light very sandy LE with scrupulous drainage, ○, rank. A bush-form Papaveracea from California, on steep banks of water courses (the Matilija poppy). Fringed, silvery, gray-green foliage on slender stalks with pendulous summits, and creeping rhizomes in all directions; stalks surmounted by enormous, shallow, cup-shaped flowers with crinkly, solid, silk-white petals, a large tuft of golden pistils, a faint Centifolia odor. — Seed in the mixture above, moderately moist; germination slight and slow, often no more than one or two kernels of a whole pinch of seed; seed directly from habitat, imported, presumably more reliable; cultivate with extreme care, thin out with a prong into pots only when the seedlings are securely rooted, always transplant to garden site with their whole clump of earth. Rhizomes, set singly, die. A royal plant that demands a throne of its own, since it rankly expands in all directions; no strong colors in the near vicinity.

Roscoea P, rhizomed, rich YD, ○ and ◐, ca. 35 VIII-IX 25, Zingiberacea of the southern Himalayas, of Southeast Asia, alpine dwarf resembling Alpinias and so forth, on the yellow-violet color scale; tall, fleshy, sleeve-like shafts with panicles of bizarrely shaped blossoms in tender enamel colors; taken individually, the flowers might seem deformed. — In sd, slightly covered, pressed firmly into the ground, keep moist, good germination, thin plants once strong into pots, and then with their clumps of earth to half-sunny garden sites with the above-described mixture of soil, in groups next to taller plants; additions of moor soil are beneficial; a successor for midsummer primroses. In rough exposures with tall leafy plants, ⌒.

Salpiglossis sinuata A SD on deep, well-drained subsoil, VI-VII, Chilean Solanaceae. Next to the tall and widely known cultivated forms with large flowers and gullets in brocaded moiré, there are others which ought not to be forgotten: smaller, with richer color schemes, highly variable wiles of the species, more voluminous, with simpler bearing, more severe. Greenish-yellow, black, pure pink, scarlet, sulphur colors, for a unique sight in the first phase of blossoming, especially in extensive groups; barely 40 cm tall.

Salvia carduacea A S ○ 40 V 20 Labiata of the California deserts. A woolly, thistle-like plant, grayish pink throughout, with lilac, pinkish, bluish, gullet-shaped flowers with abundant red filaments. — In pure s, thinning strengthens seedlings and slows rapid growth, additive nutrients for longer life and blossoming. A defining presence of sandy locales. The species' only annual worth cultivating. For more temperate zones: the *azurea grandiflora* APh ○ up to 110 VIII 40, North America, a ground-hugging umbel surmounted by long, pendant, very gracious stalks thick with large, nodding, pale blue flowers in panicles, a magnificent form with dark green foliage; *nutans*, somewhat smaller, extremely shy of moisture, dies in winter if its soil is less than perfectly drained, perhaps even more beautiful, with pure, shining, somber amethyst flowers; *hians*, from the foothills of the Himalayas, 45 VIII 40, stiff bearing, hairy, a strong round rosette of large, rising leaves and a branching, candelabra-like shaft with panicles of strong pale lilac to light blue flowers, small bracts of a dull pinkish hue; *verbascifolia syria spec.* B (or P?) 100 VI, whitish gray and woolly throughout, rapid growth, with erect, naked, verticillate shoots covered with large, colorful blossoms, their upper lips pale lilac, the lower lips with eloquent, dark violet markings, from Syrian semi-deserts, a grandiose plant that typifies its landscape; *jurisicii* AP, of unknown origin, k SY with reclining growths of medium violet flowers; *dichroa*, a smaller version of *verbascifolia*, but free from wool, with smaller, multicolored blossoms. Subtropical: *patens* A P tu ⌒ ○ 50 VIII 40, arrow-shaped leaves, somewhat downy, sparse blossoms, but very large, and velvet fleur-de-lys blue, long, fleshy rhizomes, to be kept dry in winter, seldom seen in full, satisfying bloom; *coccinea* AP ⌒, thoroughly perennial if protected in winter under glass, of constantly increasing beauty, native to Florida, slender and light in bearing, loose inflorescences of pale scarlet reddish somewhat floppy blossoms; *roemeriana*, Brazilian, 25 AP, with a thick stand of crimson reddish blossoms that often refuse to open out of their buds, a recalcitrant dwarfish growth; *splendens*, well-known for flower beds. — All species of *Salvia* in sr, and will bloom the first year if properly thinned at the right time, tropical species with abundant additions of light DML. To be placed in consideration of their individual features. A habit with possibilities that remain to be fully exploited and revealed, true pearls of poorer soils.

Scabiosa caucasica AP KSR over deep gravel, 50–60 VIII 30, magnificent oriental Dipsacacea; large, pure-amethyst, composite blossoms with large, gracious, especially sprightly flowers at their rims, by no means easy to raise; the enormous, pure-colored hybrids with enormous blossoms are more beautiful than the natural species. The cliff-side forms *graminifolia, lucida, parnassiaefolia*, of the Mediterranean countries, on the pinkish, bluish, yellowish scale, with noble colors and fine tissues, build cushions over stiff, strong, ground-hugging foliage: extremely fond of chalky soils, especially beautiful; *reuteriana*, of unknown native habitat. The annual form, with long, stiff stalks, a very delicate blue, now no longer in commerce, was once a fine cut flower.

Schizanthus retusus A (? P?) SD ○ up to 50 VI 40, Chilean Solanacea. With finely cut and lance-shaped leaves, a thick, arborescent and presumably perennial ground-level stem, and deep pink mask-like flowers showing pointed, conjoining roof petals with an eloquent, eye-shaped marking, golden-yellow, the family's finest species. The *pinnatus*, *gracilis* and the lovely *papilionaceus*, so hybridized as to make true seed a rarity, the hybrids well-known prodigies of color. — Seed in sh, thin when the plants show two true leaves, continue cultivation of the stronger seedlings, transplant to sites that run no risk of excess moisture; the plants don't need, as mistakenly recommended, heavy terrain, but deep, humus-rich soil that's able to nourish their luxuriant, foamy, sap-green foliage while also securing their deep, fleshy roots against all danger of rot.

Solanum The enormous masses of leaves of the woody Solanaceae are the midway point in the garden's floral landscape between the flowers and the leafy trees, and with care and due precaution can be every year revived in only a matter of months, since they need no more than moderate winter protection. It's sad that the seed (formerly supplied by Haage & Schmidt) of the truly giant forms, *giganteum* from southern Africa, and *aculeatissimum*, from South America, are no longer found in commerce. Of the largest available species, *robustum,* Ph RDM ○ 120–150 in all directions, with strong defenses and rust-brown hair, and *warscewiczii*, with leathery, large-lobed leaves, heavily thorned, are more ghastly than engaging. The *laciniatum*, 180 in all directions, New Zealand, with large, hanging, deep lilac-colored potato flowers in the midst of highly indented dark green foliage, is a thoroughly gracious, if somewhat empty plant; the *atroporpureum* a worthless weed;

the *marginatum*, from Abyssinia, everywhere fringed with flour white and very roundly built, is a plant of desert rock slides, to be planted in isolation from any- and everything else, and cultivated like tomatoes. — Seedlings take immediate root, once transplanted from the seed bed. Dry leaves and all prunings containing the large-sized thorns that, needle-like, remain a danger throughout the year should be burned immediately. Transplant to pots in fall, and keep frost free, prune back to a handspan tall. Of the climbing varieties, *jasminoides*, with tufts of moderate-sized, whitish to bluish nightshade flowers, is beautiful only when free to climb supports, and dangling from trees; the *seaforthianum*, with fine blue, faintly-scented flowers, somewhat bare; the wonderful *wendlandii*, from Costa Rica, with mammoth, purely-colored, dark-lilac chalices, like smaller field bindweed, unsuitable for outdoor cultivation.

Stephanophysum longifolium bushy A, ⌒, DRMS, ○ and ◐, 100 VII 30, South American Acanthacea. Deep dark-green lustrous foliage, abundant, flexible, noded stems with longish, pointed, narrow, opposing leaves, an umbrella of tubular, pure scarlet blossoms. — Sprouts quickly in warm or tepid hs, grows rapidly and healthily, is everywhere at home, one of the least known, most overlooked plants for open fields, far more rewarding than many of the prides of the old, tropical garden bed.

Stevia serrata PA suffrutex YS ○ 50 VIII 50. Composita, from Mexican mountain terrain, a modest, stiff, candyleaf plant with a clear linear structure, a thick growth of parallel branches, and heaps of tiny white sweet-smelling star-shaped flowers; for rock-garden corners, space-filling. — Normal seeding, without thinning, in rs.

Stokesia cyanea P LESK tr ○ 30, VII and later, 30, North American Composita, also known as the "fleur-de-lys aster," but more on the order of a thornless, pale-blue ground thistle with an ample growth of fluted, dark green leaves and flat, broad, short-stemmed thistle flowers, in a lovely pale blue. — Normal seeding; thin; transplant robust seedlings to dry rock-garden site.

Streptocarpus PA SHT with additions of loam, ◐ 20/40, South African Gesneriacea, native to cliff-side fissures. Resembles the Haberlea, though of normal size: a crude, exterior umbel of leaves, powerfully and abundantly nerved and swollen with lymph, and a large protruding central leaf, flanked by a flower with one or a number of lilac trumpets, tending to white or reddish. — In sy, do not cover, in shade beneath a sheet of glass; air daily, keep dry, seeds sprout thickly and must be left undisturbed; thin out the erupting whip-shaped leaves, which then quickly develop in peat soil with additions of m. Tolerates planting in half shade in the open air better than begonias; deep, loose, rich soil as above gives magnificent flowering, also with large-blossomed hybrids. For warm, half-shady gullies rich with humus and charged with gravel, along with carpets of Torenia baillonii.

Tagetes patula arborea A (B?) SLEM 180–200 IX 150, a Composita found in Mexico's flowering grassland, but said to be originally Australian, still awaits clarification. The arboreal form of *Tagetes patula*, which with commercially available seed reaches the height of at most a meter: a larger version, of identical structure, branches departing from the trunk always at the very same angle, very fragile, lax, ending in long-stemmed, well-filled blossoms, butter yellow with glistening crimson brown. In full bloom, an imposing sight. Before nights grow cool, carefully dig up the encircling soil, freeing the roots and their surrounding clod of earth, then tightly wrapping the whole in a sack before removing the plant to protection, where it then will continue to bloom into winter. — Normal seeding, without thinning. Only for ample spaces, its mass of flowers as a colorful background setting for Tithonia, Cosmos aurantiacus, Trachelium.

Tecophilaea cyanocrocus P bu, half L, half loamy R, a measure of S, ◐ 30 V 30, a Chilean Amaryllidea. A wonderful bluish-violet, at times nearly pure-blue pseudo-crocus with a paler gullet, a loose crown with several petals with rounded points, lax, narrow, lanceolate foliage, a flimsy, unclear, hidden structure, the odor of a violet. — The flat seeds, in well-drained sh, often lie dormant for months; keep uniformly lukewarm and moderately moist; as soon as the seedlings show their first leaves, thin out into small pots of the same mixture, spray with water, place in shadow; when shoots appear, bring more out into the light, small tubers soon develop; water only as needed, then suspending all moisture as soon as the plants have withered; store tubers dry in ash or sawdust until September, then again into pots with additions of loam, continue cultivation as above, place outdoors in shade, in the second September plant in a half-shady place, will bloom the third or fourth year.

Thalictrum dipterocarpum P LRK, well drained, ◐ and ○, up to 100 VII 40, Tibetan Ranunculacea. Fresh, delicate, fernlike foliage with roundish splits, robust stalks with abundant terminal ramifications into towers of pendulous, pale lilac bell-shaped flowers with golden anthers, blooms repeatedly. — In sl, press down firmly, not too moist, on the appearance of their first true leaves thin out the seedlings into rows in trays with additions of R, keep soil loose, the trays in shade in the open air, the stronger plants then transplanted to garden site. A wonderfully handsome plant in isolation among contrasting growths, never in groups.

Thunbergia gibsonii P ⥉ swampy L and deep RM, ◐ VIII rank 180, an Acanthacea of southeast Africa. The rounded pointed leaves, dark green and mirror bright, of the plant's ground-level growth rise in their second year onto climbing tendrils with round, glowing, orange-colored, mask-like flowers with no dark eye, in great abundance. — The large bizarre looking seeds go into warm sl, germinate quickly, can soon be potted, keep warm and tend assiduously, full sun, the stronger seedlings to a protected spot in the garden, in harsher climes ⊓ for the winter months. Only in abundant groups, never espalier, allow the young bushes to climb young trees, among Piptanthus nepalensis.

Tigridia pavonia P bu LESL ○ 40 VII, spread considerable. A Mexican Iridacea. The lax, sheath-like, somewhat crepe-like leaves rise in quantity from thick knots of tubers, packed together three by three, and issue stems with short-lived, giant, three-petaled blossoms, their centers a cup-like depression, from dull to saturated yellow with vehement crimson eyes and markings; other varieties in reds and whites; continues to bud and bloom till frost. — In sr, germinates rapidly, develops quickly, blooms the second year, store small bulbs dry, plant in large numbers the second year directly at garden site. One of the easiest bulbs to grow from seed, and with almost shocking forms and colors. In raw locales winter with ⌂, or beneath a bed of leaves, or wrapped, doesn't sprout before the end of May.

Tithonia speciosa A (?) strong LE, well manured and drained, worked to a minimum depth of 50 cm, ○, 200 and more, end VII, 200 in all directions. A tree-like Composita of the flowering Mexican grasslands. Dark, branching shafts with large, dark, black-green leaves, lobed and rough at the edges, always rising at same inclination, and with new growths of leaves on powerful foot and side shoots; general construction in the shape of a crude rhomboid; late summer flowers at branch tips, on long, black, arrow-straight stems covered with slippery, silky down, corollas perched like crowns over thick cup-shaped calyxes, the blooms to as much as 10 cm across in glowing nasturtium colors around a golden disk. All shoots equally charged with flowers, the plant becomes a fire tree, to which no other temperate flora bears resemblance. — Cultivation exactly the same as for zinnias and marigolds, with the young plants moved out early to the open air, protect against snails. Effective only in large-scale spaces, flowers late. Lasts up to ten days in water.

Torenia fournieri A DSHR, thoroughly worked and loose, ◐ to ○, 40 in all directions, VII, annual Scrophulariacea of the Nam Ky region of Vietnam. With a loose construction of paired, fresh colored leaves on soft shoots, widely branching from the ground up and tipped with winged, sky-blue flowers, on every wing a blot of velvet blue, yellow gullets, blossoms abundant, stronger colors for the larger-flowered garden forms, the white form dirty and grows unsightly when allowed to grow tall, must be pruned, among the handsomest tropical flowers for open summer spaces. — In warm hs, thin out with the growth of its second pair of leaves, tend carefully before transplanting. *Baillonii* the same as above, creeping, carpeting, flowering basal shoots that only slightly rise from the ground, smaller flowers, golden yellow wings with brown velvet spots, same cultivation as above, more demanding, blooms VIII and later, very beautiful.

Trachelium coeruleum P RSK ○ 100 in all directions VII, suffrutescent Campanulacea of Sicily and northern Africa. A veil-like construction of masses of tiny, pale violet flowers in umbrella-shaped clumps. — Normal seeding, very thin, keep dry, transplant repeatedly, young plants repeatedly pruned, to obtain a bushy form. In multitudes among large flowering trees.

Trachymene coerulea, the blue lace flower, or "blue calf's head," A SD, with additions of R, deep, ○ 30–40 VII 20, California Umbellifera, the only blue flower of the family. A loosely built summer flower with mediocre tissues, satisfies only with excellent care, spare foliage, soft and fluffy, upright stems with pale blue umbrellas of flattened, half-spherical flowers, the color effective only in masses, in the company of conspicuous neighbors. — Hard seeds that only slowly germinate, in hsr, thin out early, prune for promotion of branching, in the mixture above richly nourished with liquid manure, nitrogen offering the only course to abundant branching, adequate roots, effective colors: an otherwise anemic creature.

Tradescantia virginiana P DLSR ◐ 50 in all directions VII, a Commelinacea from Virginia. A bright green bush with straggling shoots, leaves that wrap around their stems, sheath after sheath from joint to joint, uncommonly abundant three-petalled flowers in glowing violet; a plant that needs shade and moisture. The *reflexa*, lax, ground-hugging, carpet forming, dark blue, requires admixture of moor soil. — In ls, seed sprouts quickly, leave potted till the vases are full of roots, remove from vases, somewhat prune the roots, plant in the mixture above, soil deep, in shade.

Ursinia A S, tu 50% moor HT, old M O up to 40 VI 20, South African Compositae, on long, thin, tough stalks, with their own scale of yellows, orange browns with lovely darker zones, disks brown or blue and paling out to dusty golden tones, or leather brown with crimson brownish zones. The *anethoides* and *anthemoides* 30, *pulchra* 20, lovely garden forms seen more and more each year. In warmer climes to be sown in the open air, otherwise normal seeding in sr, promptly transplanted to sand garden, wonderfully beautiful in large groups with Heliophila, Lobelia ramosa, Phacelias.

Venidium fastuosum A rich R with abundant D and S O up to 80 VI 80, South African Composita. A strong, lax, pendulous structure with soft gray-green foliage, deeply slit, long stems with enormous orange-colored star-shaped flowers with double rows of petals, the outer well extended, the inner almost upright, burnished deep brown disk with a bluish haze, gradually growing more golden, inexhaustible flowering. — In sandy normal earth, seeds and seedlings very small, development quick after thinning; transplant hardy plants to the open air; create broad planting mound, enrich the soil to considerable depth with D and old M, plant seedlings on its summit, water carefully, at the base of the mound, in fullest sunlight. The commercially available hybrids, resulting from a cross with *V. calendulaceum*, an unattractive plant with small white blossoms, grow with little vigor and till now have been disappointing.

Verbascum mainly B dry LES high in K O, old-world Scrophulariaceae. The giant forms called “King’s candle” (*giganteum,* up to 300, modest flowering; *vernale,* up to 200, with rich, grandiose inflorescences; the *Harkrell hybrid,* with great, primrose yellow flowers on enormous, panicled shafts, the whole growth imposing; *olympicum* (in reference to the Olympus mountains in Asia Minor) thick and woolly white with dark yellow blossoms) are all without exception for only the driest, hottest exposures, preferably stony. The smaller *phoeniceum,* up to 100, native to Mediterranean shores and available as colorful hybrids, tolerates richer and damper terrain; the small, lovely *wiedemannianum,* violet and in hybrid colors, 60–70 V, normal needs, very beautiful in the company of columbine. — In sandy, normal earth, normal cultivation, quickly out into the open air, the plants then seed spontaneously.

Verbena bonariensis AP LRS ○ 100 VII 80, Verbenacea of Argentinean heathland. Stiff, stiffly branched and rebranched stems, linear construction, lilac reddish umbrella-like blossoms on all sides in all directions, in ever greater number, and with all side shoots concurrently covered with similar blooms; a Statice-like effect; flowers till frost; cut stems last at great length in water. — Normal seeding in rows, normal earth, seedlings quick to sprout, leave unthinned transplant directly to garden site. A splendid new introduction, extremely undemanding. The *venosa,* rank, 40, redder, with uncommonly abundant blossoming, builds thick color fields, same cultivation; a first-class plant for dry stone walls and fissures in rock, never in open spaces.

Veronica P SR, the New Zealand species with additions of moor soil, and L; Scrophulariaceae from all around the world. The New Zealand varieties, shrubs, mostly ⊓, and tolerant of transplanting, with opposing, leathery, dark green leaves on slack stems, and pinkish violet grapelets of flowers sprouting out of their axils, whitening as they wilt, are defining features of their natural landscape. — Warm in hs, prompt germination, in pots until strong. The tall *exaltata,* 90 and *michauxia,* 150, from North America, build thick stands of hard, pliant stems, studded with copious bunches of small-sized fleur-de-lys blue or light violet flowers; strong, stiff foliage, bush-like structure, woody. — In sl, thin out the sprouts into low trays, arranging the seedlings in rows; undemanding, tough, quick development, bloom soon after being transplanted. A grand display on gentle, heathlike slopes.

Viola nigra P LR ○ and ◐ 10 V 10, Bowles black pansy, presumably of hybrid origin, with small clumps of miniature, nearly black violets. Beautiful in larger numbers only if scattered singly among white, vermilion pink, and yellow plants. — In sandy l, to garden site when its form grows bushy, amid Nycterinia, Schizopetalum, Anomatheca.

Zauschneria californica P SLEK tr ○ 50 and more, highly rank IX; an Onogracea of dry California mountain terrain and stony mountain wasteland. Loose, pendulous, downy, gray-green shoots resembling those of willow herb, in abundance from creeping rhizomes, the branches tipped with brick red to grayish red to orange reddish tubular flowers of a partly open trumpet shape, in form and color like the desert mallows. — In sandy earth in rows, erratic germination, into well-drained pots, clip tips to encourage new shoots, move promptly into the open air, often blooms first year. Hybrids of varying worth. An invaluable late-blooming rock-garden plant.

Zinnia Herbaceous plants with small flowers, from high, dry Mexican elevations: *linearis,* deep yellow with darker zones; *mexicana,* straw-colored with crimson zones; *haageana (mexicana)* with hybrid colors; abundantly blossoming bushes, 40 cm tall; normal seeding as with Zinnias in general; invaluable flowers, with strong character, for bare, dry exposures later in the year; in multitudes.

Notes

CHAPTER I

PAGE 5, Malvolio: Shakespeare, *As You Like It,* Act II, scene 5; Act III, scene 2.

P. 5, the philistinism of eating symbolic fruits: Genesis 3.

P. 5, the garden of Eden was square: Genesis 2, 8–15.

P. 6, one of the plants still commonly grown today: the fig: Genesis 3, 7.

P. 6, the shade of Ajax: see *Odyssey,* XI, 539, and Ovid's *Metamorphoses,* XIII, 1–398.

P. 6, the importation from China of oranges: oranges were first introduced into Europe, from China, in 1548.

P. 6, "Eurypides' *Hippolytos* contains...": such a promise to those who have never broken their word is found in Pindar, *The Oympian Odes,* II, 109–140; Eurypides' *Hippolytos,* 73–83, speaks of a field of which only those who were virtuous in life are permitted to pluck the flowers.

P. 6, The Island of Calypso: *Odyssey* V, 63–74.

P. 7, Kundrie's garden: Richard Wagner, *Parsifal,* Act II; Armida's garden: Torquato Tasso, *Gerusalemme liberata* X, 62–65.

P. 7, the parable of the sower: St. Matthew 13, 3–8; of the grain of mustard seed: St. Matthew 13, 31 ff.; of the lilies of the field: St. Matthew 6, 28 ff.

P. 8, the garden in Gethsemane: St. Matthew 26, 36–46.

P. 8, Christ as gardener: St. John 20, 14–17.

P. 8, Diocletian as gardener: Aurelius Victor, Epitome 39, 6, reports that Diocletian, on being asked after his resignation again to take command of the troops, responded: *Utinam Salonae possetis visere olera nostris manibus instituta, profecto numquam istud temptandum iudicaretis.* (If here in Salona you saw the plants which I have set with my own hands, you would know straightaway why no such thing could ever tempt me.)

P. 12, "Euclid alone has looked on Beauty bare": Edna St. Vincent Millay, *The Harp-Weaver*, Part Four, no. XXII, London 1924, p. 80. Borchardt worked extensively on the translation of the poetry of Edna St. Vincent Millay, and an assessment of her work, "Die Entdeckung Amerikas: Die Poesie von Edna St. Vincent Millay," written in 1935, is to be found in his collected essays: *Gesammelte Werke, Prosa III*, Stuttgart, Klett 1965-2000, pp. 429–472.

P. 13, "image of the soul": Goethe's poem "Words are an image of the soul," from the cycle "Rhein und Main," W. A., Vol. IV, p. 71.

P. 13, Demeter's child: Persephone: *Homeric Hymn to Demeter*, V, 1–16. Borchardt's translation of the *Homeric Hymn to Demeter* is found in *Gesammelte Werke, Übertragungen*, Stuttgart, Klett 1965-2000, p. 7 ff.

P. 14, the legend of Hyakinthus: Ovid, *Metamorphoses*, X, 162–219; the legend of Narcissus: Ibid., III, 339–510; the legend of Adonis and the "Adonis flower" (the anemone): Ibid. X, 708–739.

P. 14, "Our Lady's Little Glass": from Grimm's *Fairy Tales*: "Marienglas": *Kinder und Hausmärchen.* Gesammelt durch die Brüder Grimm. Große Ausgabe, 7th printing, 1857, Vol. II, p. 478: Kinderlegenden No. 7, "Muttergottesgläschen."

P. 15, Lenau discovered the primrose,...: Lenau's poem "Primula veris," Cotta edition 1857, Vol. I, p. 187; ...Platen the honeysuckle,...: Platen's poem "An eine Geisblattranke" ("To a Vine of Honeysuckle"), also found in *Ewiger Vorrat deutscher Poesie*, selected by Rudolf Borchardt, 4th edition, Stuttgart 1956, p. 356; ...Goethe once again the hyacinth: Goethe's poem "An Frau von Stein" ("To Madame von Stein"), W. A., Vol. IV, p. 211.

P. 15, Goethe could close the Helen act: *Faust*, Part II, Act III, 9985–10,038.

P. 15, Möricke discovered the *Datura suaveolens*: Möricke's poem "Datura suaveolens," *Mörike's Werk*, Harry Maync (ed), Vol. I, p. 84.

P. 16, a new Peregrina: Möricke's poem, "Peregrina I," Ibid., p. 97

P. 16, Goethe's archetypal plant, or *Urpflanze*: see *Italienische Reise* (*Journey to Italy*), Naples, March 25, W. A., Vol. XXXI, p. 75.

P. 16, Novalis' blue flower: *Heinrich von Ofterdingen*, Part I, ch. 1.

P. 16, Goethe's "ulterior" rose, or *durchgewachsene Rose*: *Die Metamorphose der Pflanzen*, paragraph 103 ff., W. A., Part II, Vol. VI, p. 80 ff.

P. 16, Jean Paul's astonished floral faces: see *Blumen- Frucht- und Dornenstücke aus Jean Paul's Werk,* Gesammelt von Richard Benz, Munich, R. Piper & Co. 1924.

P. 17, like Ophelia: Shakespeare, *Hamlet,* Act IV, scene 5

P. 20, "How beautiful she was, how good!...": Goethe's poem, "Lili's Park," W. A., Vol. II, p. 87, (also found in *Ewiger Vorrat deutscher Poesie,* op. cit., p. 80.)

P. 20, "This nosegay I have picked…": Goethe's poem "Blumengrus" ("Floral Greeting"), W. A., Vol. I, p. 79.

P. 21, where Persephone vanishes beneath the ground: *Homeric Hymn to Demeter,* V, 1–14. For Borchardt's translation, see *Gesammelte Werke, Übertragungen,* op. cit.

P. 21, where Sappho plaits garlands with her lost love in her thoughts: Sappho: Fragment 94 (Lobel-Page)

P. 21, where the powerful Pindar's odes celebrate the infant hero: Pindar, *The Olympian Odes,* VI, 91–95 (the saga of Iamus, Apollo's son by Evadne, daughter of Poseidon). For Borchardt's translation, see *Gesammelte Werke, Übertragungen,* op. cit., p. 128.

P. 22, the garden of hell…where plants live and bleed: Dante, *Divina Commedia,* Inferno, Canto XIII; the heavenly garden of the enormous Centifolia tree: Paradiso, Cantos XXX–XXXII; the alpine garden where the shades of princes sit: Purgatorio, Canto VII; the magnificent grove of earthly paradise: Purgatorio, Cantos XXVIII–XXXIII; *Manibus date lilia plenis* ("Fill my hands with lilies"): Virgil, *Aeneid,* VI, 883 and Dante, *Divina Commedia,* Purgatorio, Canto XXX, 21.

P. 23, as Werther he cultivated peas: Goethe, *Die Leiden des jungen Werthers,* June 21, W. A., Vol. XIX, p. 39.

P. 24, *Elective Affinities*: Goethe's novel *Die Wahlverwandschaften,* W. A., Vol XX.

P. 24, "Zephyr, take this upon your wings…": Goethe's poem "Mit einem gamalten Band" ("With a painted ribbon"), W. A., Vol. I, p. 74, (also found in *Ewiger Vorrat deutscher Poesie,* op. cit., p. 120.)

P. 24, "Rose of the Heath": Goethe's poem "Sah ein Knab ein Röslein stehn" ("A boy saw a rose bush standing"), W. A., Vol. I, p. 152; the *Ginkgo biloba* which we find in his *Divan*: Goethe, *West-östlicher Divan,* Suleika, Book VIII, "Gingo biloba,"; Germany's first exhibition of dahlias: this exhibition took place in Jena, in 1836, and Alexander von Humboldt was one of its participants.

P. 24, "Ganymede": Goethe's poem "Ganymed," W. A., Vol. II, p. 79.

P. 24, "The starry skies above me...": Immanuel Kant, *Kritik der praktischen Vernunft, Beschluß (Critique of Practical Reason, Conclusion).*

P. 25, "*Urworte*": Goethe's poem, "Urworte. Orphisch," W. A., Vol. III, p. 95.

P. 25, Marco's speech: Dante, *Divina Commedia*, Purgatorio, Canto XVI.

P. 25, "Oh star and flower...": Clemens Brentano's poems "Widmung" ("Dedication"), also found in *Ewiger Vorrat deutscher Poesie*, op. cit., p. 332, and "Es ist ein Schnitter, der heißt Tod" ("There is a reaper, whose name is Death").

CHAPTER II

P. 28, While leading his campaign against the Greeks, Xerxes called his hordes to a halt...: Herodotus, VII, 31.

P. 33, the tune of Goethe's maiden and its shameless parody...: Goethe's poem "Haus-Park" ("House Park"), W. A., Vol. III, p. 54.

P. 34, the Vicar of Wakefield: Oliver Goldsmith, *The Vicar of Wakefield*, London 1766.

P. 36, much as huts of mud and dung had at Tacitus' time protected women and children: Tacitus, *Germania*, chapter 16. For Borchardt's translation, see *Gesammelte Werke, Übertragungen*, op. cit., p. 193.

P. 37, Horace: *Carmen* I, 38

P. 42, "Fair daffodils we weep to see": Robert Herrick (1591–1674): "To Daffodils," also found in *The Oxford Book of English Verse, 1250–1900.* Chosen and Edited by A. Y. Quiller-Couch, Oxford 1908, p. 268.

P. 43, Clusius' epoch-making treatise on plants: *Rariorum plantarum historia*, Antwerp 1601, Lib. III, Cap. IX, *auricula ursi.*

P. 43, Tournefort's description of his voyage (1700–1702) through Greece and Asia Minor was posthumously published in the form of a series of letters, in three volumes: *Relation d'un voyage du Levant*, Lyons, 1717.

P. 44, "For my heart....": from Goethe's poem "Sendschreiben," ("Open Letter.") W. A., Vol. II, p. 190.

P. 45, In doctors' gardens in Breslau: the reference is to Lorenz Scholz (1552–1599), the medical doctor from Breslau (now Wroclaw, Poland) whose *Catalogus arborum, fruticum ac plantarum tam indigenarum quam exoticarum horti medici Laurentii Scholzii* appeared in 1594.

P. 50, Jean Paul: the "Blumenbühl" appears in his novel *Titan*, and

"Maienthal" in the thirteenth *Hundsposttag* ("dogpostday" is one of Jean-Paul's many humorous coinages), of the novel *Hesperus. Flegeljahre* is again the title of one of his novels.

P. 50, "There is a reaper whose name is Death": Clemens Brentano's poem "Es ist ein Schnitter, der heißt Tod."

P. 51, Eichendorff: "Valleys wide, and heights," from the poem "Abschied. Im Walde bei Lubowitz," *Eichendorffs Dichtungen*, Insel-Verlag, Leipzig, Vol. I, p. 93; "Crown imperial and red peonies,..." and "A woman sits there dozing,..." from the poem "Der Alte Garten," Ibid., p. 250.

P. 51, Leipzig tailors' pranks: see Goethe's poem "Haus-Park," W. A., Vol. III, p. 54: "Leaves drop from shears / Flowers drop, how the pain grows rank! / Dearest Cousin Asmus / Calls it purest tailors' prank." "Lili's Park": op. cit. Cf. the poem by Matthias Claudius (1740–1815, nicknamed "Asmus") "Serenate im Walde zu singen."

P. 51, the flowered couplets of "The Four Seasons": Goethe's poem "Vier Jahreszeiten," 1–18 ("Frühling"), W. A. Vol. I, pp. 345–347.

CHAPTER III

P. 66, classics of German literature: see Borchardt's anthology *Der Deutsche in der Landschadft*, Munich, Verlag der Bremer Presse 1927, or Frankfurt am Main, Suhrkamp Verlag 1953.

P. 75, Albert Rausch: see Henri Benrath (Albert H. Rausch), *Evocation d'un poète*, Paris 1936, p. 136.

CHAPTER IV

P. 87, Nietzsche remarked...that the human being is only a moment of transition: *Also sprach Zarathustra*, Prologue, paragraph 4.

P. 89, in Schiller's words: Schiller's poem "Das Höchste": "Are you seeking the highest, the greatest? A plant can teach it to you. / You must willfully be what it is will-lessly—that's the way!" *Samtliche Werke in zwölf Bänden*, Stuttgart and Tübingen 1838, Vol. I, p. 411.

P. 96, Lili's suitor: see Goethe's poem "Lili's Park," op. cit. Goethe was betrothed in 1775 to Lili Schönemann, 1758–1817.

CHAPTER V

P. 98, "Oh, to be in England now!": Robert Browning's poem "Home-

Thoughts from Abroad," also found in *The Oxford Book of English Verse, 1250–1900,* op. cit., p. 866.

P. 111, "as these lines are being written": the summer of 1938.

P. 131, Solomon in all his glory: St. Matthew 6, 28 ff.

P. 134, "the dissector of his own delights": from Goethe's poem "Die Freuden" ("The Pleasures,") W. A., Vol. I, p. 62.

P. 136, "They appear to flee each other…": from Goethe's sonnet "Natur und Kunst, sie scheinen sich zu fliehen" ("Nature and art, they appear to flee each other") in the cycle "Was wir bringen" ("What we contribute,") W. A. Vol. IV, p. 129.

CHAPTER VI

P. 154, a great American poetess: Borchardt here toys with lines from various poems by Edna St. Vincent Millay, most of which he refers to in his essay on her work: "sang her savage dirge to the weeds and multicolored herbs," see the poem "In the Grave no Flower"; "to the mullein and the flowering bliss of mountain pastures," see "Pastoral"; "springtime garden shrubs," see "Spring in the Garden"; "the *Iris chrysographes,*" see " Epitaph for the Race of Man, VIII"; "from the window of a slowing train," see "From a Train Window": *Collected Poems,* edited by Norma Millay, New York, Harper & Brothers 1956.

P. 165, The middle…holds…the problem: Goethe, *Maximen und Reflexionen,* No. 134, *Schriften der Goethegesellschaft,* Vol. XXI, edited by Max Hecker.

P. 166, the "dual meanings of the elementary words": "Über den Gegensinn der Urworte" is the title of a study published in Leipzig in 1884 by the German philologist Carl Abel (1837–1906). Abel discusses the ways in which the words of the earlier stages of language can take on two opposite meanings. (The Latin *altus,* for example, means both "tall" and "deep.") Sigmund Freud refers to Abel's study in an essay (1910) of the same title (*Gesammelte Werke,* Vol. VIII, London 1943, pp. 214–221). Abel's title appears to derive from Goethe's phrase "Jedes ausgesprochene Wort erregt den Gegensinn" ("Every spoken word calls up its opposite") which appears in Ottilia's diary in the fourth chapter of the second part of Goethe's novel *Wahlverwandschadten* (*Elective Affinities*), and as well from his poem "Urworte. Orphisch," op. cit.

CHAPTER VII

P. 172, "Feed the grape and bean…": from Edna St. Vincent Millay's poem "Feast" (see note to p. 54).

P. 181, what Goethe calls "the whole circle of creation": a reference to Goethe's poem "Sendschreiben," op. cit.: "Wer mit seiner Mutter, der Natur, sich hält, / Find't im Stengelglas wohl eine Welt."

POSTSCRIPT

P. 194, Schreber gardens are small recreational gardens on the outskirts of many German and Swiss cities. Provided by the municipalities, they stem from the ideas of the nineteenth-century pedagogue Daniel Gottlieb Moritz Schreber.

P. 195, the Dives of the Gospel: the parable of the banquet, St. Luke 14, 15–24.

P. 200, friends…whom…he himself was the first to note…: the reference is to Karl Förster, the breeder and gardening writer to whom Borchardt dedicated the essay "Gartenphantasie" (1925), *Gesammelte Werke, Der leidenschaftliche Gärtner*, Stuttgart, Klett 1968, pp. 17–40.

P. 202, In Schiller's terms: the reference is to Schiller's essay "Über naïve und sentimentalische Dichtung" ("On Naïve and Sentimental Poetry.")

P. 208, "the little fox that lost its tail": from Goethe's poem "Zueignung," W. A., Vol. IV, p. 88 ff., and finally from Aesop's fable αλωπηξ χολορος (Vol. I, Part 1, no. 17, Hausrath edition), of which a translation is found among Goethe's schoolwork (*Der junge Goethe*, edited by Max Morris, Leipzig 1909, Vol. I, p. 74).

P. 213, the words of the old Greek prophet: Hesiod, *Works and Days*, 40.

CATALOGUE

P. 215 "today": Borchardt wrote these lines in the summer of 1938.

P. 259, *Leonotis leonorus*: Borchardt was quite correct to question the attribution of this plant to a native California habitat. Recent botanical literature finds its original home in the tropics and South Africa.

Glossary

ACHERON, *mythological.* A river in Hades. "Acheron," which traditionally means "River of Woe," is also the name of a river in Epirus: an oracle of the dead was located on its banks.

Adanson, Michel, 1727–1800. French botanist, explored widely in Africa.

Addison, Joseph, 1672–1719. English essayist, dramatist and statesman; lived from 1711 until the end of his life at Bilton, his country home near Rugby, in England's West Midlands.

Adonis, *myth.* Son of the Syrian king Theias and his daughter Myrrha; a youth of remarkable beauty, loved by Aphrodite, and killed by a boar sent by the jealous Ares. Ovid (*Metamorphoses,* X, 708–739) recounts that the anemone sprang from his blood.

Aeolian lyric. The poetry of Sappho and Alcaeus.

Ajax, *myth.* The Greek hero in the battle of Troy who took his life in a fit of rage when Achilles' arms were awarded not to him but to Odysseus. See *Odyssey,* XI, 539 ff., and Ovid's *Metamorphoses,* XIII, 1–398.

Akademos. A Greek hero worshipped in a sacred olive grove near Athens; it was in a garden adjacent to this grove that Plato, in 387 BC, founded his Academy.

Alemannia. The portions of southwest Germany, Alsace, and Switzerland occupied in the late fifth century AD by the Germanic tribe of the Alemanni.

Alexandria, Egypt. The capital of the high Hellenistic culture that marked the Ptolemaic dynasty, 300–47 BC.

Altai. Central Asian mountain range between Siberia and Mongolia.

Amur Basin. The basin of the Amur River, which runs along the border between Siberia and Manchuria.

André, Edouard François, 1840–1911. French landscape gardener, explored in South America.

Antioch. Near the mouth of the Orontes River, now in Turkey; one of the largest ancient cities in the area of the Mediterranean, founded by the Greeks in 300 BC, and capital of the Syrian Seleucid Kingdom until 64 BC.

Arends, Georg, 1863–1952. German gardener and breeder.

Aristotle, 384–322 BC. Greek philosopher.

Armida. The sorceress in Torquato Tasso's *Gerusalemme liberata.*

Arthaber, (presumably) Rudolf Edler von, 1795–1867. Viennese silk manufacturer and patron of the arts.

Aschaffenburg. Bavarian city in the district of Unterfranken, once the residence of the electors of Mainz.

Athenaeus, third century AD. The author of *Deipnosophistai* ("The Gastronomers"), a widely ranging work in the form of an aristocratic symposium.

Atlas Mountains. Mountain range in northwest Africa, running generally northeast to southwest through the three countries of the Maghreb: Morocco, Algeria, and Tunisia.

Augustan verse. The poetry of Catullus and Horace.

Avestan. The eastern Iranian language of the *Avesta,* the sacred book of Zoroastrianism. It ceased to be spoken in about 400 BC.

Azores. Group of nine major islands in the North Atlantic Ocean, at a minimum of 740 miles west of Portugal, to which they belong.

Babel, Babylon. The capital of the ancient Babylonian empire in Mesopotamia, from the beginning of the third millennium to 539 BC.

Banks, Sir Joseph, 1743–1820. English explorer, in Newfoundland and Labrador in 1766, circumnavigation with James Cook 1768–71, in Iceland in 1772.

Bassa. A Greek corruption of the Turkish "Pascha."

Bath. City near Bristol in western England.

Bath. The English nursery R. H. Bath, at The Floral Farms, Wisbech, Cambridgeshire.

Baumann, an Alsatian family of gardeners: Augustin, 1779–1867 and his son-in-law August Napoleon, 1804–1884.

Bedford, John Russel, sixth duke of, 1766–1839.

Benary. Seed supplier in Erfurt, founded in 1843 by Ernst Benary, 1818–1893, now, since 1952, in Hannoversch–Münden.

Bermuda. Archipelago of seven main islands and some 150 smaller islands and groups of rocks in the western North Atlantic Ocean, about 570 miles east of Cape Hatteras (North Carolina, USA); a self-governing British colony.

Bertran de Born, ca. 1140–ca. 1215. Provençal troubadour, viscount of Hautefort, and vassal to Richard the Lion-Hearted, duke of Aquitaine and later king of England.

Blackmore and Langdon. English seed nursery in Bath, near Bristol, specialized in delphiniums.

Boboli, Giardino di. Florentine park in the purest Italian style, constructed and planted in 1550 behind the Pitti Palace; commissioned by Eleanora de Toledo, wife of Cosimo Medici I; designed and planted by Niccolò Raffaello de' Pericoli (also known as Tribolo).

Bogazköy. The site of the excavation of Hattusa, the ancient capital of the Hittites, in central Turkey, of the second half of the second millennium BC.

Böhme, Jakob, 1575–1624. German philosophical mystic who greatly influenced such later intellectual movements as Idealism and Romanticism.

Bolle, Carl August, 1821–1909. German botanist, founder of the dendrological gardens in Scharfenberg, near Berlin.

Bonpland, Aimé Jacques Alexandre, 1773–1858. French botanist who accompanied Humboldt to South America.

Bouché. A Berlin family of gardeners: Pierre, 1703–1784; Jean David, 1747–1819; and many others.

Brentano, Clemens, 1778–1842. Poet, novelist, and dramatist, one of the founders of the Heidelberg Romantic school, the second phase of German Romanticism.

Breslau. Now Wroclaw, Poland.

Brancion, Jean de. Belgian botanist of the sixteenth century.

Brockes, Barthold Heinrich, 1680–1747. Poet and city councilman in Hamburg; his collection of poetry, *Irdisches Vergnügen in Gott, bestehend in physikalish- und moralischen Gedicthen,* (*Earthly Pleasure in God, Consisting of Natural-Philosophical and Moral Poems)* nine volumes, appeared in 1721–48.

Browning, Robert, 1812–1898. Late Romantic and Victorian English poet.

Brueghel. A family of Dutch painters: Pieter the Elder, ca. 1530–1569; Jan the Elder, 1568–1625; Pieter the Younger, 1564–1638; Jan the Younger, 1601–1675.

Brunfels, Otto, 1464–1534. German doctor and botanist, author of *Herbarum vivae eicones*, 1530.

Bunge, Alexander von, 1803–1890. Russian doctor and botanist, traveled in China and Central Asia.

Bunyan, John, 1628–1688. Celebrated English minister and preacher, author of *The Pilgrim's Progress*, 1678–84, the epitome of the Puritan religious outlook.

Busbecq, Ogier Ghislain de, 1522–1592. French diplomat and writer who served as envoy from the German King Ferdinand to Sultan Suleiman II, in 1554 in Amasya, and after 1555 in Constantinople; in addition to the tulip, which he discovered in 1554, he also introduced the lilac into Europe.

Bute, John Stuart, third earl of, 1713–1792. Secretary of State and First Lord of the Treasury (effectively prime minister) under England's George III, as well as botanist, author of *Botanical Tables, Containing the Different Families of British Plants...*, 1785.

Calypso, *myth.* A nymph who kept Odysseus imprisoned on her island.

Camell (or Camellus, or Kamel), Georg Joseph, 1661–1706. Moravian Jesuit, missionary in the Philippines.

Canaries. A group of seven main islands, forming two Spanish provinces, off the western coast of Africa at the latitude of southern Morocco.

Candolle, Augustin Pyramus de, 1788–1841. A great botanist, from Geneva, Switzerland; his major work, *Prodromus systematis naturalis regni vegetabilis,* nineteen volumes, appeared in 1824–74.

Capitulare de villis. An edict issued in 795, during the reign of Charlemagne, on the practice of agriculture on royal domains: it counseled the cultivation of kitchen and medicinal herbs, and of several breeds of flowers.

Carboniferous period. The fifth oldest of the eleven periods in the Earth's geological history, directly after the Devonian and previous to the Permian, between 285 to 360 million years ago; includes the era of the great swamp forests and the formation of coal.

Carter. (Presumably) the founder of the English seed nursery Carter's Ltd., Raynes Park, London.

Channel Islands. The islands in the English channel: Alcerney, Guernsey, Jersey, Sark, and various lesser islets.

Charlemagne, 742–814. King of the Franks in 768, Holy Roman emperor in 800.

Chatsworth. The estate of the dukes of the Devonshire, near Sheffield in South Yorkshire, in central England.

Chelsea. A quarter of the city of London, where a botanical garden was founded in 1673.

Chimborazo. One of the highest peaks of the Andes (6247 m), in Ecuador, climbed by Alexander von Humboldt in 1802.

Chou-san archipelago. Group of more than 400 islands off the northern coast of Chekiang Province, China.

Cilicia. Ancient district of southeast Anatolia, Turkey, bounded on the north and west by the Taurus mountain range, on the east by the Anti-Taurus, on the south by the Mediterranean.

Cliffort (or Clifford), Gerard George, 1685–1760. Dutch merchant and proprietor in Hartekamp near Haarlem of collections in the natural sciences and a botanical garden which at one point was supervised by Linnaeus.

Clusius, Carolus, or Charles de l'Ecluse, 1525–1609. Dutch botanist, professor in Vienna and Leiden, and author most notably of *Rariorum plantarum historia,* 1601, and *Exoticorum libri decem,* 1605.

Cobe, Barnabas Cobo, 1582–1657. Spanish Jesuit, missionary, and naturalist in Mexico and Peru.

Constance, Lake. Borders Switzerland, Germany and Austria, occupying an old glacier basin at an elevation of 1300 feet, and forming part of the course of the Rhine. Some forty miles long and up to eight miles wide, and with an average depth of 295 feet, the lake both stores and reflects heat, thus ameliorating the climate along its shores.

Dante Alighieri, 1265–1321. Italian poet, author of *La Divina Commedia.*

Demeter, *myth.* The earth goddess, mother of Persephone.

Devonshire, William George Spencer Cavendish, sixth duke of, 1790–1858. President of the Royal Horticultural Society.

Diadochi. The Macedonian generals who succeeded Alexander the Great.

Dietrich. A German family of botanists: Adam, 1711–1785, a farmer, the Ziegenhain botanist with whom Linnaeus corresponded; Johan Adam, d. 1799; Johann Gottlieb, 1768–1836, court gardener at Eisenach and professor of botany; Nathaniel Friedrich David, 1800–1888; Alfred Gottfried, 1795–1856.

Diocletian, Gaius Aurelius Valerius Diocletianus, 245–313. Roman emperor after 284, reorganized the empire, resigned in 305, and lived thereafter in the Dalmatian city of Spalato (now Split).

Dioscorides, Pedanius, ca. AD 40–90. Greek physician and pharmacologist whose work *De materia medica* was the foremost classical source of modern botanical terminology and the leading pharmacological text for sixteen centuries.

Dippe, Gustav Adolf, 1824–1890. Seed grower in Quedlinburg, proprietor of the firm Gebrüder Dippe.

Douglas, David, 1799–1834. Scottish naturalist, traveled widely in North America.

Dürer, Albrecht, 1471–1528. German painter and printmaker.

Dyck, Antonius van, 1599–1641. Flemish painter.

Earthly paradise. The garden Dante places at the summit of the mountain of Purgatory as the place of transition and final cleansing of the soul that makes its passage into heavenly paradise.

Ecklon, Christian Frederik, 1795–1868. Danish botanist, active in southern Africa along with Karl Zehyer, with whom he co-authored the *Enumeratio plantarum Africae australis.*

Eichendorff, Joseph Freiherr von, 1788–1857. German poet.

Elliott. Botanist and explorer active in South America in the mid-nineteenth century.

Elliott's Sevenhills Nursery. English gardening company in Stevenage, Hertfordshire.

Engadine. The Romansch-speaking upper valley of the River Inn (which continues on to Innsbruck, Austria) in the Swiss Canton of Graubünden.

Engler, Adolph, 1844–1930. Geographer and botanical taxonomist in Kiel, Breslau, and Berlin, the author, among other works, of *Versuch einer Entwicklungsgeschichte des Pflanzenreiches* (*Towards a History of the Development of the Realm of Plants*), 1879 and 1882.

Eünoè and Lethe. The two rivers in Dante's earthly paradise; the waters of the Eünoè restored the dead to the knowledge of their virtuous deeds in life; the waters of Lethe renewed their knowledge of the evils they had performed: Purgatorio, Canto XXXIII.

Farrer, Reginald John, 1880–1920. English explorer and botanist.

Fendler, August, 1813–1883. German botanist.

Ferdinand I, 1503–1564. Holy Roman emperor (1558–1564), king of Bohemia and Hungary from 1526, and regent, from 1521, of the hereditary Habsburg lands.

Fintelmann. A Berlin family of gardeners: among others, William, d. 1816, a commercial gardener; Ferdinand, 1774–1863, court gardener at Charlottenburg; Friedrich, nineteenth century, director of the Berlin Zoo.

Flora, *myth.* The Roman goddess of the flowering of plants.

Fuchs, Leonard, 1501–1566. Doctor and botanist in Tübingen.

Geert, Auguste van. Belgian botanist, author of an *Iconographie des azalées de l'Inde,* Ghent, 1882.

George, Stephan, 1868–1933. Lyric poet largely responsible for the revival of German poetry at the close of the nineteenth century, both a Symbolist and a proponent of a new classicism.

Gerard, John, 1545–1612. English breeder and writer, cultivated plants in Fetter Lane and Holborn in London; the author of *Catalogus arborum, fruticum ac plantarum tam indigenarum quam exoticarum,* 1596, and *Herball, or Generall Historie of Plants,* 1597, illustrated by over eighteen hundred woodcuts.

Gesner, Konrad, 1516–1565. Doctor and professor of philosophy in Zurich, referred to as "the German Pliny." His botanical works remained unpublished until the eighteenth century.

Ghent. Flemish city, the center of Belgium's cultivation and commerce in flowers, with a state-operated gardening school (founded in 1847) and a large quinquennial flower show.

Gibson, John. Nineteenth-century English botanist, director of a London garden, collected in India.

Goes, Hugo van der, 1440–1482, Dutch painter.

Goethe, Johann Wolfgang von, 1749–1832. German poet, dramatist, novelist, statesman and natural scientist.

Goldsmith, Oliver, 1728–1774. English writer, author of *The Vicar of Wakefield.*

Goya, Francisco, 1746–1828. Spanish painter.

Grashoff, Martin Jakob, 1797–1866. Founder of the Quedlinburg seed nursery.

Gray, Thomas, 1716–1771. English scholar and lyric poet.

Griffith, William, 1810–1845. English doctor and botanist in India.

Guianas. Region on the north central coast of South America, comprised of the Co-operative Republic of Guyana (formerly British Guiana), the Republic of Suriname (formerly Dutch Guiana), and French Guiana.

Haage. A German family of gardeners: Johann Heinrich, b. ca. 1735; Johann Nikolaus, d. 1878, partner of the Erfurt commercial gardening company Haage und Schmidt, which today specializes in the breeding of cacti; Friedrich Adolf, 1796–1866.

Hadrianople. Now Edirne, city in the European part of Turkey.

Haenke, Thaddäus, 1761–1817. Bohemian botanist.

Hayler. Bavarian court gardener in Schleißheim, near Munich, at the end of the eighteenth century.

Heem, Jan Davidsz de, 1606–1683. Dutch flower painter; his son, Cornelius, 1631–1695, painted in a similar manner.

Heldreich, Theodor von, 1822–1902. Director of the botanical gardens in Athens.

Hérouard, Jean, d. 1627. Personal physician of the French king Louis XIII, who entrusted him with the founding of the Jardin des Plantes.

Herwart, Johann Friedrich. Augsburg patrician of the sixteenth century.

Hesperides, *myth.* The daughters of the Night, and custodians of the gardens at the western edge of the world where golden apples grew, stolen by Hercules.

Hildebrandt, Johann Maria, 1847–1881. German botanist and explorer in eastern Africa and Madagascar.

Hirschfeld, Christian Cay Lorenz, 1742–1792, professor of philosphy in Kiel, and author of *Theorie der Gartenkunst,* 1779–85.

Hölderlin, Friedrich, 1770–1843. German poet.

Holocene. More recent of the two epochs (the other is the Pleistocene) that comprise the Quaternary Period, and the latest interval of the Earth's geologic history, the last ten thousand years to the present. The first half of the epoch was marked by great warming and far wetter climates than those of today.

Homer, ninth or eight century BC. Greek poet, presumed author of the *Iliad* and the *Odyssey.*

Hooker, Sir William Jackson, 1785–1865. English botanist, director of the Kew Gardens.

Horace, Quintus Horatius Flaccus, 65–8 BC. Roman poet.

Houtte, Louis van, 1810–1876. Belgian botanist and gardener who traveled widely in Brazil, and proprietor of a commercial gardening company in Ghent, where he was also director of the school of garden construction.

Hügel, Carl Alexander Anselm Freiherr von, 1795–1872. Austrian diplomat and natural scientist.

Humboldt, Alexander von, 1769–1859. Natural scientist, geographer and botanist, friend of Schiller and Goethe, traveled from 1799 to 1804 throughout South and Central American: the fruits of his voyages are recorded in a monumental work in thirty volumes, 1814–34; he is also the author of *Ansichten der Natur*, two volumes, 1808, and *Kosmos, Entwurf einer physischen Weltbeschreibung*, five volumes, 1845–62.

Humboldt, Wilhelm Freiherr von, 1767–1835. German statesman and scholar, the author late in life of his masterpiece *Über die Kawi-Sprache auf der Insel Java*, three volumes, 1836, with the introductory essay, "Über die Verschiedenheit des menschlichen Sprachbaues und ihren Einfluß auf die geistige Entwicklung des Menschengeschlechts." He was the elder brother of Alexander von Humboldt.

Hyakinthus, *myth.* A boy loved by Apollo, and accidentally killed by the god while they were playing at throwing the discus: he was then transformed into a dark flower, on which the written words "AI AI," sounds of lament, are said to be recognizable. See Ovid, *Metamorphoses*, X, 162–219.

Indus. The river at the western border of India.

Ionian epic. Homer's narrative poems.

Ipswich. City on the eastern coast of central England.

Isfahan, or Esfahan. City in west central Iran, the major center of the Seljuq Turks (eleventh to twelfth century) and of the Persian Safavid dynasty (sixteenth to eighteenth century).

Islands of the Blessed. The Azores and Canary Islands. (The "Isles of the Blessed" are also the Elysion in Greek mythology.)

Ithaca. Odysseus' native island, off the western coast of Greece.

Jacquin, Nikolaus Joseph von, 1727–1818. Dutch botanist, traveled extensively in the West Indies and South America.

Jardin des Plantes. Now Musée national d'histoire naturelle, founded in Paris in 1626 by Jean Hérouard, personal physician of Louis XIII.

Jekyll, Gertrude, 1843–1932. English writer, resided at her country home Munstead, authored numerous essay and books on gardening, among others: *Home and Garden*, 1900, *Children and Gardens*, 1908, *Colour in the Flower Garden*, 1908, *A Gardener's Testament*, 1937, published by her sister Francis Jekyll.

Jost, Franz, 1814–1862. Gardener of Count Thun in Tetschen, Bohemia.

Jussieu, Bernard de, 1699–1776. Established a natural system for the ordering of plants and implemented it at the Trianon: "the old Jussieu system." His nephew, Antoine Laurent, 1748–1836, director of the Jardin des Plantes after 1778, established "the new Jussieu system."

Kamchatka. Peninsula in northeast Asia, between the Sea of Okhotsk on the west, and the Pacific Ocean and Bering Sea on the east.

Kant, Immanuel, 1724–1804. German philosopher.

Karl V, 1500–1558. Holy Roman emperor, 1519–1556, king of Spain (as Carlo I), 1516–1556, heir to a Spanish and Habsburg empire extending from Spain and the Netherlands to Austria and the kingdom of Naples and reaching overseas to Spanish America.

Karoo. An arid to semi-arid region of the interior of Cape Province, South Africa, occupying about one third of the country's total area.

Kashubian. The Kashubians, a Slavic people in western Prussia.

Kent, William, 1686–1748. Classical English architect, painter and landscape gardener.

Kepler, Johannes, 1571–1630. German astronomer who discovered that the Earth and planets travel around the sun in elliptical orbits.

Khwarezm. A strip of land southeast of the Caspian Sea.

Knight, (presumably) Joseph, 1781–1855. English botanist.

Kundrie. Herald of the Grail in Wolfram's *Parsifal*, both herald of the Grail and sorceress in Richard Wagner's.

Lake Thun. In the Canton of Bern, Switzerland.

Lehmann, George Christian, 1792–1860. Director of Hamburg's botanical gardens.

Leichtlin, Max, 1831–1910. City councilman in Baden-Baden and proprietor of a private botanical garden.

Leiden. Dutch city; the university was founded in 1575, the botanical gardens in 1587.

Lenau, Nikolaus (Niembisch von Strehlenau), 1802–1850. German poet.

Lenné, Peter Joseph, 1789–1866. Descendent of a Lüttich gardening family, and director of the royal gardens of Prussia.

Lethe. See Eünoè and Lethe.

Liguria. The region on the northwest coast of Italy, from the French border to Tuscany.

Linden, Jean Jules, 1817–1898. Luxemburg botanist, traveled in Brazil and Mexico.

Lindheimer, Ferdinand, 1801–1879. German botanist.

Lindley, John, 1799–1865. English botanist, author of *Natural System of Botany*, 1835.

Linnaeus, Carolus (Carl von Linné), 1707–1778. Swedish botanist, explorer and physician, the first to frame principles for defining genera and species of organisms and to create a uniform system for naming them; author, among other works, of *Systema naturae* (1735), *Genera plantarum* (1737), and *Species plantarum* (1753).

Loddiges, William, d. 1849. Proprietor of the old commercial gardening company Conrad Loddiges and Sons, in Hackney, near London.

Lorrain, Claude, 1600–1682. French painter.

Louis. The three Louis, kings of France: Louis XIII, 1610–1643; Louis XIV, 1643–1715; Louis XV, 1715–1774.

Lucullus, Lucius Licinus, ca. 115–57 BC. Roman politician, proverbial for his wealth and unlimited pursuit of pleasure.

Lüttich. City in eastern Belgium.

Luzon. The largest and most important of the Philippine islands.

Macoy, Jacob. Gardener in Lüttich.

Mainau. Island in Lake Constance with a splendid park, laid out in 1853 by the Grand Duke of Baden.

Marco, Marco il Lombardo. A penitent in the circle of wrath in Dante's Purgatorio, Canto XVI: the poet entrusts him with a theological explanation of freedom and necessity.

Marias. The three Marias: see St. Mark, 16, 1, where subsequent to His resurrection, Christ appears to Mary Magdalene, Mary the mother of James, and Salomé.

Markgrafschaft. The margraviate of Baden, to the north of Freiburg in Breisgau.

Martius, Carl Friedrich Philipp von, 1794–1868. German botanist, traveled in Brazil.

Matilija. Presumably a river in southwest California.

Mattioli (Mattiolus), Petrus Andreas, 1500–1577. Italian doctor and botanist, personal physician to Emperor Maximilian.

Maximowicz, Karl Johann, 1827–1891. Russian botanist, traveled in eastern Siberia and Japan.

Mecheln. Belgian city in the province of Antwerp where in 1570 a merchant by the name of Georg Rye succeeded in breeding tulips.

Michaux, André, 1746–1806. French botanist, collected in Persia, North America, Teneriffe and France.

Millay, Edna St. Vincent, 1892–1950. American poet.

Montdidier. City in the French Department of La Somme.

Möricke, Eduard, 1804–1875. German poet.

Müller, Ferdinand Baron von, 1825–1896. German-Australian botanist, director of the botanical gardens in Melbourne.

Muskau. See Pückler-Muskau.

Namaqualand. Region of southwestern Africa, home of the Khoikhoin (or Hottentot) Nama people, extending from near Windhoek, Namibia, into Cape of Good Hope Province, South Africa, and from the Namib desert eastward to the Kalahari.

Narcissus, *myth.* A beautiful youth who rejected the love of the nymph Echo, and who as punishment fell in love with his own image, which he saw reflected in a pool of water; on attempting to embrace it, he fell into the water and drowned. But, rather than a corpse, he left behind the flower that bears his name. See Ovid, *Metamorphoses*, III, 339–510.

Nassau-Siegen, Fürst Johann Moritz von, 1604–1679. Viceroy, from 1636 to 1644, of the Dutch colonies in Brazil.

Natal. The smallest of the four provinces of the Republic of South Africa, bounded on the east by the Indian Ocean, on the south by Cape of Good Hope Province, on the northwest by Transvaal Province.

Neubronner. Gardening company in Ulm.

New Granada. Old name for the country of Colombia, in South America.

New Holland. Old name for Australia.

Nietzsche, Friedrich, 1844–1900. German philosopher.

Novalis (Friedrich Leopold, Freiherr von Hardenberg), 1772–1801. German Romantic poet; the visions of the hero of his mythical romance *Heinrich von Ofterdingen* center on a blue flower, which subsequently became a symbol of longing among German Romantic poets.

Numidia. Ancient expression for North Africa.

Olbrich, Josef Maria, 1867–1908. German architect.

Olympus. Greece's tallest mountain, on the border between Macedonia and Thessaly, and the seat in Greek mythology of the celestial gods. Olympus, however, is also the name of various other hills and mountains both in Greece and in Asia Minor.

Omar Khayyam, 1034–1122. Persian mathematician and poet, author of the *Rubáiyát.*

Optimates. The oligarchic nobility that dominated the Senate during the later Roman Republic and the civil wars of the first century BC.

Orbigny, Alcide Charles Victor Desalines d', 1802–1852. French botanist.

Oreads, *myth.* Mountain nymphs.

Ossian. Legendary bard whose writings were claimed to have been found by the Scottish writer James MacPherson, 1736–1796; the works MacPherson published, 1760, were later proved to be forgeries.

Otto, Karl Friedrich Eduard, 1812–1885. German botanist, collected in Venezuela, director of the botanical gardens in Hamburg.

Parkinson, John, 1567–1640. English botanist, author of *Paradisus terrestris*, 1656, and *Theatrum botanicum*, 1640.

Parnassus. A chain of mountains to the north of Delphi, sacred to Apollo and seat of the muses.

Passaeus (van de Passe). A Dutch family of copper engravers of the sixteenth and seventeenth centuries, especially Crispyn van de Passe, 1590s–1670, whose *Hortus floridus*, 1614, was published in Arnheim.

Patagonia. Semiarid, scrub plateau in southern Argentina, the largest desert in the Americas, bounded on the north by the Rio Colorado, on the east by the Atlantic, on the south by the Rio Coig, on the west by the Andes.

Paul, Jean (Johann Paul Friedrich Richter), 1763–1825. German novelist.

Paxton, Sir Joseph, 1802–1865. English gardener and designer of hothouses in the service of the Duke of Devonshire; he also designed the Crystal Palace for the Great Exhibition of 1851.

Persephone, *myth.* Proserpina in Roman mythology, daughter of Demeter, abducted by Hades (Pluto) into the netherworld.

Pfau, (presumably) Riccardo, d. 1897 (in Costa Rica). Botanist.

Pfeiffer, Ludwig, 1805–1877. German doctor and botanist.

Pfitzer. Large seed nursery in Fellbach, near Stuttgart.

Pindar, ca. 520–after 442 BC. Greek poet.

Platen, August Graf von, 1796–1835. German poet and dramatist.

Plato, 427–347 BC. Greek philosopher.

Pliny, Gaius Plinius Secundus, 23–79 AD. Roman officer, public administrator, and writer who died in the eruption of Vesuvius, author of *Naturalis historia*, in thirty-seven books.

Plumier, Charles, 1646–1704. French Franciscan monk, botanist, collector of America flora.

Poeppig, Eduard Friedrich, 1798–1868. German zoologist and botanist, active in South America.

Poiteau, M. A., 1766–1854. French botanist, collected in Santo Domingo and the Guianas.

Pomona, *myth.* Roman goddess of gardens and fruit trees.

Pontic. Refers to the region on the borders on the Black Sea (Pontus Euxinus).

Pope, Alexander, 1688–1744. English writer, lover of gardens and proprietor of a small estate on the Thames, at Twickenham.

Poussin, Nicolas, 1594–1665. French painter.

Proserpina. See Persephone.

Pückler, Hermann Fürst von Pückler-Muskau, 1785–1871. Laid out an exemplary English park at his estate Muskau in Schlesia; the author, among other works, of *Briefe eines Verstorbenen* (*Letters from a Man Deceased*), 1830, and *Andeutungen über Landschaftsgärtnerei* (*Thoughts on Landscape Gardening*), 1836.

Quedlinburg. City in the western part of eastern Germany, on the Bode River, in the northern foothills of the Lower Harz Mountains, once a favorite residence of the Saxon emperors and the site of an imperial abbey.

Rausch, Albert H., 1882–1849. German poet and novelist, wrote after 1931 under the pseudonym Henri Benrath.

Regel, Albert, 1845–1908. Eldest son of Eduard August Regel, researched the plants of Central Asia.

Regel, Eduard August, 1815–1892. German botanist, director of the St. Petersburg botanical gardens after 1855.

Reichart, Christian, 1685–1773. Founder of the Ehrfurt flower nursery.

Reichenbach. A German family of botanists: Heinrich Gottlob Ludwig, 1793–1879, director of the Dresden botanical gardens; Heinrich Gustav, 1823–1889, director of the botanical gardens in Hamburg.

Rinz, Sebastian, 1782–1861. Landscape gardener, municipal gardener for the city of Frankfurt, court gardener in about 1800 to the Bishop of Würzburg.

Rio de la Plata. Large estuary of roughly triangular shape on the southeastern coast of South America, with Uruguay to the north and Argentina to the south, fed by the Parana and Uruguay Rivers.

Ritter, Karl, b. 1800. German botanist and traveler.

Rivoire et Fils. Seed nursery in Lyon.

Rodigas, Franz Karl Hubert, 1801–1877. Dutch botanist.

Roezl, Benedikt, 1824–1885. Bohemian botanist, traveled widely in North and South America.

Roman elegy. Catullus, Propertius, Ovid.

Roxburgh, William, 1759–1815. Scottish botanist, director of the botanical gardens in Calcutta.

Royal Horticultural Society. Founded in 1804, the RHS operates experimental gardens at Wisley, to the south-west of London; its official organ, the *Journal of the Royal Horticultural Society*, has been published since 1866.

Royle, John Forbes, 1799–1858. English botanist, director of the botanical gardens in the Indian city of Saharumpore.

Ruprecht, F., 1814–1870. Botanist from Prague; collected in Russia.

Ruysdael (Ruisdael), Jakob van, 1628/29–1682. Dutch landscape painter.

Salm-Reifferscheidt-Dyck, Fürst und Altgraf Joseph zu, 1773–1861. German plant collector, especially of succulents.

Salvaticus Matthias (Matteo Silvatico, Mattheus Sylvaticus). Born end of thirteenth century in Mantua, and active in Salerno after 1297, where he founded the botanical gardens, d. in Salerno in 1342, author of *Pandectae Medicinae.*

Santo Domingo. District of the Dominican Republic, on the island of Hispaniola, the second largest island of the West Indies, in the group of the Greater Antilles.

Sappho, ca. 600 BC. Greek lyric poet.

Scharfenberg. Island in Tegel Lake in the vicinity of Berlin, site of the dendrological gardens founded by Carl August Bolle.

Schiller, Friedrich von, 1759–1805. German dramatist, poet and literary theorist.

Schleißheim. Castle of the Bavarian royal family, north of Munich.

Schomburgk, Sir Robert Herman, 1804–1865. German botanist, collected in the northern parts of South America.

Schöner Busch. The park of the Brentano family in Aschaffenburg.

Schott, Heinrich Wilhelm, 1794–1865. Austrian botanist, collected in Brazil, director of the imperial gardens at Schönbrunn.

Schwetzingen. Castle of the Electors Palatine, constructed in the seventeenth century.

Scipios. The noble Roman Cornelius family, especially its major members of the third and second century BC: Publius Cornelius Scipio Africanus maior, 235–183, who defeated Hannibal; Publius Cornelius Scipio Aemilianus Africanus minor, 185–129, who destroyed Carthage, and was a friend of Greek culture.

Sckell, Ludwig von, 1750–1825. German landscape gardener, designed parts of Schwitzinger Park and the English Garden in Munich.

Seljuq Caliphate. The earliest Turkish empire, from the tenth to the thirteenth century.

Sello. A German gardening family, in service from 1698 to 1891 as court gardeners of the Prussian royal family: Johann Samuel, b. 1712, in service at Rheinsberg and Sanssouci; Karl, 1754–1796, at Sanssouci; Louis Samuel Christian, 1775–1837, at Sanssouci; Hermann Louis, 1800–1876, at Charlottenhof and Sanssouci; Emil Ludwig Walter, 1816–1893, at Neuer Palais in Potsdam.

Semiramis. Legendary Assyrian queen, ca. 2000 BC, said to have created the hanging gardens of Babylon, one of the seven wonders of the world.

Serenissma. The Republic of Venice, 1140–1797.

Sevenhills Nursery. See Elliott's.

Shiraz. City in the Zagros Mountains in south central Iran, birthplace of the Persian poets Sa'di and Hafez, whose garden tombs lie on its northern outskirts.

Sibthorp, John, 1758–1796. English botanist.

Siebold, Philipp Franz von, 1791–1866. German doctor, researched the botany of Japan, and also introduced Japan to Western scientific method.

Silvaplana. Village in the upper Engadine, in the Swiss Canton of Graubünden.

Skinner, George Uren 1804–1868. Scottish natural scientist, lived and collected in Guatemala.

Smith, (presumably) John Donnel, 1829–1928. American botanist.

Solander, Daniel, 1735–1782. Swedish zoologist, librarian after 1773 of the British Museum.

Sparmann, Anders, 1748–1820. Swedish botanist, student of Linnaeus, accompanied Cook on his second voyage, author of *Iter in Chinam*, 1768.

Spee, Friedrich von, 1591–1635. German poet, author of *Trutz-Nachtigall oder Geistlichs-Poetisch Lust-Wäldlein*, 1639.

Stern, Colonel Sir Frederick Claude, b. 1884. English garden lover and botanist.

Strawberry Hill. The estate of Sir Horace Walpole, 1717–1797, near Twickenham, west of London, not far from the home and garden of Alexander Pope.

Susa. The capital city of Elam (Susiana) and administrative center, starting in 522 BC, of the Achaemenian king Darius I and his successors, at the foot of the Zagros Mountains in the Khuzistan region of Iran.

Sutton and Sons. English seed nursery in Reading, Berkshire.

Sweerts, Emmanuel, 1552–1612. Dutch seed merchant, botanist, and copper engraver, publisher of a *Florilegium*, Frankfurt am Main, 1612.

Tacitus, ca. AD 55–120. Roman historian.

Tartariya. An old term for Central Asia.

Tasso, Torquato, 1544–1595. Italian poet, author of *Gerusalemme liberata*.

Taurus. A great chain of mountains in southern Turkey, running parallel to the coast of the Mediterranean and extending in the east to the upper reaches of the Euphrates.

Teniers, David, the younger, 1610–1690. Flemish painter.

Tetschen. Northern Bohemian city, Czechoslovakia, in the gorge of the Elbe River, and site of the eighteenth-century castle of the counts of Thun and Hohenstein.

Theophrastus, ca. 372–287 BC. Student of Aristotle, author of numerous scientific treatises.

Thompson and Morgan. English seed nursery in Ipswick, Suffolk.

Thunberg, Karl Per, 1743–1822. Swedish botanist, researched in southern Africa, Java and Japan.

Tournefort, Joseph Pitton de, 1656–1708. French botanist, author of *Institutiones rei herbariae*, three volumes, second edition 1700.

Tovar. City in western Venezuela.

Transvaal. The northernmost and second largest province of the Republic of South Africa, containing both Pretoria and Johannesburg.

Trianon. Two pleasure palaces in the Park of Versailles: Grand Trianon, constructed under Louis XIV; Petit Trianon under Louis XV.

Uckermark. Region to the north of Berlin.

Veitch. English gardening family, proprietors of the firm Veitch and Sons, Ltd. Royal Exotic Nursery in Chelsea, London: John, 1792–1863; James, 1792–1863; James (son of the former) 1815–62, who in 1853 purchased the Royal Exotic Nursery which had been founded by Knight and Perry in 1816; and John Gould, 1839–1870, who traveled in Japan, China, the Philippines and Australia.

Veltheim, August Ferdinand Graf von, 1741–1801. German botanist.

Verrières-le-Buisson. Town near Versailles, famous for its cultivations of flowers.

Verschaffelt, Ambroise, 1825–1886. Proprietor of a garden in Ghent, and an important Belgian garden impresario.

Vilmorin (L'evêque de Vilmorin). French family of gardeners and botanists: Philippe Victoire, 1746–1804; Pierre Philippe André, 1776–1862; Pierre Louis François, 1816–60; Charles Philippe Henri, 1843–99, grounded the Jardin Latil at Golf Juan, near Antibes.

Virgil, Publius Vergilius Maro, 70–19 BC. Roman poet.

Walachia. Romanian principality on the lower Danube River.

Wallich, Nathaniel, 1786–1854. Danish doctor and botanist, superintendent of the botanical gardens in Calcutta.

Wallis, Gustav, 1830–1878. German botanist, active in South and Central America.

Ward, Frank Kingdom Ward, b. 1885. English botanist.

Warscewicz, J. von, 1810–1866. Polish botanist.

Wassermann, Jakob, 1873–1934. German novelist.

Wendland. A German family of gardeners: Johann Christophe, 1755–1828, inspector of the Herrenhausen gardens, near Hannover; Heinrich Ludolph, 1792-1869, master of the Herrenhausen gardens; Hermann, 1825–1903, director of the Herrenhausen court gardens.

Wichura, Max Ernst, 1817–1866. Prussian jurist and botanist, active in India and Ceylon.

Wied, Prince Maximilian Alexander Phillip zu Wied-Neuwied, 1782–1867. German botanist, active in South and Central America, author of a *Beitrag zur Flora Barasiliens* (*Study of the Flora of Brazil*).

Willmoth, Ellen. English garden director, sister of Gertrude Jekyll, author of *Warley Garden in Spring and Summer*, 1909, and *The Genus Rosa*, 1910.

Wisley. Town in the County of Surrey, southwest of London.

Woburn Abbey. The estate of the dukes of Bedford, in Bedfordshire, in south-central England.

Xerxes, king of Persia from 485 to 465 BC. Son and successor of Darius I, invaded Greece in 480; was defeated by the Greeks at Salamis and Plataea.

Zähringer. Medieval line of south-west German princes, forebears of the margraves of Baden.

Zeyher. A German family of botanists: Johann Michael, 1770–1843, director of the gardens at Schwetzingen; Karl, 1799–1858, researched the flora of South America, co-author with C. F. Eklon of *Enumeratio plantarum Africae australis*.

Index of the Names of Plants